ANGLO-SAXONS AND THE NORTH

Essays Reflecting the Theme of the 10th Meeting
of the International Society of Anglo-Saxonists in
Helsinki, August 2001

MEDIEVAL AND RENAISSANCE
TEXTS AND STUDIES

VOLUME 364

Essays in Anglo-Saxon Studies
Volume 1

ANGLO-SAXONS AND THE NORTH

Essays Reflecting the Theme of the 10th Meeting
of the International Society of Anglo-Saxonists in
Helsinki, August 2001

Edited by

Matti Kilpiö, Leena Kahlas-Tarkka,
Jane Roberts, and Olga Timofeeva

ACMRS
(Arizona Center for Medieval and Renaissance Studies)
Tempe, Arizona
2009

Library of Congress Cataloging-in-Publication Data

Anglo-Saxons and the north : essays reflecting the theme of the 10th meeting of the International Society of Anglo-Saxonists in Helsinki, August 2001 / edited by Matti Kilpiö ... [et al.].
    p. cm. -- (Medieval and renaissance texts and studies ; v. 364)
    "The present volume consists mainly, but not exclusively, of papers presented at the tenth biennial meeting of ISAS in Helsinki, 6-11 August 2001."
    Includes bibliographical references and index.
    ISBN 978-0-86698-412-6 (acid-free paper)
    1. English literature--Old English, ca. 450-1100--Criticism, Textual--Congresses. 2. Civilization, Anglo-Saxon, in literature--Congresses. 3. Civilization, Medieval, in literature--Congresses. 4. Civilization, Anglo-Saxon--Historiography--Congresses. I. Kilpiö, Matti.
    PR179.T48A84 2009
    829.09'3584201--dc22

                                                                    2009027576

∞
This book is made to last.
It is set in Adobe Caslon Pro,
smyth-sewn and printed on acid-free paper
to library specifications.
Printed in the United States of America

TABLE OF CONTENTS

ACKNOWLEDGMENTS

First of all, our warmest thanks are due to the Arizona Center for Medieval and Renaissance Studies (ACMRS) and its Director and General Editor Professor Robert E. Bjork for including the present volume in their series Medieval and Renaissance Texts and Studies, for skilfully turning the manuscript into a book and, not least, for showing patient confidence in a positive outcome for our project. Of the highly professional staff of ACMRS we would like to single out Managing Editor Roy Rukkila and the copy-editor of this volume, Leslie S. B. MacCoull, for special thanks.

At the Helsinki end, we are particularly grateful to Marianna Hintikka, who did an excellent job as the editorial secretary of this volume at the earlier stages of the editing process. Our grateful thanks go to Bethany Fox for language checking.

The editorial work was supported in part by the Academy of Finland Centre of Excellence funding for the Research Unit for Variation, Contacts and Change in English (VARIENG) at the Department of English, University of Helsinki.

M.K.
L.K-T.
J.R.
O.T.

Abbreviations

ASE	Anglo-Saxon England
ASPR	Anglo-Saxon Poetic Records
CLCLT	CETEDOC Library of Christian Latin Texts
CPL	Clavis Patrum Latinorum
EEMF	Early English Manuscripts in Facsimile
EETS	Early English Text Society
Gmc	Germanic
IE	Indo-European
LG	Low German
MLG	Middle Low German
ModE	Modern English
ModHG	Modern High German
ModIr	Modern Irish
OE	Old English
OFris	Old Frisian
OGNS	Ordbog over det Gamle Norske Sprog
OHG	Old High German
OIcel	Old Icelandic
ON	Old Norse
OS, OSax	Old Saxon
OSw	Old Swedish
OWN	Old West Norse
PL	Patrologia Latina
PrGmc	Primitive Germanic
WGmc	West Germanic

INTRODUCTION

MATTI KILPIÖ

The present volume consists mainly, but not exclusively, of papers presented at the tenth biennial meeting of ISAS in Helsinki, 6–11 August 2001. The theme of the conference was "Anglo-Saxons and the North", a theme that readily suggested itself to the organizers because of the lively reciprocal traffic of people, goods, and ideas, between the British Isles and the Nordic countries from the early Middle Ages to the end of the Anglo-Saxon period—and even later, if we consider the important role of English missions in the Christianization of the Nordic countries, including Finland. These contacts, peaceful or warlike, were appropriately enough the topic of many papers given at the Helsinki meeting. Most of them concerned the vertical dimension, the contacts between the Nordic countries and the more southerly Anglo-Saxon England. ISAS 2001, however, also had a horizontal dimension, reflected in the post-conference symposium in St Petersburg on 12–13 August, in the twin exhibitions of manuscripts organised by the National Library of Russia and Helsinki University Library,[1] and also in two papers included in the present volume.

The volume of scholarly work on various aspects of "Anglo-Saxons and the North" since the early modern period is enormous: the number of books and articles on *Beowulf* alone rises to more than 1,500 items in Greenfield and Robinson's bibliography.[2] Today, the number must be considerably higher. The presence of the Vikings in England, to mention just one other area of research, has also given rise to a large literature, partly because the foci of interest are so many: language, literature, place-names, farming, settlement history, political history, legislation, art, and so on.

Before we survey the contents of the present volume, let us have a look at where Anglo-Saxon studies began in Finland. The Finnish scholar who anticipated the theme of ISAS 2001 by more than two centuries was H.G. Porthan.

---

[1] See *Ex Insula Lux: Manuscripts and Hagiographical Material Connected with Medieval England*, ed. Matti Kilpiö and Leena Kahlas-Tarkka (Helsinki, 2001).

[2] Stanley B. Greenfield and Fred C. Robinson, *A Bibliography of Publications on Old English Literature to the End of 1972* (Toronto, Buffalo, and London, 1982).

In the wake of Ohthere and Wulfstan[3]

Henrik Gabriel Porthan (1739–1804), humanist and professor at the University of Turku, the former capital of Finland, was a man of the Enlightenment, a great scholar, whose research interests ranged from Finnish folk poetry and the Finnish language and its linguistic relatives to history and geography, to mention only a few.[4]

It was probably Porthan's interest in geography that gave him the impetus to study the geographical interpolation in Orosius's world history. Porthan produced two studies in which this interpolation is found in part or in its entirety:

> 1. *De antiqva gente Qvenorum* 'About the ancient nation of the *Cwenas*' [A dissertation formally defended by one of Porthan's students, Henr. Wegelius, but mostly or entirely written by Porthan]. Turku, 1788.[5]

> 2. *Försök at uplysa konung Aelfreds geographiska beskrifning öfver den europeiska Norden.* 'An attempt to give an account of King Alfred's geographical description of the European North.' Kongliga Vitterhets Historie och Antiquitets Academien. Handlingar, Del 6. 1800.

The doctoral dissertation *De antiqva gente Qvenorum* is a short study which, as its name suggests, concentrates on the people called *Cwenas*. The passage cited from the Ohthere-Wulfstan interpolation is very brief:

> Donne is to gemnes thæm lande sudveardum, on odre healfe thæs mores, *Sveoland*, [oth thät land nordveard]. And to emnes [An *gemnes*? (Porthan's

---

[3] The following sources have provided useful information for the section on Porthan: the entry on Porthan by Rafael Koskimies in vol. 6: cols. 1443–45, of *Otavan Iso Tietosanakirja (Encyclopaedia Fennica)*, 5th ed.; Nils Erik Enkvist, "English Studies in Finland, 1890–1940: The Era of Uno Lindelöf" [accessed on 16 June 2006 at www.eng. helsinki.fi/main/news/ESSE-2000/nils.erik.enkvist.htm]; *Henrik Gabriel Porthan: Valitut teokset*, ed. and trans. Iiro Kajanto, Suomalaisen Kirjallisuuden Seuran Toimituksia 373 (Helsinki, 1982); M.G. Schybergson, *Henrik Gabriel Porthan: Lefnadsteckning, Senare delen*, Skrifter utgifna af Svenska Litteratursällskapet i Finland 98 (Helsingfors, 1911). For a richly analytic account of early Anglo-Saxon studies in Scandinavia, see Robert E. Bjork, "Nineteenth-Century Scandinavia and the Birth of Anglo-Saxon Studies," in *Anglo-Saxonism and the Construction of Social Identity*, ed. Allen J. Frantzen and John D. Niles (Gainesville, FL, 2000), 111–32.

[4] See also Minna Skafte Jensen, "Scandinavia," in *A Companion to the Classical Tradition*, ed. Craig W. Kallendorf (Oxford, 2007), 252–64, here 261.

[5] The majority of the dissertations defended by Porthan's students followed the same pattern: Porthan himself was responsible for the substance of the thesis; the role of the respondent was mainly restricted to showing that he was able to use Latin for scholarly argumentation.

footnote)] thæm land nordeveardum, *Cvena land*. Da *Cvenas* hergiad hvilum on tha *Nordmen* ofer done mor, hvilum tha Nordmen on hy. And thær sint svide micle meras fersce geond tha moras. And berad tha *Cvenas* hyra scypu ofer land on tha meras, and thanon hergiad on tha *Northmen*. Hy habbad svide lytle scypa and svide leohte.[6]

What, then, were Porthan's conclusions concerning the *Cwenas*, the main topic of the study? On the basis of the evidence presented by Ohthere, Porthan rejected the idea that the homeland of the *Cwenas* lay in what is present-day Finland, east of the Gulf of Bothnia, arguing that most of the *Cwenas* lived in what in Porthan's own time were the Swedish provinces of Hälsingland, Jämtland, Medelpad, Ångermanland, and Västerbotten. He was of the opinion that their language was not related to Finnish but was Germanic.

Porthan took his Old English text from Langebek's *Scriptores rerum Danicarum medii aevi*. He found it necessary to take a stand on the meaning of a word that occurs three times in the short citation: the noun *mor*. He did not accept the interpretation of this word as 'moor' presented by the German scholar Forster. Instead, he, correctly, sided with 'the Oxfordians' who translated this word by *montes* in the version of the Ohthere-Wulfstan interpolation in Spelman's life of King Alfred; he also appeals to Junius' *Etymologicum Anglicum* and other authorities in defence of his view. Another point connected with the Old English passage is that Porthan had problems with the meaning and function of the prepositional phrase *oth thät land nordveard*, and suggested that it would best be omitted.

The second, later study, the *Försök*, is an altogether more ambitious piece of research, which, fifteen years after its appearance, earned the praise of the famous Danish scholar Rasmus Rask. In the process of writing the *Försök*, Porthan had realised how defective his knowledge of Old English was and tried to make up for this deficiency. During his stay in Stockholm in the summer of 1795 he wrote to the University Librarian of Uppsala, P.F. Aurivillius:

> As I did not have the opportunity during my short visit to Uppsala to see you, Professor, I now take the liberty to inquire in writing if the academic library there has an Anglo-Saxon dictionary (e.g. by Somner, Benson or Lye). For a study on the well-known geographical chapter in Alfred's Orosius which I am now working on I would need to consult such a dictionary which is to be found neither at home in Turku nor here in Stockholm.[7]

---

[6] The text has been cited from the photostatic edition of *Henrici Gabrielis Porthan Opera Omnia* 9, ed. Heikki Koskenniemi et al. (Turku, 1993): 419–37. This passage corresponds to 15.31–38 in *The Old English Orosius*, ed. Janet Bately, EETS s.s. 6 (Oxford, 1980).

[7] Translation mine; the Swedish original is cited in Schybergson, *Porthan*, 42–43.

Porthan received a dictionary on loan and was later even successful in acquiring a copy of Somner for the library of his home university, and the notes of the *Försök* attest to the use of both Lye and Somner.

Försök at uplysa konung Aelfreds geographiska beskrifning öfver den europeiska Norden[8] is considerably more substantial than *De antiqva gente Qvenarum*. It is best described as "an annotated edition of the Ohthere-Wulfstan interpolation."[9] Its base text is that of Daines Barrington, *The Anglo-Saxon Version from the Historian Orosius, by Ælfred the Great, Together with an English Translation from the Anglo-Saxon* (1773), an edition not very highly rated by Porthan. All the same, he had at least secondary access to the manuscript evidence for both the Cotton and the Lauderdale versions; this is evident from his notes to Barrington's text.

In the *Försök* Porthan's Old English text begins with *Nu ville ve ymbe Europe land gemaere reccan, sva mycel sva ve hit fyrmest viton.*[10] It ends with the closing words of Wulfstan's narrative: *hy gedoth thaet other bith oferfroren, sam hit sy summor, sam vinter.*[11] A Swedish translation is given synoptically in the right-hand column.

The edition of this excerpt is richly annotated: the main emphasis is on geographical questions. Geography was clearly Porthan's forte, and his confidence is clear from the way he argued with the work of other scholars. What is for a historical linguist more difficult to anticipate is the rather skilful way in which Porthan deals with linguistic matters. Not only does he give variant readings from the Lauderdale and Cotton manuscripts but occasionally he also makes sensible comments on syntactic matters. For example, for the sentence *North Dene habbath be him northan, thone ilcan saes earm, the man sae haet Ost.*[12] Porthan has the following comment: "[p]erhaps the word-order here has been disturbed (*rubbad*) in the text, so that one has to read: *the man haet Ost sae* or *the sae man haet Osti?*" Porthan's first conjecture in fact restores the better manuscript reading. The second *thonne* in the sentence *Thonne is an port on sutheveardum thaem lande, thonne man haet Sciringes-heal*[13] receives the following comment: "*Thone?*", and this successfully restores the reading *þone*, which is attested in the Lauderdale manuscript but not in the Cotton manuscript.

Porthan's contributions to Anglo-Saxon studies are impressive, particularly considering the fact that, being far away from the libraries where the original medieval manuscripts were kept, he had to make do with what was available to him. Although he humbly says in the *Försök* regarding Barrington's edition:

---

[8] The edition I have used is *Henrici Gabrielis Porthan Opera Selecta, Pars qvinta*, Suomalaisen Kirjallisuuden seuran toimituksia 21:5 (Helsingfors, 1873), 43–99.

[9] Enkvist, "English Studies in Finland."

[10] Corresponds to 12.14–16 in *The Old English Orosius*, ed. Bately.

[11] Corresponds to 18.1–2 in *The Old English Orosius*, ed. Bately.

[12] Corresponds to 13.19–20 in *The Old English Orosius*, ed. Bately.

[13] Corresponds to 16.2–3 in *The Old English Orosius*, ed. Bately.

"Men vi få emellertid vara nögde med hvad vi fått, och tacka derföre" ('But we must, however, be satisfied with what we have got and be grateful for it'), he was well aware of the higher standards required for the elucidation of such a difficult text as the Ohthere-Wulfstan interpolation. Nevertheless, it seems appropriate to re-assess Porthan's contribution to the theme "Anglo-Saxons and the North," at the outset of the volume from the ISAS 2001 conference.

From Rök to the Reorganization of Arable Land: The Nine Essays

In this section I provide a brief introduction to each of the essays contained in this volume. It is difficult to do justice in a few lines to studies which are full of detailed analysis and theoretical insights. My notes are designed just to whet the appetite of readers, and I shall draw attention to some of the more striking thematic links between individual essays.

Some twenty years ago, I had occasion to read a sizable collection of articles by Joseph Harris, and I still remember my excitement when I realized that Old Norse literature provided far more parallels for Old English poetry than I could have anticipated.

The theme of Harris's essay in this volume is the Rök stone in Östergötland, Sweden. This stone bears a long runic inscription that has challenged the interpretative abilities of generations of scholars. Harris concentrates on the first two narrative sections of the inscription, finding West Germanic materials in both. The first section contains verse connected with a certain Theodoric, identified as Theodoric the Great by Harris and a majority of scholars. There is a fascinating link between this Rök text and the equestrian statue of Theodoric brought to Aachen in 801; Harris is inclined to believe that the exact description of the statue in the Rök text goes back to an eye-witness report by a Gautish visitor to Aachen. Throughout his essay, Harris establishes links between the Rök text, which he views as literature, and other early Germanic texts and genres. One example is the close connection he sees between the first narrative section and the Old English poem *Deor*. The second narrative section poses many problems of interpretation, but the personal names it contains are either definitely or possibly West Germanic, and all could have been names of Frisians. I cite part of Harris's conclusions on this part of Rök: "[f]or Rök's section on the twenty kings we can hold fast to the West Germanic source of many or all of the names and perhaps to some parallels in *Zeitgedichte*; anything beyond this is very uncertain. But I have tried to imagine a historical situation (involving a Frisian or partly Frisian trading brotherhood and its demise in battle) passing into historically-based fiction, i.e. legend, in a form that preserved some hints of the *Zeitgedichte* that first recorded it."

Frank Battaglia's essay takes us even further back than Harris's in the cultural milieu of early Scandinavia. He points out in his essay that the use of bogs and lakes for religious offerings ended in Scandinavia around the year 500, and that bogs as sites for rituals later began to be replaced in this function by large buildings. In the words of Battaglia, "[t]he halls created new sacral relationships and memorialized the centralization of power that was responsible for them." Rich documentation, most of it archaeological, is marshalled in the essay as material for an updated analysis of "the cultural landscape and geography of power in South Scandinavia in the mid–first millennium." The closing part of the essay is dedicated to possible implications of the deepened understanding of the Scandinavian milieu for the interpretation of *Beowulf.* Just one example of the suggestions Battaglia makes in this section is that the monsters in the poem, all of them connected with watery places, are possibly related to earlier practices when bogs and lakes functioned as religious sites.

Geoffrey Russom analyses the metrical differences and similarities among the three Norse metres, *fornyrðislag, ljóðaháttr,* and *málaháttr.* As a point of comparison he uses the metre of *Beowulf.* Russom points out that Sievers's system of scansion sits very uncomfortably with Eddic metres, and uses instead the word-foot theory in which "the basic or paradigmatic expression of each verse type is a pair of words." This theory accommodates the verse types, both old and new, of Norse Eddic poetry in a much more natural way than Sievers's system. Russom's judicious use of quantification in the metrical analysis of his select corpus enables him to create a general picture in which the three Eddic metres on the one hand and that of *Beowulf* on the other each have a distinct profile of preferred metrical solutions. One of the results of the quantificational analysis is that *málaháttr* emerges as "a well-defined verse form with a distinct purpose: to accommodate traditional types and variants excluded by the other Eddic meters."

If H. G. Porthan had been able to use a time machine to travel to the early twenty-first century and read the essays in the present volume, he would certainly have appreciated Jonathan Roper's essay on differences and similarities between Finnic and Germanic versification. Porthan's major scholarly works include *De poësi Fennica,* one of the earliest studies to pay serious attention to Finnish folk poetry. Lauri Honko praises the skill Porthan shows in analyzing the traditional alliterative meter.[14]

Jonathan Roper comes to the conclusion that Finnic alliterative verse provides relevant comparative material for Old English and, to some extent, Middle English, alliterative verse. Comparison becomes relevant precisely because of the non-identity of the English and Finnic material: there are similarities but also differences. One particularly intriguing observation Roper makes is that the

---

[14] Lauri Honko, "Porthan suomalaisen runouden ja mytologian tutkijana" ['Porthan as a student of Finnish poetry and mythology'], in *Porthanin monet kasvot,* ed. Juha Manninen (Helsinki, 2000), 87–99.

'informal' style of Old English verse shows more obvious affinity with Finnic verse than with the 'classical' style of Old English verse. This can be seen, for example, in the genre of Old English charms with orally-based features. Roper ends his essay by suggesting new ways to interrogate the Anglo-Saxon poetic corpus. We know that in the Finnic tradition alternate singing is the rule. Was this also the case with the Anglo-Saxons? Roper asks further questions concerning genres that may have existed in the Anglo-Saxon period but have not survived, and concerning melodies used in the performance of Old English verse. In relation particularly to the process of metrical death and the adoption of end-rhyme, couplets, and stanzas, which took place in both the Finnic and the Anglo-Saxon culture, the more recent and well-documented Finnic development can possibly throw light on similar developments in England in the late Middle Ages.

It is probably fair to say that Russian scholars have so far played a minor role in the interpretation of early medieval Germanic literatures, although there are signs that the situation may change with the new rising generation. Jonathan Wilcox examines an interesting medievalist of the Soviet period, M.I. Steblin-Kamenskij, in order to explore "how Steblin-Kamenskij's discussions of Old Norse saga literature might be of value for interpreting Old English literature." Wilcox finds no real counterpart in Old English literature for the sagas. However, his tentative application to Old English literature of some of the key concepts of Steblin-Kamenskij yields interesting results. These concepts include the non-identity hypothesis, together with the terms 'syncretic truth' and 'ecclesiastical truth', the view of time as a continuum embracing the past, the present, and the future, and the concept of 'unconscious authorship'. Some of Steblin-Kamenskij's theoretical constructs sit uneasily when applied to Old English literature, while others provide useful insights. Wilcox concludes his essay with a criticism of Steblin-Kamenskij's analysis of medieval laughter.

It is mainly thanks to the efforts of the passionate collector Peter Dubrovsky (1756–1816) that the National Library of Russia in St Petersburg now boasts a marvellous collection of medieval insular manuscripts, including the so-called 'Leningrad Bede'.[15] George Hardin Brown's essay on this manuscript is an account of state-of-the-art research, by himself and other scholars, on this manuscript, one of the most valuable treasures of the National Library of Russia in St Petersburg. The essay also discusses previous research into the *Historia Ecclesiastica*, and includes discussion of editions. The gradually growing appreciation of the 'Leningrad Bede' as the most important and reliable witness of Bede's text is made very clear in Brown's discussion.

The vantage-point from which Barbara Yorke examines the Anglo-Saxons and the Vikings in her essay is different from that of the other essays in this

---

[15] See Margarita Logutova, "Insular Codices from Dubrovsky's Collection in the National Library of Russia," in *Ex Insula Lux: Manuscripts and Hagiographical Material Connected with Medieval England*, ed. Kilpiö and Kahlas-Tarkka, 93–98.

volume in that she analyses the attitudes of the Victorian period to the Anglo-Saxons in general and King Alfred in particular on the one hand, and on the other to the Vikings and their legacy. It turns out that the nineteenth century was full of conflicting ideas about the Vikings. The essay also shows in a fascinating way how Alfred and the Vikings were utilized according to the needs of Victorian politics, and how they were deployed in various attempts to build a national identity for Britons. For someone like Porthan, who was instrumental in creating the incipient Romantic feeling of Finnish nationhood, many of the Victorian sentiments discussed in Yorke's essay would probably have had great resonance.

The essays by Katrin Thier and Debby Banham have largely to do with the material culture of Anglo-Saxon England as compared with that of Scandinavia, though both cast their nets more widely, covering related practices and terminology elsewhere in Europe too and expanding the time-span of their discussion both forwards and backwards in time when necessary.

Of these two essays, Thier's is the more linguistically oriented, in its *Wörter und Sachen* type of approach. She subjects the technical terms connected with ships to close scrutiny, recognising cognates and more or less certain lexical borrowing between the Scandinavian languages and Old English. This borrowing takes place in both directions, albeit usually from Old Norse into Old English. Attention is also given to semantic borrowing, semantic change, and borrowing involving languages outside the Germanic group.

The purpose of Banham's essay is, according to her own formulation, "to assess the evidence for Scandinavian influence on Anglo-Saxon agriculture during the period of Viking settlement in England." The main emphasis of the essay is on the possible role of the Scandinavian settlers in reorganising arable land into open fields. Banham addresses a number of interrelated questions, discussing changes both in agricultural technology and the choice of crops as well as the introduction of the open field system and the motivation behind this innovation. After a rigorous analysis of both written and archaeological evidence, Banham is compelled to admit that Scandinavian innovativeness in Anglo-Saxon farming is hard to prove. Engagingly, she concludes her essay as follows: "[w]hile I would not like to suggest that Anglo-Saxon influence on Scandinavian agriculture is any more than a possibility, it does seem to me at least as plausible as that the major influence was in the opposite direction."

At the beginning of this introduction, I referred to the breadth and depth of the contacts between medieval Scandinavia and Anglo-Saxon England. Sometimes indeed these contacts are carved in stone, as for example the Scandinavian pronoun form *hanum* on the Aldbrough sundial. Quite often they have left traces which are difficult to interpret and evaluate—witness the ambiguity of Banham's conclusions. All the same, even if we term these traces "bad data," they have been an incentive, rather than an obstacle, to Anglo-Saxonists interested in different aspects of the theme "Anglo-Saxons and the North." The essays of this volume, varied as they are in their topics and approaches, all add to our understanding of variation and change within a culture as well as change and exchange resulting from contacts between cultures.[16]

---

[16] A recent—and monumental—addition to our knowledge of Ohthere's and Wulfstan's travels in their contexts is Irmeli Valtonen's dissertation *The North in the* Old English Orosius: *A Geographical Narrative in Context*. Helsinki: Mémoires de la Société Néophilologique de Helsinki LXXIII. 2008.

The Rök Stone through Anglo-Saxon Eyes

Joseph Harris

The Rök stone is a mighty slab of granite bearing a long inscription—the longest of any rune stone—in about 750 runes, with a text of interest to Anglo-Saxonists. It was raised as a memorial in the first half of the ninth century, as generally dated, or perhaps more precisely 810–820.[1] It stands now on the western edge of East Gautland (Östergötland, Sweden) near the great central lake Vättern; the chances are that it was originally positioned beside a segment of the royal route, the Eriksgata, where it crossed a small stream just north of the stone's present position in the churchyard of Rök, but a number of factors, including local place names apparently echoed in the inscription, make it unlikely that it has ever been moved far from its origin.[2]

An Anglo-Saxonist might be forgiven for assuming that this time and place—almost in the center of the old cultural settlement areas of Viking Age Sweden some three centuries before its conversion—would be an unlikely spot to find influence from the mainstreams of European civilization, but in this short contribution to our theme of Anglo-Saxons and the North, I will argue that as much as two-thirds of the narrative content of the inscription is ultimately due to West Germanic oral sources; I will not be concerned here with the last, purely native part of the inscription. These foreign elements are chiefly Low German,

---

[1] Ottar Grønvik, *Der Rökstein: Über die religiöse Bestimmung und das weltliche Schicksal eines Helden aus der frühen Wikingerzeit*, Osloer Beiträge zur Germanistik 33 (Frankfurt am Main, 2003), 92. This edition largely subsumes Grønvik's earlier article "Runeinnskriften på Rök-steinen," *Maal og minne* 3–4 (1983): 101–49 (on dating 139–40). I wish to thank the Netherlands Institute for Advanced Study where this article was conceived and written in 2005.

[2] Touched on by a number of scholars, e.g., Rune Palm, *Vikingarnas språk 750–1100* (Stockholm, 2004), 25; most fully by Bengt Cnattingius, "Var har Rökstenen ursprungligen stått?" *Fornvännen* 25 (1930): 116–19; more recently, see Jan Paul Strid, "Rökstenen, götarna och goterna," in *Språkets vård och värden: En festskrift till Catharina Grünbaum*, ed. Unn Hellsten (Stockholm, 2004), 286–96. A good website, "Eriksgatan i Östergötland," is to be found at <http://www.kulturarvostergotland.se/eriksgata/index.htm>.

Frankish, or Frisian, but Old English, too, has some indirect light to shed on this rich inscription.

Very little of my material here is unknown to Rök scholarship and much is debatable—*and debated* in the enormous scholarship on and around this famous text. I have read the major contributions—going back to the infinitely inventive Bugge and including the other pillars of Rök scholarship, von Friesen, Höfler, and Wessén[3]—many lesser contributions, and the most influential recent ones by Grønvik, Lönnroth, and Widmark, the three recent predecessors with whom I will most often agree or disagree here.[4] Except for popularizing writings and more or less objective surveys,[5] every interpreter has a somewhat, or radically, different take on the inscription as a whole and on indeterminable details. Many alternatives and almost all the strictly runological matters will have to be avoided

    [3] Sophus Bugge, *Der Runenstein von Rök in Östergötland, Schweden*, ed. Magnus Olsen, with contributions by Axel Olrik and Erik Brate (Stockholm, 1910); Otto von Friesen, *Rökstenen: Runstenen vid Röks kyrka Lysings härad Östergötland* (Stockholm, 1920); Otto Höfler, *Der Runenstein von Rök und die germanische Individualweihe*, Germanisches Sakralkönigtum 1 (Tübingen and Münster, 1952); Elias Wessén, *Runstenen vid Röks kyrka*, Kungl. vitterhets historie och antikvitets akademiens handlingar, filol.-filos. ser. 5 (Stockholm, 1958).

    [4] Grønvik, "Runeinnskriften"; idem, *Rökstein*; idem, "To viktige ord i Rök-innskriften: norr. gjalda vb og minni n.," *Arkiv för nordisk filologi* 105 (1990): 1–40; Lars Lönnroth, "The Riddles of the Rök-Stone: A Structural Approach," *Arkiv för nordisk filologi* 92 (1977): 1–57; Gun Widmark, "Varför ristade Varin runor? Tankar kring Rökstenen," in *Saga och Sed*, Kungl. Gustav Adolfs Akademiens årsbok 1992 (Uppsala, 1993), 25–43; idem, "Vamod eller Vämod," in *Nordiska orter och ord. Festskrift till Bengt Pamp på 65-årsdagen den 3 november 1993* (Lund, 1993), 210–12; idem, "Tolkningen som social konstruktion: Rökstenens inskrift," in *Runor och ABC: Elva föreläsningar från ett symposium i Stockholm våren 1995*, ed. Steffan Nyström (Stockholm, 1997), 165–75.

    [5] Sweden, where Rök is an industry, has produced quite a few learned and well-illustrated popular treatments; one very good one is Gun Widmark, "Varför Varin ristade: Rökstenens hemlighet," *Forskning & Framsteg: Populärvetenskapligt magasin* 5 (juli 1998): 16–22. Among surveys I mention in particular Thomas Birkmann, "6.2.5 Rök," in *Von Ågedal bis Mal: Die skandinavischen Runeninschriften vom Ende des 5. bis Ende des 9. Jahrhunderts*, Ergänzungsbände zum Reallexikon der Germanischen Altertumskunde 12 (Berlin and New York, 1995), 290–314; Hermann Reichert, "Runeninschriften als Quellen der Heldensagenforschung," in *Runeninschriften als Quellen interdisziplinärer Forschung: Abhandlungen des Vierten Internationalen Symposiums über Runen und Runeninschriften in Göttingen, 4–9 August 1995*, ed. Klaus Düwel et al. (Berlin and New York, 1998), 66–102; and Helmer Gustavson, "Rök," in *Reallexikon der Germanischen Altertumskunde* 25 (Berlin and New York, 2003), 62–72. The official website for Rök of the national antiquities office is <http://www.raa.se/sites/rokstone.asp>; but better views of the inscription are to be found on the Vadstena site <http://www.illustrata.com/pages/vadstena/vadstenakarta.html>. Also useful are the runology links of Uppsala University: <http://www.nordiska.uu.se/forskning/runlink.htm>.

here: one of the difficulties in writing economically about Rök is that so much that we "know," we know only through the scholarship; and it is difficult to say *anything* without saying *everything*.

Despite all differences of opinion, however, Rök scholarship does constitute an optimistic, even triumphant, tale of the gradual unlocking of an impressive word-hoard, and there is considerable agreement to build on. I see no reason for a literary Anglo-Saxonist to despair of arriving at a useful understanding.[6] The history of Rök scholarship shows two main interpretative trends; according to one the inscription is functional, an extended speech act of dedication, warning, incitement, or cursing; according to the other it is language with its illocutionary force suspended—that is, literature. My allegiance is to this second approach, along with most who have written since Wessén's trend-setting book of 1958, *Runstenen vid Röks kyrka*. The fact that we are dealing with literature is important too in explaining why the hermeneutics of Rök will continue to vary, perhaps evolving with the needs of the times and of the explicators.

The following outline of the contents and structure of Rök is strongly influenced by Lönnroth ("question/hint," or simply "question," substitutes for Lönnroth's "riddle"); the line numbers are those of Wessén:

Dedication (1–2): The stone is raised in memory of Vamoð[7] by his father Varin.
First narrative section (material about Theoderic) (3–11):
    First question/hint (3–5): Which two spoils were twelve times taken . . .?

---

[6] Cf., e.g., Gustavson, "Rök," 71; Reichert, "Runeninschriften," passim.

[7] I am persuaded by Widmark, "Vamod eller Vämod," to adopt this form of the son's name (representing what would be *Vámóðr in classical ON), rather than the more frequently used *Væmod* (=*Væmoð, Vémóðr, Vämod*, etc.). Widmark convincingly argues that a derivative of the root known in WScan as *vé* would have to be *vi-* in Östergötland. In fact, that root is so realized in Rök itself (*viavari*). Widmark (and Bugge, *Runenstein*, 3–4, before her) recognize problems with *wā-* as the root, however, and make no firm etymological proposal with a good parallel. In my opinion *wā-* 'woe, ill luck' (from a PrGmc *waiwō-*) is not semantically likely. I would propose instead the root surviving in Gothic *waihjo* 'kampf' and probably in ON *veig* 1 'kraft' (cf. Jan de Vries, *Altnordisches etymologisches Wörterbuch*, 2nd rev. ed. [Leiden, 1962], s.v.), with onomastic parallels like *Hermóðr*; cf. the probable etymology of *Váli* (*waihalaʀ, 'der kleine kämpfer' [de Vries, *Wörterbuch*, s.v.]). The unique name would thus be one of the "Gothic" relics (such as *Hraiðgutum*) in evidence in Rök. I adopt the OSw text (with changes where my interpretation demands them) from Wessén along with his conventions—vowel length is not marked—but also find it helpful occasionally to use OWN or OIcel. (ON) forms (following especially Grønvik). The translations in this article are my responsibility; in the text (only sporadically in the footnotes) I translate modern foreign languages except when reference to form or style (rather than content) predominates or the context is self-explanatory.

Second question/hint (5–8): Who died with the Hreiðgoths nine ages ago . . .?

Answer (9–11): Theoderic ruled . . . now he sits on his Gothic steed . . .

Second narrative section (unknown story of a battle and a brotherhood) (12–19):

First question/hint (12–14): Where is the battlefield on which twenty kings lie dead?

Second question/hint (14–17): Which twenty kings occupied Zealand four winters . . .?

Answer (17–19): List of five Valkis, etc. (totaling twenty plus four 'fathers')

[Line 20: damaged; perhaps an introduction to the third section]

Third narrative section (much disputed; probably a myth in a local form) (21–28):

First question/hint (21–22): Who among the Inguldings was compensated for . . .?

Second question/hint (23–24): To whom was an heir born . . .?

Answer (24–28): [content depends on order of lines and other factors]

As this overview suggests, Varin's memorialization of his son takes the form of a small anthology—not as grand as Charlemagne's famous lost collection of heroic poems presumably was, but at least preserved. How to begin appreciating it?

Anglo-Saxonists are accustomed to thinking in terms of thematic unity as an overriding quality of an art work composed out of disparate elements. We seek and find such unity in the Franks Casket's pictorial program, for example. That the programs propounded in detail disagree with each other does not undercut the principle; and some comfort for the discouraged resides in the common method and the occasional interpretive overlaps. If we are willing to see any cultural object as a "work of art," we have already assumed some degree of unity. Close behind the Casket comes *Deor*, with its panel structure and content echoes of the Casket. Here the refrain guarantees some kind of unifying principle in the selection of thumbnail narratives, whether of the optimistic troubles-overcome variety or of a darker vision of tragedy which passes away only because time sweeps all things away.[8] In *Widsith* the narrator's frame and the "yed," as Malone called the scop's autobiography, provide more organic unity, but encasing even more heterogeneous materials in the thulas and brief narrative vignettes.[9] Even when we are dealing with a "collection" (say, the *Beowulf* manuscript) rather than a "work of art," we are reluctant to yield too much to chance, and nothing as fine as the Exeter Book could be *entirely* random. Not that Nordicists do not also manifest the same rage for order and with similar reason; in its context and *in parvo* the Rök Stone is arguably almost as much a *summa litterarum* as *Beowulf*: it

---

[8] Joseph Harris, "'Deor' and Its Refrain: Preliminaries to an Interpretation," *Traditio* 43 (1987 [1989]): 23–53.

[9] Kemp Malone, *Widsith*, rev. ed., Anglistica 13 (Copenhagen, 1962).

gathers several genres in into one literary utterance, and it stands alone, without peers or imitators, in literary history.[10]

The stone has five inscribed faces, front, right side, back, left side, and top. What one might call the current standard edition (Grønvik, *Rökstein*) labels them A–E and numbers the lines by face (e.g., C1); I follow instead Wessén, who numbers the lines in a single series, a clearer model especially for textual study, but also labels the faces A–E, occasionally reminding us where the line is located by adding A–E to the line numbers. Like the Franks Casket, however, the faces do not align exactly with the "panels" or communicative units, and content is not neatly confined to either communicative units or to faces of the stone.

Two larger segments can be recognized depending on whether the rune carver employed the normal script of the time and place, a branch of the six-teen-rune futhark known as short-twig runes, or else employed some form of cipher. Lines 1–20 on sides A (1–10), B (11), and C (12–20) are in normal runes, but the ciphered sections begin also on C (21–22; 23–25 [with some short-twig exceptions]), continuing on D (26), and E (27 together with the top of C, line 28). There are, roughly speaking, three types of cipher used: C 21–22 are not in a genuine cipher at all but in the older, twenty-four-character futhark, though the rune carver has introduced distortions or arbitrary signs wherever a rune of the old series coincided exactly with one of the normal sixteen-character series and line 21 is upside-down—all presumably features designed to make read-ing more difficult. Line 23 is consistently in a type of cipher in which each rune stands for the rune following it in the fixed futhark order (as if A stood for B, B for C, etc.); line 24 complicates things by using normal runes in its first half and the shifted cipher in the second; line 25 also begins with normal runes, then passes into cipher, but now coordinates or numerical cipher, and the whole line is entered upside-down. In coordinates or numerical cipher the futhark is divided into three "families"; each rune can be designated by its coordinates, its position or number in the numbered "families." In l. 25 the realization of numerical ci-pher is fairly straightforward, but the remaining lines, all in number cipher, are increasingly tricky.

The runology of these encrypted lines, which was for the most part solved long ago by Bugge, is not our remit, nor is any detailed consideration of the arrangement of lines. It is evident, however, that while the first segment in normal runes (1–20) is meant to be relatively easily read, the second is arranged in increasingly difficult cipher. The order in which lines are to be read is of course a crucial part of a literary interpretation; but I believe that the standard order following Wessén's numbering is the most natural and best adapted to the stone and to the types of lettering. In

---

[10] Joseph Harris, *"Beowulf* in Literary History," in *Interpretations of Beowulf: A Critical Anthology*, ed. R. D. Fulk (Bloomington, 1991), 235–41 (original publ.: *Pacific Coast Philology* [1982]: 16–23).

FIGURE 1
Rök Stone, Side A (front), lines 1–8 vertical, 9–10 horizontal.
© Antikvarisk-topografiska arkivet (ATA), Riksantikvarieämbetet.

FIGURE 2
Rök Stone, Side B (right edge), line 11 (read from bottom).
© Antikvarisk-topografiska arkivet (ATA), Riksantikvarieämbetet.

8 JOSEPH HARRIS

FIGURE 3
Rök Stone, Side C (back), vertical framed lines = 12–20; horizontal bottom line = 21,
left vertical line (reading up) = 22; three up-slanted framing lines = 23–25; top line
with windmill runes = 28.

© Antikvarisk-topografiska arkivet (ATA), Riksantikvarieämbetet.

FIGURE 4
Rök Stone, Side D (left edge), line 26 (reads down).
© Antikvarisk-topografiska arkivet (ATA), Riksantikvarieämbetet.

FIGURE 5
Rök Stone, Side E (top), line 27.
© Antikvarisk-topografiska arkivet (ATA), Riksantikvarieämbetet.

any case, it carries us down almost to the conclusion of the ciphered section with little controversy—well beyond the concerns of this essay.

The bipartite character of the script, normal or ciphered, corresponds not only to legibility but to the comprehensibility of contents and to a division into something like heroic and religious material. The easily read first section is relatively uncontroversial, clearly dealing with humans of ancient times, not gods, while the murkier content of the enciphered part is generally understood to treat religious mysteries expressed in myth. This arrangement, but reversed with mythological poems followed by heroic poems, is found in the bipartite *Poetic Edda*, which Nordicists have not hesitated to interpret as a thematically organized "work of art" in our terms;[11] the Edda's twenty-nine fully quoted poems obviously contrast with the much smaller number of allusively invoked stories on Rök, but the principle of unity and the dual structure are similar. Rök has been frequently compared to the Gotland picture stones (especially of Period III, c. 800–1000) where a lower human and an upper divine register often dominate the picture field;[12] this comparison is perhaps the most revealing for Rök, but the thematic organization of the picture stones seems to be chiefly funereal, having to do with death and the afterlife even where they clearly integrate heroic stories such as that of Wayland.

The second narrative section

It is in the first and second narrative sections, the heroic part of Varin's anthology, that our West Germanic influence seems to occur. I begin with the second, where scholars have found a mixture of clarity and obscurity that seems to lead to no certain conclusions but where at least the West Germanic borrowings are simpler:

> First question/hint (12–14): *Þat sagum tvalfta, hvar hæstR se GunnaR etu vettvangi a, kunungaR tvair tigiR svað a liggia?* 'This I pronounce as twelfth: where does the steed of Gunn see food on the battlefield which twenty kings are lying on?'

> Second question/hint (14–17): *Þat sagum þrettaunda, hvariR tvair tigiR ku-nungaR satin at Siolundi fiagura vintur at fiagurum nampnum, burniR fiagu-*

---

[11] Heinz Klingenberg, *Edda—Sammlung und Dichtung*, Beiträge zur nordischen Philologie 3 (Basel, 1974); Joseph Harris, "Romancing the Rune: Aspects of Literacy in Early Scandinavian Orality," in *Atti*, Accademia Peloritana dei Pericolanti, classe di lettere, filosofia e belle arti 70, Anno accademico 265: 1994 (Messina, 1996): 109–40; Frands Herschend, "Codex Regius 2365, 4to—Purposeful Collection and Conscious Composition," *Arkiv för nordisk filologi* 117 (2002): 121–43.

[12] E.g., Wessén, *Runstenen vid Röks kyrka*, 70–72.

rum brøðrum? 'This I pronounce as thirteenth: which twenty kings sat on
Zealand for four winters under four names, sons of four brothers?'

Answer (17–19): *ValkaR fim, Raðulfs syniR, HraiðulfaR fim, Rugulfs syniR,
HaislaR fim, Haruðs syniR, KynmundaR fim, BernaR synir.* 'Five Valkis, sons
of Raðulf; five Hraiðulfs, sons of Rugulf; five Haisls, sons of Haruð; five
Kynmunds, sons of Bern.'

The first question/hint here (i.e., the 'twelfth'—my interpretation of the puzzling
enumeration with its gaps is close to that of Lönnroth and will become clear) essentially asks where the battlefield is (or will be) on which twenty kings are slain.
The steed of the valkyrie Gunn ('battle') is a wolf; the kenning is part of the beasts
of battle topos familiar in both Old English and Old Norse and later also in Middle High German. The syntax has been variously rendered (e.g., ". . . auf dem
Schlachtfeld sieht: so daß zwanzig Könige dort liegen"; "battlefield, where"[13]). The
relative is *svað*, as in 1. 4 and regularly in poetry ("so daß" seems questionable),
but *svað* is here postposed to follow the subject of the relative clause. This seems to
foreground the kings and to be a vestige of poetic usage.[14] The second question is
not explicit in asking the names of precisely the twenty dead kings of the preceding
question, but that is the inevitable interpretation; the question complicates the issue, however, by presenting them before death when they occupied (*satin*) Zealand
and by defining them through their organization and naming pattern. The answer
lists the names in language that approaches verse.

The treatments of this puzzling textual section in Rök literature are very
inconclusive (and are likely to remain so). Grønvik finds recent history here and
connects it with the death of Vamoð; the present tense in *liggia* (but this verb
depends for tense on *se*) is neither historical present (so Bugge and Wessén) nor
a future (in the magical revenge theory of von Friesen) but rather indicates "that
the battle mentioned here has just recently taken place and further that Vamoð
has fallen in this battle . . . Remarkably enough, Vamoð's fall is not explicitly
mentioned here."[15] Remarkable indeed, and I agree rather with Wessén that the
image of the battlefield and its present tenses is typical of *literature*;[16] yet Wessén
has relatively little to say about this section *as* literature.

Far better, and in fact the best that has ever been written about it, are Lönnroth's pages, although Höfler has also made important contributions to its piece-
by-piece elucidation.[17] Lönnroth assembles materials to argue that the twenty or,

---

[13] Grønvik, *Rökstein*, 61; Wessén, *Runstenen vid Röks kyrka*, 25; Lönnroth, "Riddles
of the Rök-Stone," 6 and, more poetically, 30.

[14] Bugge, *Runenstein*, 66.

[15] Grønvik, *Rökstein*, 62.

[16] Wessén, *Runstenen vid Röks kyrka*, 47.

[17] Lönnroth, "Riddles of the Rök-Stone," 32–38; Höfler, *Runenstein*, 296–344;
Höfler's original article on the Trelleborg analogy is not available to me: "Die Trelleborg

with the "fathers," twenty-four 'kings' (generally agreed to indicate 'sea-kings,' each commander of a ship, rather than national kings in a modern sense)[18] constitute berserk bands with animal affinities. Half the fathers' names contain the element 'wolf'; the other half, he argues, show bear affinities. A number of *fornaldarsagas* or narrative materials of this kind tell of similar bands; and one such tale (in *Hervarar saga, Ǫrvar-Odds saga*, and Saxo's *Gesta Danorum*) also preserves a thula of the names of the dead berserks quite comparable to Rök's: *Hervarðr, Hjǫrvarðr,/ Hrani, Angantyr*, etc. The 'two Haddingjar' of this thula (also in *Hyndluljóð*) are like-named brothers (or "brothers") resembling those of Rök. Wessén had spoken briefly and, as it seems, condescendingly of the material in this section as oral literature: "The whole was a narrative stuff which must have sufficed for tale-telling on many a winter evening." Lönnroth has strengthened the comparative material greatly and made the best effort yet at identifying "the general tale-type" to which it would have belonged.[19]

Lönnroth prudently does not give this "tale-type" a genre name, but he can only be speaking of a preliterary *fornaldarsaga* that was never recorded in writing (except here). His evidence is all at least four hundred years later than Rök (Saxo, c. 1200, being the earliest in writing), and the circumstances of his implicit story seem to reflect the high Viking Age. Höfler, for whom the inscription reflects not literature but life, was closer to the age of Rök in claiming that the mathematical organization of Viking Age fortresses of the Trelleborg (Zealand) type lay behind the symmetry and numbers of the kings. But if Rök is as early as generally thought and if its story material is as conservative as the context seems to imply, we are transported to a time before or at the beginning of the Viking Age as generally understood. Höfler's insight is of value but hard to integrate.

More important, in my opinion, is the fact, noticed by Höfler and others, if not in exactly these words, that the identical names of the "brothers" and the relationship to a common "father" reflect a social organization that substitutes for the family a *Männerbund*,[20] whether that of a war-band or a trading

---

auf Seeland und der Runenstein von Rök," *Anzeiger der Österreichischen Akademie der Wissenschaften*, Phil.-hist. Klasse, 85, Jahrgang 1948, Nr. 1 (Vienna, 1949): 9–37.

[18] See Grønvik, *Rökstein*, 66 for an explicit reference to a custom of according the viking ship's captain this title (though it contains the assumption that the persons so called are of royal blood, an unlikely criterion for the West Germanic 'kings').

[19] Wessén, *Runstenen vid Röks kyrka*, 49; Lönnroth, "Riddles of the Rök-Stone," 37. But in what follows on p. 37 Lönnroth pushes the riddling aspect to philologically unacceptable overinterpretation (as also on p. 29).

[20] Höfler, *Runenstein*, 296–344, esp. 302; Grønvik, *Rökstein*, 65. On *Männerbünde*, see for references Joseph Harris, "Love and Death in the *Männerbund*: An Essay with Special Reference to the *Bjarkamál* and *The Battle of Maldon*," in *Heroic Poetry in the Anglo-Saxon Period: Studies in Honor of Jess B. Bessinger, Jr.*, ed. Helen Damico and John Leyerle, Studies in Medieval Culture 32 (Kalamazoo, 1993), 77–114.

company—raiders and traders sometimes being two sides of the same group in our period. Such organizations submerge individuality to some extent, including onomastically; Grønvik sums up this aspect: "Saxo and modern Icelandic folktales, however, also tell of men who have joined together into a group where they may bear the same name."[21]

Probably the "hardest" evidence concerning this section is that on the origin of the names, which show at least a strong West Germanic strain. Von Friesen, whose extensive work on the names I depend on here, goes further: ". . . it seems that one should . . . draw the conclusion that the twenty kings [in fact he includes the 'fathers' here, for an actual total of twenty-four] are of non-Nordic origin."[22] I select just a few details. *Valki* (**ualkaʀ**) is very probably Frisian or North German; evidence for it in Scandinavia appears to begin in Schleswig in the fifteenth century, and it is very common in Frisian as far back as records go.[23] Rök's form **kunmuntaʀ** is almost equally conclusively West Germanic; the name appears once in Scandinavia as **kunimu(n)diu** on the Tjurkö bracteate of about 500,[24] but a highly portable object like a bracteate cannot show that a name is native to the place it was found. Otherwise, name types in **kunja-* and this particular name are very common in West Germanic. On **hraiþulfaʀ** the sources say "not found on Old West Norse ground in the older time but quite common in Norway after 1300" and unattested in Denmark; two Swedish rune stones have a form that von Friesen thinks may represent this name;[25] it is found 700–900 in middle

---

[21] Grønvik, *Rökstein*, 64 (and see references there to Höfler).

[22] Von Friesen, *Rökstenen*, 81; followed by Grønvik, "Runeinnskriften," 120–21.

[23] Von Friesen, *Rökstenen*, 76–78. Höfler, *Runenstein*, 337, n. 265 (and elsewhere), seeking animal-names for the kings, considers it possible that *Valki* belongs to *valr* m., poetic for 'hawk,' followed by Lönnroth, 33, n. 56 (with more Höfler citations); de Vries too (*Wörterbuch*, s.v. *Valki*) considers a *-ki* construction to *valr* possible. Rikard Hornby, "Fornavne i Danmark i Middelalderen," in *Personnavne*, ed. Assar Janzén, Nordisk kultur 7 (Stockholm, 1947), 210–11, just comments on the difficulty of telling Danish *-ki* diminutives from German *-ke*. But if Frisian, it is likely to be from the root of OHG *wala* 'choice' (not **walha-*), cf. Wala, abbot of Corvey, and Ansgar's superior (see below, nn. 32–33).

[24] Von Friesen, *Rökstenen*, 79–80; Wolfgang Krause and Herbert Jankuhn, *Die Runeninschriften im älteren Futhark*, I: Text, Abhandlungen der Akademie der Wissenschaften in Göttingen, Philol.-hist. Kl., 3. Folge, Nr. 65 (Göttingen, 1966), 272–74 (no. 136).

[25] Von Friesen, *Rökstenen*, 78–79, says of these forms, **hriþulfs** and **riþulf**, that they could "well go back to **Hræiðulfʀ* rather than to *Hríðulfʀ*" (78). But to have the i-rune here represent the diphthong *ai* would seem to call for more evidence. Note that names built on **hraip-* 'nest' in upper Germany run counter to von Friesen's (and Malone's) reservation of that name element to the old home and that *hríð* f. 'storm; attack' forms a satisfactory name element here; cf. the *Weder-Geatas* 'Storm-Geats' of *Beowulf*. Niels Åge Nielsen, *Runerne på Rökstenen*, Odense University Studies in Scandinavian Languages 2 (Odense, 1969), 29, finds this a better etymology than 'nest' for **hraiþ-*.

and upper Germany but apparently not in north Germany.[26] The name **haislaʀ** seems to have no other attestations; Bugge convincingly sees it as a compound with *-gisl* as the second element and *hanh-* as the first; continental names like *Hangbert* are "perhaps related."[27] Von Friesen finds its closest match in a German *Hahkis*. Among the fathers, **raþulf-** and **haruþ-** are well attested in Scandinavia but also in Anglo-Saxon and Old High German; **rukulf-**, for *Rugolf,* is not encountered as a proper name in the North but occurs in West Germanic, specifically Old High German.[28] The form **birnaʀ** is a special case discussed at length on runological grounds: obviously *Bjǫrn* is very common in the North, but von Friesen favors the idea that this form with **i** may represent the name found in older German *Berinus, Beren, Bern* and OE *Beorn.*[29] Thus two of the fathers' names are probably West Germanic, while the other two are attested in both north and west; the sons show two definitely West Germanic names and two where the evidence is inconclusive but compatible with West Germanic origin.[30]

Since all of these West Germanic names were or could have been carried by Frisians, von Friesen continues his explication of the second narrative section with the historical backgrounds of Frisian sea-enterprise and Frisian-Swedish

---

[26] Von Friesen, *Rökstenen*, 79, could be wrong in taking Frisian names like *Redulf* for an "umlauted by-form of *Rodolf*"; OE *Hrēda* (*Widsith* l. 120; Malone, *Widsith*, 174) from **hraið-* implies an OFris form that could be represented by *Red-*.

[27] Bugge, *Runenstein*, 78–79.

[28] Von Friesen, *Rökstenen*, 75.

[29] Von Friesen, *Rökstenen*, 73–75.

[30] Von Friesen, *Rökstenen*, 81. The problematic form for the island seat of the twenty kings, **siulunti**, ought at least to be mentioned here. The chief discussions are Grønvik, *Rökstein*, 90; with further bibliography in "Runeinnskriften," 138, 147, n. 88 (esp. Nielsen there); and Bugge, *Runenstein*, 69–71. The etymology must go back to **selh-undi* 'seal-island' to explain early forms like skaldic *Selund*; later folk-etymology substituted both parts of the compound resulting in 'sea-land,' ON *Sjóland* etc. But Rök's **iu** cannot represent *jǫ*, the breaking of *e* before *-u-*, because Rök spells that diphthong **ia** (e.g., *fiaru*); so Grønvik accounts for **siulunti** as a transitional form in which folk-etymology has already replaced the first element but not yet the second. This is plausible, but it would be expected that the first element to be replaced would be the unanalyzable *-und-*, known only as a place-name element for islands but having no free morphemes to be related to. (Cf. Eva Nyman, *Nordiska ortnamn på -und*, Acta Academiae Regiae Gustavi Adolphi 70 [Uppsala, 2000], 156, 460–64.) An alternative explanation: an English (OE *seol* < **selh-*) or Frisian etymology, where *e* breaks before l+consonant, would produce the correct phonology for the Rök spelling. However, OFris breaking is assumed rather than attested (Wilhelm Heuser, *Altfriesisches Lesebuch mit Grammatik und Glossar*, Sammlung germanischer Elementarbücher, 3. Reihe [Heidelberg, 1903], §24). Von Friesen, *Rökstenen*, 69–71, attempts, torturously and unsuccessfully, to derive **siulunti** from the border district of Frisia and Jutland, called in OE *Sillende* and in Carolingian Latin *Sinlendi*; the WGmc connection is worth noting.

trade.[31] Some main points, partly from von Friesen: "the seafaring, trade- and piracy-practicing Frisians" had an important role in early Sweden, perhaps as founders of Birka, certainly as major players in trade and religion there in the eighth and ninth centuries. The *Vita Ansgarii* speaks of Swedes visiting Dorestad, the great "emporium" of the Rhine-mouths region in the eighth and ninth centuries, which enjoyed an established trade connection with Birka. In particular Rimbert lets an individual speak in the Swedish assembly in favor of allowing Ansgar's priests to remain; this elder happens to mention that "[s]ome of us who on various occasions have been to Dorstadt have of our own accord adopted this form of religion . . .," casually suggesting the frequency of such contacts in human rather than archeological (coins, import wares) terms.[32] The route between Dorestad and Birka lay through Haithabu, where an early colony of Frisian settlers is attested; Ansgar himself, after starting from Cologne, traveled this route as far as Denmark on his first mission (chap. 10) and later. In the life of Ansgar we read not only of the Swedish "ambassadors" who came to Louis the Pious requesting a missionary in 829 (chap. 9), but also of Ansgar's return from Birka bearing written royal documents in Swedish characters to the emperor and a similar "token" to the Swedish king entrusted to Ansgar by his friend the Danish king in Haithabu.[33] Ansgar and his associates ministered to the Christians in Birka; and the story of a wealthy Christian woman there, Frideburg, who sent her daughter to Dorestad to expend moneys for the soul of her mother (chap. 20), illustrates the cultural connections to Frisian territory. More recent treatments of "Friesenhändel" and "Birka" generally support the views briefly sketched from von Friesen or directly from Rimbert.[34]

Von Friesen modulates from history to his own fiction as he imagines an actual group of Frisian merchant-venturers, who like guild-men had taken oaths

---

[31] Von Friesen, *Rökstenen*, 81–83.

[32] Charles H. Robinson, *Anskar: The Apostle of the North*, Lives of Early and Mediæval Missionaries (London: Society for the Propagation of the Gospel in Foreign Parts, 1921), 93 (chap. 27); *Vita Ansgarii auctore Rimberto*, ed. G. Waitz, Scriptores rerum Germanicarum in usum scholarum ex Monumentis Germaniae Historicis recusi (Hannover, 1884; repr. 1977), 58 (chap. 27).

[33] *Vita Ansgarii: et cum litteris regia manu more ipsorum deformatis* (chap. 12, p. 33); *iam dicti regis Horici missum pariter et signum secum habuit* (chap. 26, p. 55); Robinson, *Anskar*, 49; 89.

[34] Among many possible works on this large background subject, I name: St[éphane] Lebecq, "Friesenhandel," in *Reallexikon der Germanischen Altertumskunde* 10 (Berlin, 1998), 69–80; B[irgit] Arrhenius and E[mil] Schieche, "Birka," in *Reallexikon der Germanischen Altertumskunde* 3 (Berlin and New York, 1978), 23–28; Herbert Jankuhn, "Karl der Große und der Norden," in *Karl der Große: Lebenswerk und Nachleben*, ed. Helmut Beumann (Düsseldorf, 1965), 1: 699–707. See now Michael McCormick, *Origins of the European Economy: Communications and Commerce, A.D. 300–900* (Cambridge, 2001), 562–64, 606–13, 670–74.

of brotherhood: perhaps it was on their trade mission to the Swedish coast that matters turned violent and Vamoð fell. (Grønvik adopts this fiction without the Frisian emphasis.) Von Friesen attributes the numerical symmetries "perhaps" to the runemaster: "and [this] can very well be his way of conceiving and representing the information he happened to have picked up about [the Frisians]."[35] But the text makes no connection between Vamoð and the "Frisians" or sea-kings, and the symmetrical patterning is more satisfactorily explained as an oral-literary layer than by personal psychology.

That we are dealing with literature rather than real life is made highly likely by the thula of names, a genre very old in West Germanic oral literature and well known to Anglo-Saxonists from *Widsith*. The one literary model Rök scholarship has so far offered, Lönnroth's, is arguably anachronistic and unsuited to incorporate the Frisian, or at least West Germanic, names (a feature unmentioned by Lönnroth); its internal evidence of wolf and bear affinities is very debatable, and it is just this feature that connects best to the *fornaldarsaga* "tale-type." Most damaging of all, however, it does not accommodate the feeling many scholars have had that some trace, proximate or distant, of a historical reality underlies the hints of proto-Trelleborg type organization, the typical *Männerbund* features, the setting on Zealand, and the fact that the only actual event is a single devastating battle.

We might just consider as an alternative model a form of oral-literary tradition grounded in reality and contemporary with Varin, praise-poetry about contemporary events and the oral information required to understand it — better known under the German terms *Preislied/Zeitgedicht* and *Begleitprosa*. Of course, this would depend on an exercise unpopular today, a Heuslerian comparative/reconstructive approach from preserved descendants in skaldic poetry and in West Germanic, chiefly *The Battle of Brunanburh* and OE chronicle verse; *The Battle of Maldon*; and *Ludwigslied*.[36] But such a model would account for the slightness of a "story" that focuses on one battle and a few attendant facts, as well as for the distinctly skaldic "steed of Gunn" and the beast(s) of battle; in particular the careful numbering of the dead kings and their naming is reminiscent of this literary milieu. *Brunanburh* (which also pictures the beasts *after* battle as in skaldic verse)[37] specifies that *Fife lægun / on þam campstede, cyningas giunge, / sweordum aswefede, swilce seofene eac / eorlas Anlafes, unrim heriges, / flotan and Sceotta* (28b–32a; 'Five young kings lay dead on that battlefield, put to sleep by swords, likewise seven of Anlaf's earls as well, a countless number of the host, of shipmen

[35] Von Friesen, *Rökstenen*, 82.

[36] Andreas Heusler, *Die altgermanische Dichtung*, 2nd rev. ed. (Potsdam, 1941), esp. 123–50.

[37] Joseph Harris, "Beasts of Battle, South and North," in *Source of Wisdom: Old English and Early Medieval Latin Studies in Honour of Thomas D. Hill*, ed. Charles Wright et al. (Toronto, 2007), 3–25.

and Irishmen') and names two of the defeated allies, Anlaf and Constantine—a fairly close content analogue to our first question/hint.[38] The *Maldon* poet presumably did not know any of the vikings' names and gives no body count, but he does memorialize the English by name. Among the skaldic poems of this type, I think first of the fragmentary *Eiríksmál* (c. 954), which breaks off when Eric Bloodaxe is quizzed at the door to Valhǫll about the dead who accompany him after his last battle: *Konungar eru fimm*—*sagði Eiríkr*—, / *kenni ek þér nafn allra, / ek em hinn sétti siálfr* (st. 9; 'Five are the kings, said E., I will teach you the names of all; I am myself the sixth')—if the poem were complete the five kings would have been named. The "Battle of Hafrsfjǫrð"-section of the composite and fragmentary *Haraldskvæði* (the single poem Heusler nominates as most likely to be representative of the common Germanic eulogistic type) names *Kjǫtvi* and *Haklangr* (only the latter explicitly dead) but generalizes *Valr lá þar á sandi* (st. 12; 'The dead lay there upon the sand').[39] In the Rök text the numerical arrangement has been stylized by oral transmission and any actual *Zeitgedicht* absorbed into its story or at least not cited (unless in the kenning and diction of the first question/hint).

The recapitulating thula seems at first glance an excrescence, not a feature of the *Zeitgedicht* style but of the related historical *Merkdichtung*. But let us pause on the *Widsith* analogy. Widsith is the type of the early Germanic court poet, South Germanic ancestor of the skald; his trade is praise of kings, which is echoed (along with praise of such poets) by the framework of the poem *Widsith*. No single example of a *Preislied/Zeitgedicht* is quoted, however, and the bulk of the poem *Widsith* is comprised of thulas, historical name lists. Who was the audience for such a verse catalogue? Heusler seems to think that the catalogues themselves were presented in the halls;[40] I am not so sure, since the thula (which, by the way, can be used to systematize *any* set of nouns, not only of historical significance) is by nature a retrospective memorial device, hardly entertaining to a king though perhaps presentable as the *Programmheft* of heroic, historical material to follow. In any case, it is clear that in *Widsith*, as in the second section of Rök, the *Zeitgedicht* and its normally elite milieu converge with the humble thula in a single literary context.

The West Germanic names have survived as a set because somewhere behind this Rök passage there was an actual event, something like the end of a Frisian

[38] Egil Skalla-Grímsson's long praise-poem (*drápa*) on Æþelstan after the same battle mentioned only three dead kings, to judge by the single preserved stanza. A full survey of skaldic praise-poems which are also *Zeitgedichte* would be useful in the present argument but has not been possible in the time available.

[39] Heusler, *Die altgermanische Dichtung*, 128. Skaldic poems are quoted from Jón Helgason, *Skjaldevers*, Nordisk filologi, ser. A, 12 (Copenhagen, 1962), Old English from ASPR, 6.

[40] Heusler, *Die altgermanische Dichtung*, 89, 92.

trading post. Heusler expressed in various places a skeptical interest in putative transformational relationships between praise-poetry/*Zeitgedichte* and heroic poetry, how presumably occasional and descriptive poems passed into narrative legendary fiction.[41] Possibly in this section of Rök we have a record of a medial stage of material that never became fully-fledged legendary fiction or was unrecorded at that stage. I can point to only one study of this kind of transformation in the early Middle Ages, namely Heusler on the transmission of knowledge about Hygelac's raid on the Rhineland,[42] and of course the difference is that *Beowulf* did record the final phase of development. But imagination of the afterlife of *Preislieder/Zeitgedichte* need not be limited to the strict realm of the Heuslerian heroic poem; traditions in ordinary language (saga) and chansons de geste have both been linked to such historical poems.[43]

The first narrative section (Theoderic)

First question/hint (3–5): *Sagum mǫgminni þat: hværiaʀ valraubaʀ vaʀin tvaʀ þaʀ, svað tvalf sinnum vaʀin numnaʀ at valraubu, baðaʀ saman a ymissum mannum?* 'I pronounce this *mǫgminni*: Which were the two war-spoils which, both together, were taken twelve times in booty-taking from different men?'

Second question/hint (5–8): *Þat sagum annart: hvaʀ fur niu aldum an urði fiaru meðʀ Hraiðgutum, auk tomiʀ en umb sakaʀ?* 'This I pronounce as second: Who became without life (died) among the Hreiðgoths nine ages ago, and yet his affairs are still under discussion?'

Answer (9–11):   *Reð Þioðrikʀ hinn þurmoði,*
                  stilliʀ flutna, strandu Hraiðmaraʀ.
                  Sitiʀ nu garuʀ a guta sinum,
                  skialdi umb fatlaðʀ, skati Mæringa.

---

[41] For example, Heusler, *Die altgermanische Dichtung*, 156–57, 162. Heusler was unwilling to draw Tacitus's Arminius passage into the picture (124), but others have seen the 'still sung' historical poems as the kernel of the Sigurd tale.

[42] Heusler, *Die altgermanische Dichtung*, 125. A contemporary approach and recent bibliography may be found in Augustine Thompson, "Rethinking Hygelac's Raid," *English Language Notes* 38 (2000–2001): 9–16.

[43] Cf. Hermann Schneider, *Germanische Heldensage*, 3 vols., Grundriß der germanischen Philologie 10/1–3 (Berlin and Leipzig, 1928–1934), 1: 15–19; 2.2: 137 (mostly skeptical).

'ÞioðrikR the bold, ruler of sea-warriors, (once) ruled the shore of the Gothic Sea. Now he sits outfitted on his Gothic steed, with his shield buckled
on, prince of the Mærings.'

This is the most familiar part of the Rök inscription to Anglo-Saxonists; one
learned intervention by our own Kemp Malone gives a characteristically intri-
cately reasoned alternative to the usual reading. But the widely accepted interpretation of the answer here yields Theoderic the Great, the Dietrich von Bern of
later heroic legend, as the subject of the poem. The structural logic of the whole
section means that the questions must have to do with the far-flung material associated with him.

I begin with the second question/hint, which, as I understand it, asks the
essential question that the Rök collector sees in the Theoderic material: Who
died nine ages ago but is still hotly debated today? Almost every element here is
controversial. The word *fiaru*, for example, is genuinely ambiguous; formally it
could be ON *fiara* 'shore' or ON *fjǫr* (OE *feorh*), a u-stem. The preposition gov-
erning this noun, *an*, could be 'on (the shore)' or 'without (life),' but *urði* (or *yrði*)
'became' fits better into a periphrasis for 'died.' (Höfler offered a third interpretation that also is not impossible: 'he became on life' = he was born.) The temporal
relationships in the verse answer (he 'ruled'; now he 'sits') argue strongly for 'died'
in the second question, which, as I interpret it, contains the same opposition and
sense of wonder: he died nine ages ago, and (yet) something concerning him still
(*æn*, ON *enn*) goes on.

After *auk* the rune sequence **tumiRąnubsakaR** has been transcribed and divided into words in two main ways: **tu miR ąn ub sakaR** or **tumiR ąn ub sakaR**.
The first yields Wessén's *do meðR hann umb sakar* 'died with (them = *Hraiðgutum*)
he for his offence'; here there is no contrast of tenses and a superfluous and awkward "hann." More recent expositors have followed Höfler in interpreting the
second transcription as ON *dœmir enn um sakar*, but this improved syntax, which
also gives the rhetorical contrast of then and now, can still be variously interpreted according to an overall view of the section and the text as a whole. Lönnroth
(whose pages on this section are again the richest in analogues), seeking an ap-

propriate meaning for *dæma um sakar* and choosing his words carefully, finds 'put up a fight' in relevant eddic phrases.[44] But on the same page his final phrasing has become "and still (yet) is ready for battle"; this clearly anticipates the poem (in his interpretation) rather than reflecting the question. To 'put up a fight' or *deila sakar* (which is approximately 'get into a violent quarrel') is easily distinguished from 'be ready for battle' (cf. *garuʀ*), and I must also doubt the interpretation of the eddic passages.

Here I prefer Grønvik, who looks closely at the eddic and other evidence and comes to the conclusion: (1) that *dæma* in several comparable passages means 'speak about some subject, discuss something, make judgments' and (2) *sǫk* means 'matter under dispute, legal case' while (3) the verb here is impersonal: 'and there is still discussion of his affairs.' This can be taken simply to mean that though Theoderic died long ago, he still lives in the memory of tale-tellers, which certainly fits with that hero's huge reputation. But *dæma um sakar* tempts one to sharpen the meaning. Theoderic had a mixed reputation, condemned by the church (he was an Arian, executed Boethius, etc.) but celebrated in oral tradition (unfairly exiled, justly reconquers, kills monsters, etc.). In some cases the church's attitude reaches into vernacular literature (an example below), and the Rök stone's formula *dæma um sakar* may well indicate an awareness of these disparate opinions.[45]

In view of the very close relationship we will see between *Deor* 18–19a and Rök's Theoderic verse, it seems to me worthwhile to speculate further over the possibility of a link between 19b: *Þæt wæs monegum cuþ* and the idea of *dæma um sakar*. The OE certainly means that Þeodric's affairs (*sakar*) were well known; but the tense is past, so the phrase cannot easily mean 'were well known and still are.' If the thirty years of *Deor* 18b refer to the legendary exile (rather than to the historical rule), then the tone is probably sympathetic; but the next stanza concerns another Gothic king, Eormanric, who was 'grim,' and the public mentioned there (24–26), structurally comparable to the public in *monegum*, wishes him dead. In that light, could 19b imply 'known to many (to their cost)' and so

---

[44] Wessén, *Runstenen vid Röks kyrka*, 25; Höfler, *Runenstein*, 37–42; Lönnroth, "Riddles of the Rök-Stone," 26.

[45] Grønvik, *Rökstein*, 54–55 concludes: "Die Rökinschrift kann an dieser Stelle vielleicht so ausgelegt werden, daß die Häuptlinge von Östergötland über diesen Konflikt zwischen volkstümlicher und kirchlicher Tradition bezüglich Theoderichs des Großen vermutlich gut unterrichtet waren, insbesondere daß seine 'Sachen' und Streitigkeiten noch immer in Gespräch seien." The point is supported by Erik Brate, "Rökstenen och Teoderikstatyn i Aachen," *Eranos: Acta Philologica Suecana* 15 (1915): 71–98, at 74, despite a different interpretation of the other debatable passages here. Earlier Grønvik, "Runeinnskriften," 139–40, was still more emphatic about all the Aachen connections: "Denne overraskende presise opplysning ['nine generations'] stammer sikkert ikke fra hjemlig sagntradisjon, men fra latinkyndige klerker og historiografer."

reflect Theoderic's divided fame? Answerable perhaps only in the context of an interpretation of *Deor* as a whole.

The phrase 'nine ages (or generations) ago' is remarkable in that it is close to the truth. Theoderic died in 526; at 30 years per generation, we arrive at 796; at 33 per generation, at 823. These facts are uncontroversial in Rök scholarship unless we relate them (with Brate) to the hypothetical visit to Aachen (below) as a part of the Frankish influence.[46] 'Nine ages' certainly has a folk-poetic ring, but I cannot believe that the accuracy is accidental: heroic tradition has here been tainted by some brush with historical lore.

Once the first question/hint is firmly attached to Theoderic the Great, it seems less cryptic. For as Lönnroth so well shows, early Germanic literature is full of allusions to war-booty (OE *wæl-reaf* = *val-raub-*), technically the war-gear a victor strips from the dead body of a victim—the swords and treasure that have complex histories of their own—like the torque given by Wealhtheow to Beowulf, by him to Hygd and by her to Hygelac, stripped from Hygelac by Dæghrafn and from him again by Beowulf. The scene of the stripping of armor is a deeply moving one, as its reflection in the *Hildebrandslied* (55–62) suggests. Lönnroth makes it probable that the treasures alluded to in the first question are Theoderic's sword Mim(m)ing and his horse Falka, but the section refers "to a legend not only about Theoderic himself but also about the two spoils mentioned in the first riddle. It does not matter whether we think of these spoils as 'horse and shield' or 'sword and shield.'"[47]

The verse, often said simply to be a stanza of *fornyrðislag*, does fall within the attested parameters of that meter, but it is noteworthy that its first half-line seems to have three syllables. It has been suggested that this is a transitional stage toward *kviðuháttr* (a 3-syllable on-verse followed by a 4-syllable off-verse); and one might suppose that a funerary nexus links this line to the *kviðuháttr* poems *Ynglingatal* and *Sonatorrek*.[48] But a more direct tie is the diction and content of a passage of *Ynglingatal* regularly compared with our stanza: *Réð Óláfr / ofsa forðum / víðri grund / of Vestmari . . . Nú liggr gunndiarfr / á Geirstǫðum / herkonungr / haugi ausinn.* 'Olaf ruled extremely (?) long ago the broad land about Vestmar . . . Now the battle-bold one lies at Geirstaðir, a warrior-king buried in his mound.'[49] The contrast of then and now, the ruler and his resting place, offer seductive parallels to Rök, and the verb *réð* (from *ráða* 'to rule') persuades most Rök scholars

[46] Grønvik, *Rökstein*, 59; Brate, "Rökstenen och Teoderikstatyn," 75.

[47] Lönnroth, "Riddles of the Rök-Stone," 28–29; 29–30.

[48] Hallvard Lie, "Kviðuháttr," in *Kulturhistorisk leksikon for nordisk middelalder* 9 (Oslo, 1964): coll. 559–61, at 561. In fact, Lie considers l. 5 also to have three syllables, thus: "the first verse in each half-strophe has three syllables"—an observation that strengthens the idea of a transitional form. But see note 62 below.

[49] *Ynglingatal* in Snorri Sturluson, *Ynglingasaga*, ed. Elias Wessén, Nordisk filologi, ser. A, 6 (Copenhagen, 1954), 51 (st. 35–36).

that Rök's *raið* here has to be explained philologically as equivalent to *réð*. Von Friesen has an extensive discussion of such spellings, but Grønvik holds to the verb *ríða*.[50] I have been tempted to think of the (vastly later, of course) ballad formula where a song opens with a hero riding over the strand; the overall sense of the stanza and section would be little changed with either verb. But the majority of Rök scholars are convinced by *réð* in the *Ynglingatal* parallel.

The *Hreiðgotar* are well known to Anglo-Saxonists; the *Hrǣda* gen.pl. of *Widsith* 120 is short for **Hrǣdgotan* and the exact OE equivalent of Rök's *Hraiðgutum*. The OE names in *hrēð-* 'honor' (related to *hrōðor*, *hrōð-* by i-umlaut) represent a separate etymological family but are probably confused in the two spellings of Hreðel's name with the *hrǣd-* root.[51] The honoring epithet *hrēð-* is applied to Eormanric in *Widsith* 7 (*Hrēðcyninges* gen. sg., probably from a **Hrēðgotena cyning*) and directly to his Goths in l. 57. Malone holds that *Widsith* makes the distinction between the 'nest-Goths' (so von Friesen's persuasive etymology of **hraiþ-*), who remained behind in the ancient "nest" of the Goths at the Vistula mouth, and the *Hrēðgotan* in south-eastern Europe. When the honorific is applied to the Geats, in the *first* "nest" (*Hrēþ-manna* gen. pl. [*Beowulf* 445]), a folk etymology might be responsible.[52] Von Friesen consistently took *Hraiðmarr* to mean the sea of the 'nest'-(Goths), the Baltic, and the *Hraiðgutum* among whom the section's *Þioðrikʀ* died (or came ashore) to refer to their second "nest" on the Vistula, and Malone (consistent with his *Widsith* elucidations) followed with the east Baltic setting; but if we are dealing with the Ostrogoth Theoderic the Great—and the evidence for that is too strong to deny—then the *Hraiðmarr* has to be the Adriatic (cf. 'Vandal Sea' in *Hildebrandslied*). The explanation must be that the Goths took their "nest" terminology with them, and all tradition has not been as consistent as *Widsith*.

A similar but more complex problem is presented by *skati Mæringa*. The reminiscence of *Deor*'s *Þeodric ahte þritig wintra / Mæringa burg* (18–19a) is overwhelming, and the two Theoderics have to be the same. But Malone identified both as Theoderic the Frank, a slightly younger contemporary of Theoderic the Great, and in the windy reaches of later heroic literature both are exiles and both can be plausibly tied somehow to a fortress of the Mærings; perhaps the Frank had the earlier claim on it, but in the course of time there was a good deal of exchange between the legends. Malone has some good points, and it would take a long and intricate argument to try to refute him thoroughly, but I would like

---

[50] Von Friesen, *Rökstenen*, 42–43 (and cf. Widmark, "Vamod eller Vämod," 211); Grønvik, *Rökstein*, 57.

[51] Malone, *Widsith*, 174. I cannot accept Malone's idea of a name (*Hrēþel*) plus a surname (*Hrǣdl[a]*) in lieu of a simple confusion (174).

[52] Malone, *Widsith*, 175; von Friesen, *Rökstenen*, 108–34.

to point out two flaws that can be handled economically.[53] To construct a legend which places Theoderic the Frank in the east Baltic Malone imagined Gautish tradition as preserving an intermediate stage between, on the one hand, the historical facts of Hygelac's raid on the Rhineland, in which the Geatish king was killed by the forces of Theoderic, son of Clovis, and, on the other, the high medieval (Snorri) tradition about the death of Hugleikr at home in Sweden at the hands of the invading sea-king Haki.

The hypothetical mid-stage has Hygelac die at home in Gautland, but the invader keeps his real name. Here is Malone's translation: "This I say second, who nine generations ago landed on the shore among the Hreiðgoths and he is spoken of in a poem: Þiaurikr the bold, the sea-king, rode (or ruled) on the strand of the Hreiðmarr; now he sits on his horse, his shield slung about him, the chieftain of the Mærings."[54] We can ignore the reference to a poem, unexplained and unjustified, but not important here.[55] (1) But how could Malone have allowed "ruled" for the invader who killed the Gautish king? And why are the Gauts celebrating Theoderic at all? The constructions of legendary history were Malone's specialty, and I do not object in principle; on the contrary, the fact that his middle stage is so thin in events and fits so poorly the runic evidence proves how consistently Malone operated when trying to track a story. But the contradiction between Malone's story and the written evidence of glorification in Rök's Theoderic section is simply glaring. (2) The Rök verse is so reminiscent of a famous statue that Malone does not try to deny the resemblance. To save his argument he imagines that "the poet whom the runemaster is quoting had visited Aachen and, naturally enough, had taken for a statue of Theoderic the Frank the Theoderic statue which he saw in the Frankish capital."[56] Naturally enough? Three hundred years after the death of the lesser Theoderic? An unmotivated mistake of this scale is hardly reliable method in the study of legendary history.

In fact, the striking match between the statue and the verse constitutes a solid piece of the Rök puzzle. This connection entered the literature on Rök as early as 1889, so I will give only the briefest account. In 801 Charlemagne had a great

[53] Kemp Malone, "The Theodoric of the Rök Inscription," in *Studies in Heroic Legend and Current Speech*, ed. Stefán Einarsson and Norman E. Eliason (Copenhagen, 1959), 116–23 (originally *Acta Philologica Scandinavica* 9 [1934]: 76–84). For a good, brief account of the Mæring problem, see Anne L. Klinck, *The Old English Elegies: A Critical Edition and Genre Study* (Montreal, 1992), 165–66.

[54] Malone, "Theodoric," 117.

[55] Malone probably had in mind Hugo Pipping, "Zur Deutung der Inschrift auf dem Runenstein von Rök," *Acta Philologica Scandinavica* 4 (1929–1930): 250–51; but by 1934 Pipping had partly changed his mind: "Om Rökstenens ąnurþifiaru," *Lunder Germanistische Forschungen* 1 (1934): 265–72 (=*Studia Germanica tillägnade Ernst Albin Kock den 6 december 1934* [Lund]).

[56] Malone, "Theodoric," 118.

bronze gilded equestrian statue of Theoderic the Great moved to Aachen from Ravenna. There were actually several statues of Theoderic in Italy, but this one in particular is described by Agnellus of Ravenna as having a shield hung over the shoulder. The statue was relocated outside Charles's palace in a spot that was easily visited, as we learn from a poem, *De imagine Tetrici*, written about it by one of Louis the Pious' visiting ecclesiastics, the well-known Walahfrid Strabo; the poem, which is critical of Theoderic and his statue and perhaps by implication of Louis for tolerating it, dates from 829.[57] The statue, which must have been the first of its kind north of the Alps, is somehow, most Rök scholars would agree, the inspiration for the *fornyrðislag* stanza; the question is how to conceive that influence. Wessén thinks (like Heusler) that the stanza is not original with the Rök inscription but a quotation, but he adds that it cannot be older than 801.[58]

Lönnroth points out a passage in the great compendium of Theoderic lore and tales, the German/Norwegian *Þiðreks saga*, written about 1250, a passage about Theoderic having had statues of himself with horse and sword made in Rome. Lönnroth comments: "This story about Theoderic 'immortalizing' himself and his celebrated possessions probably existed in oral tradition long before the Rök inscription was made. The Theoderic stanza could be based on such tradition. It is thus not necessary to suppose that the author of the stanza had become acquainted with the newly erected statue in Aachen." This idea and the supporting citation are new and valuable in Rök scholarship, but I am not convinced. The late Dietrich lore is not at all untouched by ecclesiastical influence, and without the Rök stanza there would be no justification for projecting this information (hardly a story) back so far. Then too this passage concerns Theoderic's vanity whereas the Rök stanza is glorifying ekphrasis, for Heusler a *Denkmalepigramm*: "an epigram for a memorial, hardly part of a larger whole."[59]

---

[57] As far as I know, there is no connection between Strabo's poem and Rök except the possible shared experience of seeing the statue, shared knowledge of Theoderic's mixed reputation, and, if it counts, the question-answer format; but Bugge, *Runenstein*, 44, noted the first line of the poem's main description of the statue: *Tetricus Italicis quondam regnator in oris*, which he cited in the context of deciding for *réð* over *reið* in *réð Þjóðrikr . . . strandu Hreiðmarar*. Cf. Brate, "Rökstenen och Teoderikstatyn," 79–80 and passim. For some modern work on Strabo's poem see Michael Herren, "The 'De Imagine Tetrici' of Walahfrid Strabo: Edition and Translation," *Journal of Medieval Latin* 1 (1991): 118–39; idem, "Walahfrid Strabo's *De Imagine Tetrici*: An Interpretation," in *Latin Culture and Medieval Germanic Europe*, ed. Richard North and Tette Hofstra, Germania Latina 1 (Groningen, 1992), 25–41.

[58] Wessén, *Runstenen vid Röks kyrka*, 45; Brate, "Rökstenen och Teoderikstatyn," 73–76, speaks of Varin's "informant" (*hemulsman*), whose trip to Aachen reports considerably more than just a description of the statue.

[59] Lönnroth, "Riddles of the Rök-Stone," 29; Heusler, *Die altgermanische Dichtung*, 85. See Lönnroth for a more complete survey of explanations of the Theoderic stanza;

So for me (with Grønvik) a more direct form of southern influence is required. The stanza gives a vivid, ultimately eye-witness image, but its clearly
articulated theme, considered together with the questions/hints, is not that of
Lönnroth's *Þiðreks saga* passage. Grønvik's analysis of the form þiaurikʀ (for
usual ON *Þjóð-*) is valuable here. The loss of /ð/ before /r/ is "no problem" (cf., for
example, *Hrœrekr* < **Hróðrikr*); but the vowel sequence **iau** does require an explanation. Grønvik postulates Low German for the *ia* sequence: "thus in the words
thiad, *thiadan* and particularly in proper names in *Thiad-*." But the full sequence
may show Latin influence as well: "It is therefore possible that the peculiar name
form <ÞiAurikR> goes back to a half latinized, half Low Saxon form **Thiadorik*,
*Thiadurik, which, when borrowed, adjusted itself to Nordic structural rules and
emerged as Nordic **Þiaðurik* > **Þiauðurik* > **Þjaurik(R).*" The seemingly unnec-
essary stage **Þiauðurik* is explained by some problematic forms in early Danish
and Swedish phonology; Grønvik intends this as part of the adaptation to Nordic phonetic structure: "In Danish and Swedish runic inscriptions <iAu> is also
found on rare occasions for older /jó/ before a dental, especially in the word *þjóð*
f. 'nation' . . . According to [certain] grammarians, it is, however, very uncertain
how the spellings in question are to be explained and whether we really have here
a specially southern Scandinavian diphthongization." Noreen, however, regards
iau (*iǫu*) as a regular stage in the Scandinavian development of Gmc *eu*, treating it as first a falling, then "schwebende" triphthong before it became the standard rising diphthongs /jo:/ and /ju:/, depending on context. Grønvik's Latinized
stage seems, then, to be possible but not linguistically necessary, though the vanishingly small number of words attesting to the supposed triphthong stage renders any explanation chancy.[60] In any case, it is generally assumed that the name
in its usual Nordic form, *Þjóðrekr/Þjórekr*, was imported with the legend: "In a
similar way, the etymologically identical name form *Þiaurikʀ*, attested in the

since Lönnroth, see especially Kees Samplonius, *"Rex non rediturus*: Notes on Theodoric
and the Rök-Stone," *Amsterdamer Beiträge zur älteren Germanistik* 37 (1993): 21–31.

[60] Grønvik, *Rökstein*, 56; Adolf Noreen, *Altnordische Grammatik*, 5th ed. (Tübin-
gen, 1970), 1: 52–53 (§ 56), 94–95 (§ 101); cf. idem, *Altschwedische Grammatik mit Einschluss des Altgutnischen* (Halle, 1904), 113. The "grammarians" cited by Grønvik are Axel
Kock, *Svensk ljudhistoria* (Lund, 1909–1911): 329 [also relevant, 324–28, 334, 398] and
Johs. Brøndum-Nielsen, *Gammeldansk grammatik i sproghistorisk fremstilling* (Copenhagen, 1928), 1: 169, n. 1. In different ways, both undercut Noreen here, and the approximately ten further references cited by Brøndum-Nielsen leave the question very murky.
The spelling *iau* for Gmc *eu* seems to occur outside Gotland only four times (including Rök), and all may be explained without recourse to Noreen's common Scandinavian
triphthong stage (see especially Kock). Bugge (*Runenstein*, 166) tentatively proposed that
Rök's name form was borrowed from Gotland, but the Gutnish triphthong seems to
develop after the period of Rök (Kock, *Svensk ljudhistoria*, 334). Brate ("Rökstenen och
Teoderikstatyn," 80, n.) thought the whole verse was from OWN, hence that the spelling
stood for /jo:/; but the spelling itself is more or less unmotivated.

Rök inscription, has come from North Germany, bears the imprint of combined Latin and North German phonology, and has been adjusted according to Nordic sound laws."[61]

Grønvik's cautious wording is cautiously to be accepted. But if the stanza was originally composed with a Latinized Low German form like *Thiadurik*, the anomaly of its metrics may be explained. Assuming that *iau* was treated metrically as the equivalent of *jó*, the line (as pointed out above) would have been of a 3-syllable type, out of place in a *fornyrðislag* environment; but if the original form had a medial syllable as in *Thiadurik*, the line could have been intended as a normal Sievers B type.[62] This hypothesis is qualified by ignorance of how the rune sequence **iau** could have been handled metrically and of what it meant phonologically (see n. 60). If a WGmc source like OE *Þeod[ric]* or OSax *Thiad[rich]* could have produced two syllables for metrical purposes at the *iau* stage, the Latin influence would not be needed; but a glance at the plethora of trisyllabic forms of the name in Förstemann argues more strongly for Grønvik's idea of a borrowed form with a medial syllable.[63] Either way, it seems likely that the original form or earliest Swedish form of the name in this line would not have yielded a contextually anomalous three-syllable verse type. Instead of a transitional form to *kviðuháttr*, the Theoderic stanza may here reveal its foreign inspiration.

But it is worth remembering that "foreign" origins for Germanic heroic story constitute merely a normal case: the material of *Beowulf* is rooted in Danish and Gautish story, only the language being English; the Finnsburg tale must come from Frisia; *Waldere* contains continental stuff, and so on. Usually the foreign element must remain at the level of story material, but in the *Poetic Edda* Hans Kuhn was able to ferret out West Germanic models in Old Norse verse.[64] Whether foreign fingerprints survive in the language of an extant monument of

---

[61] Grønvik, *Rökstein*, 58.

[62] It would be crucial to know whether l. 5 of the Rök stanza represented a 3-syllable, *kviðuháttr*-type line (cf. n. 48); if it did, it would support (though not prove) the "transition-to-*kviðuháttr*" theory, and it certainly would have become trisyllabic after syncope (*sitr nú gǫrr*). In the extant line the first word, *sitiʀ*, is definitely subject to resolution, but *garuʀ*, I believe, is not. In principle verse-final resolution is disallowed (i.e., vanishingly rare) in *fornyrðislag* (Geoffrey Russom, *Beowulf and Old Germanic Metre* [Cambridge, 1998], 103–5) and apparently also in *kviðuháttr*. (I thank R.D. Fulk, p.c., for enlightenment on various points in this note.) Rök l. 5 would seem to fall under types discussed in Russom, *Metre*, 105–8. But it seems relevant in such an early text that *garuʀ* is etymologically *garwaʀ*; perhaps the metrical system here is archaically treating what is apparently a short syllable as still long (cf. Russom on metrical archaisms: *Metre*, 60–63).

[63] Ernst Förstemann, *Altdeutsches Namenbuch* (Nordhausen, 1856), 1: coll. 1186–90.

[64] H. Kuhn, "Westgermanisches in der altnordischen Verskunst," *Beiträge zur Geschichte der deutschen Sprache und Literatur* 63 (1939): 178–236; repr. in idem, *Kleine Schriften*, ed. Dietrich Hofmann et al. (Berlin, 1969), 1: 485–527.

this kind must depend on the medium of transmission[65] and the gestation period in the new home; and their discovery might also depend on the amount of language material available. Our stanza is certainly a *Fremdstofflied* (Kuhn's term for poems based on foreign materials), and the relevant time frame (801 to, say, 850) is relatively brief; the language material, however, in Rök's four long lines is so small that one metrical trace of a West Germanic origin, if it is accepted as such, is strong influence.

An alternative origin of the Rök stanza would obviate a West Germanic source by emphasizing the similarity to *Ynglingatal*, st. 35–36, and the Swedishness of the hypothetical eye-witness to the statue in Aachen: the Swedish poet put the Frankish scene into a mold offered by ancient Swedish genealogical verse that we find reflected in the later Norwegian *Ynglingatal* (c. 900). We have already glanced at the similarities that are available to support this theory. Both the diction around *réð* and transition to *kviðuháttr* are debatable; the "then-and-now" framework is a genuine analogy, but it depends partly on *réð* for **raiþ** and on an incomplete similarity in the "now" section, for the marvelous thing about Theoderic here is that he does *not* lie in a howe but sits like a statue. *Ynglingatal* is a genealogy that specializes in reporting each ruler's death and sometimes burial; the "then-and-now" pattern is not a predictable part of this formulaic poem, but after all it is not a rare poetic device.[66] For Wessén the relationship to *Ynglingatal* is a crucial question; and it does deserve a fuller investigation.[67] The Rök stanza stands finely balanced between two models, a hypothetical Swedish proto-*Ynglingatal* and West Germanic poems, especially *Deor*. But *Deor*, *Widsith*, and *Beowulf* all demonstrate the minor art of the heroic vignette, and, for the moment at least, I prefer to think of the Theoderic *Denkmalepigramm* as one of the import wares from Charlemagne's empire so richly attested in Birka.

The speech formula, opening frame, and overall genre

Like the Gotland picture stones, Rök is probably the product of a funeral ritual but certainly a memorial erected by a bereaved father, Varin, for his predeceased son, Vamoð. The opening lines (1–2):

---

[65] Cf. the slogan "Heldensage ist Heldenlied" (Schneider, *Germanische Heldensage* 1: 29).

[66] Heusler, *Die altgermanische Dichtung*, 85, produced, seemingly off-the-cuff, a small collection; many more instances could be found in Old Norse alone (e.g., Egil's *lausavísur* 17 and 20); in fact, the pattern is discernible also in the Strabo poem, where it takes on what we might call Ozymandian tones. Note that in *Ynglingatal* the pattern and similarities to Rök do not constitute a stanza (as several commentators assert) but extend over two.

[67] Wessén, *Runstenen vid Röks kyrka*, 45.

Aft Vamoð standa runaʀ þaʀ. Æn Varinn faði, faðiʀ aft faigian sunu. 'In memory of Vamoð stand these runes. But Varin wrote them, a father in memory of his death-doomed son.'

Like the narrator's introduction in *Widsith*, these lines constitute a frame separate from the heroic and mythic contents, the story allusions; unlike *Widsith*, no terminal frame balances the form on Rök (except in Lönnroth's reading). And these lines are Varin's only personal words (unless possibly he speaks directly in his own person in line 20) though they too participate in the poetic and hieratic diction of Rök as a whole. After this opening the remainder of the inscription is a collection of passages introduced by a ceremonial formula. This occurs in three variants (omitting the damaged 20): (1) in ll. 23 and 26 **sakumukmini**; (2) in ll. 3 and 21 **sakumukminiþat**; and (3) in 5–6, 12, and 14 **þatsakum** [+ordinal number]. The word which anchors the formula, *sagum*, is usually taken as first person plural, the word that in Old West Norse appears as *segjum* 'we tell, let us tell'; Grønvik, however, explains the Rök form without *-j-* more satisfactorily as a very old medial active, preserving the archaic *-u* of the first person singular protected by the dative personal pronoun <*-miz*—a construction perhaps once connected with a speaker's experiential involvement in an event.[68] Grønvik suggests that this "vague" sense might remain in Varin's usage, but I think that, if anything, the ancient form here contributes to Varin's disappearance into the role of traditional speaker.

More important than **saku(m)** to an interpretation is the rune sequence **(m)uk**, which recurs in four of the instances of the formula. For Grønvik the underlying form is *sagumᵘk*; *-u-* before *-k* is epenthetical, and the enclitic *-k* from *ek*, as a whole then simply 'I tell.' But recent interpreters have more frequently fallen back on the compounding form *múg-* from *múgr* 'a crowd' (cf. Sw. *allmoge*, Dan. *almue* 'common people'); thus OSw. *mog-minni* would be something like 'folk-lore' in a sense like 'national lore.' Several telling arguments have been offered against this compound, and it is my opinion that Widmark has offered the best solution.[69] She has solved (to my satisfaction) the phonological problems associated with an early suggestion of Bugge's: that we have here *mǫgr* 'son, heir, relative.'[70]

---

[68] Grønvik, *Rökstein*, 48–49, partly anticipated by Hugo Pipping, *Om runinskriften på Rökstenen*, Acta Societatis Scientiarum Fennicæ 49. 1 (Helsingfors, 1919), 17–18 (and Vigfusson cited there).

[69] Grønvik, *Rökstein*, 48–49; Widmark, "Tankar kring Rökstenen," 29–31.

[70] Her solution briefly: Rök shows no syncope of *u* after short vowel in *sunu, garuʀ, allu, iatun, fiaru* and no u-umlaut. But Widmark argues that the composition vowel in a compound **magu-minni* would have been the first to undergo syncope and that the runic **u** rightly stands for *ǫ* because the first *u*-umlauts will have occurred preceding lost *u*. These two codependent arguments could not be extended to a free-standing *mǫg* dat. sg. (later a correct form beside *megi*). Marez also comes to the conclusion that our word is

Recent scholars' opinions on the sequence **mini** have largely settled on a word for ancient lore remembered. Since modern Scandinavian languages have retained this word with meanings like 'memory, remembrance' and in compounds such as Dan. *folkeminde(r)* 'folklore,' *minni* in the Rök inscription may have a deceptive transparency; and a combination *forn minni* 'ancient lore' that seems close to the usage on the stone is attested in Snorri and earlier. But one of Lönnroth's many services to Rök explication is to have introduced (or reintroduced) OIcel. *greppaminni* (gen. pl. from *greppr* 'skald; doughty man') into the discussion.[71] This term is applied in the metrical section of Snorri's *Prose Edda* (also earlier) to a series of questions and answers in verse, and Vésteinn Ólason's study of *greppaminni* had already produced a number of parallels and analogues so that *greppaminni*'s existence as a minor, but real, generic pattern within oral poetry appears secure.

Lönnroth, whose principal method in interpreting Rök was to establish overall structure and to use structure to leverage solutions to problems of detail, seems to me to overemphasize (in the service of his modification of Wessén's repertoire theory) the specifically *riddling* aspect of *greppaminni* and of Rök; my "question/hint" is an attempt to label the structure with a neutral and descriptive (if awkward) technical term. I also doubt that *greppa-* here refers to 'skalds' rather than to ancient 'heroes': "*Greppaminni* would then be the kind of legend or myth that forms part of the repertory of the *greppar*, i.e. the skalds, and the main function of the questions and answers would probably be to test people's knowledge of this repertory."[72] True, Bugge had already translated *greppaminni* as "ancient events which are brought to mind by the poets," and the main dictionaries do give 'skald' as the first meaning of *greppr*.[73] But since *minni* refers to "legends and myths,"[74] the skaldic repertory element appears to be a gratuitous import; *greppaminni* is better understood as 'old stories *of heroes* remembered.'[75] Either way, with or without reference to a skaldic repertory, Snorri's application of *greppaminni* to the deeds of the living Duke Skúli has to be understood as an exten-

---

mǫgminni; see Alain Marez, "<sakumukmini>?—Une relecture de l'inscription de Rök," *Études germaniques* 52 (1997): 543–57. *Mǫgr* is a frequent poetic word, and the full old form *magu* acc. sg. is found in the Kjølevik inscription, the memorial of a father for a son about 500 (Krause and Jankuhn, *Runeninschriften im älteren Futhark* 1: 172–74 [No. 75]).

[71] Lönnroth, "Riddles of the Rök-Stone," 16–20; but Bugge had anticipated this too: *Runenstein*, 39, 244–45.

[72] Lönnroth, "Riddles of the Rök-Stone," 18.

[73] Bugge, *Runenstein*, 39.

[74] Lönnroth, "Riddles of the Rök-Stone," 18.

[75] Etymology does not seem particularly to support the sense 'skald'; de Vries, *Wörterbuch*, s.v., gives 'tapferer mann, held' as the first meaning, 'skald' as the second; cf. the related *garpr* 'tüchtiger mann'; a common factor may be the sounds made by a bully (de Vries relates ON *karp* 'prahlerei').

sion of *minni*, "legends and myths," to a contemporary *greppr*, 'doughty man.' And either way, the medieval term *greppaminni* does increase our confidence that in Rök's questions and answers on heroic legend and myth we are dealing with a traditional oral-literary form.[76]

The murky history of *minni* itself is a larger problem. Grønvik treats it very briefly in his edition, but at length and in convincing detail earlier.[77] Drinking and toasting the ancestors, the recently departed, and the gods was an ancient custom; the words spoken then could apparently be designated *minni*, a performed instance of old stories of heroes remembered. In the late eleventh century the German custom of *minne trinken* was introduced to Scandinavia in the context of the newly imported institution of the guild. Later instances of *minni drekka* in ON literature may be colored by the imported custom and idiom. For Rök Grønvik supposes that the inscription's *minni* are a selection from the actual toasts made at the funeral of Vamoð. To my mind the supposition of a ritual context somewhere behind the text is reasonable but does not explain the exact usage of *minni* in the inscription. Are the three "legends or myths" referred to in the inscription, each one *minni*? Or is a *minni* the question/hint that *evokes* memory of a legend or myth? Perhaps the overall difference is not great, but Rök's diction seems to favor the latter (as does one crucial piece of evidence in Grønvik's discussion),[78] which fits well with the ritual context and with the rhetoric of *greppaminni* and does not conflict with more general senses such as *forn minni*. Having avoided *minni* as a technical term to this point, I believe it would now be methodologically allowable to use it in its various ON senses: (1) memory, remembrance; (2) old myths and legends preserved in memory; (3) a stimulus to memory of old myths and legends, such as pictures, toasts, or hinting questions, especially in the playful context of *greppaminni*.

Varin's opening words put Vamoð's name first and frame the father's contribution in references to his son. This contrasts with many later memorials where the stone's raisers often devote much space to celebrating themselves and their

---

[76] Wessén, *Runstenen vid Röks kyrka*, 75, seems to imply that it is a nonce form, but his extensive comparison to *Widsith* and declaration that Varin is a *þulr* whose repertoire is on display would seem to qualify this emphasis on uniqueness.

[77] Grønvik, *Rökstein*, 49–50, 82–83; "To viktige ord," 15–35. Cf. Chr. Zimmermann, "Minne und Minnetrinken," in *Reallexikon der Germanischen Altertumskunde* 20 (Berlin, 2002), 49–56 summarizing the contemporary view (but not including Grønvik, "To vikitige ord").

[78] Grønvik, "To viktige ord," 31–32; the passage in Ulfr Uggason's *Húsdrápa* is a refrain: *hlaut innan svá minnum*. Grønvik argues strenuously but inconclusively against Klaus Düwel's translation: "Es wurde (die Halle) inwendig mit Erinnerungszeichen (Bildern?) geschmückt" (32). Widmark ("Tankar kring Rökstenen," 30) supports *"minni* as a designation for images with mythic and legendary content"; but it does not inspire confidence when she adds that *minni* is a quite unproblematic word.

monument. Varin defines his contribution narrowly (*faði*) and links his role as *faðir* with his son through an adjective carefully chosen, *faigian*. There is insufficient evidence to call Varin's posture here "modest," and tradition rather than personality probably govern; but this opening seems to me to tell against some aspects of Wessén's reading according to which Varin takes the occasion of the memorial for his son to dazzle an audience with his repertoire of stories and his command of writing. The word *faigian*, in any case, does not mean that Vamoð is dedicated to a god (or ritually dead as part of an initiation),[79] but that his human mortality—we are all *feigir*—is being emphasized. A word like *faigian* would seem to evoke pathos; the periphrasis or euphemism for "dead" is paralleled in OE in poetic diction like *feores orwena* 'despairing of life' [*Fortunes of Men* 40b] of an already dead body and of the dead Christ *limwerigne ... meðe æfter þam miclan gewinne* 'limbweary ... tired after the great struggle' [*Dream of the Rood* 63a, 65], where pathos is obvious.[80]

We should not forget that the Rök inscription is a father's memorial to a dead son; though emotion is not totally foreign to the later rune stones (of which no small number are of fathers for sons), Rök generally shares their laconic memorial discourse. In its function, purpose, and nature as literature, though, it is comparable to an *erfikvæði* or elegy such as Egil Skalla-Grímsson's *Sonatorrek*, and the comparison has been made many times. Though Rök's structure and style differ greatly from *Sonatorrek*, I think their motivation is comparable. One complaint against versions of the repertoire theory has been that there is no connection between the *minni* and the occasion, while the older scholars forced such a connection with the assumption that the stories concern ancestors of Varin. The text of the heroic part gives no solid reason for believing this, although a case can be made for the concluding myth as belonging to Varin's family.

Nor is there any textual reason to accept the still more direct connections of the revenge and dedication theories, including Grønvik's claim that real contemporary events are reflected in the *minni* of the twenty kings, specifically that Vamoð was killed in the battle in which he or his army slew the twenty. In fact, there is no textual reason to believe that Vamoð was even a full-grown man; in contrast to the custom on many of the later memorial stones, no deeds or even qualities are ascribed to Vamoð here. The expression *mǫgminni* in fact suggests a juvenile version of *greppaminni*; perhaps to translate 'a boy's ancient stories'

[79] Grønvik, *Rökstein*, 84; Widmark, "Tankar kring Rökstenen," 32 (contra); Henry Kratz, "Was Vamoð Still Alive? The Rök-stone as an Initiation Memorial," *Mediaeval Scandinavia* 11 (1978–1979): 9–29.

[80] Bugge, *Runenstein*, 8–9, anticipates my point about the emotional freight of the word and also my WGmc comparison: "Es liegt in dem Ausdrucke eine Andeutung darüber, dass der Sohn früher, als der Vater gewünscht hatte, gestorben ist. In westgerman. Dichtung wird das entsprechende Adjektiv von dem bereits gestorbenen angewendet und geht in die Bedeutung 'tot' über." He adds examples from WGmc and *Vǫluspá*.

would go too far in this direction and omit the crucial fact that the 'boy' (*mǫgr*) is a 'son, descendant.' But a funeral gift of a bouquet of stories, perhaps stories loved by the deceased and arranged in the playful question-and-answer form, is consistent with these speculations. Egil's son Bǫðvar is calculated to have been about eighteen, but Egil speaks of him chiefly in terms of unrealized potential: *Veit ek þat siálfr / at í syni mínum / var(a) ills þegns / efni vaxit, / ef sá randviðr / røskvask næði / unz her-Gauts / hendr of tœki* (11). 'I myself know this: that in my son the makings of a bad man had not waxed—if only he had been able to grow up a warrior before Odin's hands seized him.'[81] The word *efni* is especially important here: a young boy was *manns-efni* 'the makings of a man.' Perhaps Vamoð, like Bǫðvar, was still in the stage of *mannsefni*.

If we adopt the compound *mǫgminni*, we acquire the explicit connection many have found wanting between the items of oral literature and the elegiac occasion. *Mǫg-minni*, like *sona-torrek*, might be a coinage for the occasion, even a coinage that alludes to *greppa-minni*, despite structural differences. As to the numbering of the questions/hints, we might imagine that Vamoð's repertoire of favorite heroic stories and myths included at least six (thirteen questions at two or more per story would be only six), but the formal rigidity (two questions plus verse answer) implicit in Lönnroth's structural discussion cannot be supported because of the odd number of questions/hints. There have been many other speculations in this area. I like the idea that other *minni* were painted or carved on wooden tablets (rather than imagining lost companion stones), or that *minni* spoken at the funeral or later remembrance ceremony were numbered. The numbering makes it obvious that the three transmitted *minni* were chosen from a larger number. In any case the natural question for a literary person to ask is: why just these stories? In short, what is the theme and meaning of Rök? Questions for another essay.[82]

---

[81] My translation differs only in tone from E. O. G. Turville-Petre's (*Scaldic Poetry* [Oxford, 1976], 34); but his note gives an overview of another way to construe the last two lines, making Bǫðvar the subject of *tœki* and *her-Gauts hendr* (or an emendation for *hendr* to give 'shield') the object, thus meaning 'until [he] should have won the hands of a warrior' [alternatively 'a shield']—or more fully paraphrased: if only he had been able to mature, a warrior, until he had achieved the hands of a warrior. The redundancy of message argues against this understanding though I may be pushing the sense by translating 'grow up a warrior' instead of 'that warrior [=simply "he"] had been able to grow up.' The next stanza (12) does not contradict st. 11 though it speaks obscurely of strength Egil drew from his son.

[82] See Joseph Harris, "Myth and Meaning in the Rök Inscription," *Viking and Medieval Scandinavia* 2 (2006): 45–109; but also Lönnroth, "Riddles of the Rök-Stone," esp. 50–51.

Conclusion: *minni* and *memoria*

To reprise: the first two narrative sections of Varin's memorial collection are ultimately based on West Germanic materials. The Theoderic material stems from such sources just as certainly as the *Fremdstofflieder* of the *Edda* ultimately derive from continental tradition; but with Rök, the connection, paralleled by the Birka-Haithabu-Dorestad commercial and cultural axis, is less uncertainly mediated. The verse appears to be from an eye-witness of the Aachen statue, whether or not at one or two removes, and recent enough arguably to preserve a metrical fingerprint suggestive of its origin. A close connection to *Deor* through Theoderic's legendary rulership of the Mærings is certain, though how it is to be modeled is unclear; and given that certainty I am tempted to see a second link to *Deor* through the king's mixed reputation. For Rök's section on the twenty kings we can hold fast to the West Germanic source of many or all of the names and perhaps to some parallels in *Zeitgedichte*; anything beyond this is very uncertain. But I have tried to imagine a historical situation (involving a Frisian or partly Frisian trading brotherhood and its demise in battle) passing into historically-based fiction, i.e. legend, in a form that preserved some hints of the *Zeitgedichte* that first recorded it. This imagined West Germanic origin requires, I would argue, no more unmoored belief than Lönnroth's very early *fornaldarsaga* episode; both, of course, are speculations. The whole nature of Rök, however, presumes that this foreign material was not totally new but already familiar to the audience of the inscription.

The West Germanic elements that appear in the Rök text can all be attributed to "oral tradition," but oral tradition need not be a disembodied ("superorganic," in the idiom of folkloristics) force moving in mysterious waves; one conceptualizes it so vaguely only when no actual tradition-bearers are available as its vectors. With many other Rök scholars I believe a more direct connection, ultimately an eye-witness, is implicit in the relationship of the Theoderic verse and the Aachen statue. Other features, such as the Swedish monument's apparent allusion to Theoderic's compromised fame, *could* have been brought from the land of the Franks and Frisians by the kind of individual traveler quoted by Rimbert.

I want to ask in conclusion whether Varin's unique decision to record his selection of legends in writing—"a revolutionizing idea," as Preben Meulengracht Sørensen calls it[83]—could have been one of the West Germanic, specifically Frankish, influences. Other runic memorials quote appropriate verse, and myths and legends were rendered pictorially in the North; but no other rune

---

[83] P. Meulengracht Sørensen, "Der Runen-Stein von Rök und Snorri Sturluson––oder 'Wie aussagekräftig sind unsere Quellen zur Religionsgeschichte der Wikingerzeit?'" in *At fortælle Historien / Telling History: Studier i den gamle nordiske litteratur / Studies in Norse Literature* (Trieste, 2001), 131–41, at 133 (orig. publ. 1990).

stone attempts to record a collection of such *minni* in writing.[84] Our hypothetical East Gautish visitor from Birka will have traveled after 801 to Dorestad and further up the Maas to Aachen. He was curious enough about the great emperor to admire his statue of the famous and controversial Theoderic. Perhaps among the things he learned there (Theoderic's bad reputation? how long ago he lived?) one concerned the emperor's activities after 800 in improvement of native law, including having the oral laws written down. Perhaps he heard that the emperor was even having ancient oral story-telling poems collected and reduced to writing—in Einhard's famous words: '[Charles] also had barbarous ancient songs, in which the deeds and wars of the ancient kings were sung, written out for transmission to posterity':—*barbara et antiquissima carmina, quibus veterum regum actus et bella canebantur, scripsit memoriaeque mandavit.*[85] In the context of such a collection perhaps references to *memoria* reminded him of his native *minni* with a somewhat similar range of meanings centering on 'memory, remembrance.' Einhard's *memoriae mandare* is debated by specialists; but in context its meaning cannot have been far from 'preserve for posterity (in letters).' For the Swede—whose stories *were* 'memory' and 'memory,' story—the possibility of *writing* stories or poems *pro memoria* was a new idea and one from an authoritative source. But it did have a partial analogue at home where runic writing was associated with monumentalization, often to preserve the memory of individuals in stones and runes that were to last until Ragnarök. Ideas, like seeds, may fall on ready ground, or not. Did our imaginary Swedish visitor carry his new idea back with him to Östergötland, where, sometime after the death of young Vamoð, Varin applied it to a memorial, resulting in a monument unique in literary history but one with a familiar feeling for the Anglo-Saxonist?

---

[84] See Meulengracht Sørensen, "Der Runen-Stein," 132–34, on the typological isolation of Rök and the unsuitability of the rune-stone medium for recording stories.

[85] Einhard, *Vita Karoli*, chap. 29. For a recent comprehensive treatment of the "Heldenliederbuch," see Wolfgang Haubrichs, *"Veterum regum actus et bella*—Zur sog. Heldenliedersammlung Karls des Großen," in *Aspekte der Germanistik: Festschrift für Hans-Friedrich Rosenfeld zum 90. Geburtstag,* ed. Walter Tauber (Göppingen, 1989), 17–46. Einhard's reference to writing in *memoriae mandavit* is supported from many sides, including the Poeta Saxo's paraphrase of these words as *barbara mandavit carmina litterulis* . . . (quoted by Haubrichs, "Heldenliedersammlung," 18); but see Haubrichs on the complexities here. The old question of whether Charles's *barbara et antiquissima carmina* were Heuslerian *Heldenlieder* or *Preislieder/Zeitgedichte* obviously remains unaffected by the accident that Rök seems to anthologize one *minni* comprised of material of heroic legend, one *minni* of *Zeitgedicht*-material, and one *minni* of mythic/religious weight; but the comparison to Haubrichs on the genre question is interesting.

Not Christianity versus Paganism, but Hall versus Bog: The Great Shift in Early Scandinavian Religion and its Implications for *Beowulf*[1]

Frank Battaglia

The most important single change in early Scandinavian religion, reorganizing beliefs and the way people shared them, was not the change from paganism to Christianity: archaeologists have been saying this for some time. For the most part, major phenomena associated with Christianity in the high Middle Ages are now seen to have been underway before the conversion. A church being the center of religious practice, for example, continued the arrangement in which a cult place supervised by a political figure and linked to his residence was the focus of an area's ritual activity. What then can have been the watershed shift in early Scandinavian religion?

In virtually every single bog in South Scandinavia, Iron Age pots can be found in which sacrifices of food had been made.[2] Depositing votive offerings in bogs was a universal practice which went back into the Stone Age, while the

---

[1] I was honored to speak to the Helsinki meeting of ISAS and am grateful to our Finnish hosts for their relentless hospitality. My own work has benefited from research published at Åbo. Else Mundal's essay comparing place names with written records over a thousand years is fundamental to the study of Scandinavian goddesses: "The Position of the Individual Gods and Goddesses in Various Types of Sources—with Special Reference to the Female Divinities," in *Old Norse and Finnish Religions and Cultic Place Names*, ed. Tore Ahlbäck (Åbo, 1990), 294–315. *Neuphilologische Mitteilungen* is a continuing resource.

[2] Charlotte Fabech, "Samfundsorganisation, religiøse ceremonier og regional variation," in *Samfundsorganisation og Regional Variation*, ed. C. Fabech and Jytte Ringtved (Aarhus, 1991), 283–303; eadem, "Booty Sacrifices in Southern Scandinavia: A Reassessment," in *Sacred and Profane*, ed. Paul Garwood, David Jennings, Robin Skeates, and Judith Toms (Oxford, 1991), 88–99; Flemming Kaul, "The Bog—Gateway to Another World," in *The Spoils of Victory*, ed. Lars Jørgensen, Birger Storgaard, and Lone Gebauer Thomsen (Copenhagen, 2003), 18–43.

pedestrian character of some offerings suggests that any member of a population could appeal directly to the powers accessed in such places. But around 500 C.E. the use of bogs and lakes for religious offerings stopped.

"Instead," in the words of Ulf Näsman, "religious objects are found hoarded in settlement contexts, sometimes—and this is a new phenomenon . . .—in the postholes of the great halls of the magnates. This indicates a change whereby the elite has taken over the control of religion in a new way: they have made a personal institution of religious practice . . . The close link between cult and elite continued unbroken after Christianization; that is, the church was built by the magnate and on his ground, . . . a cult-site continuity from the pagan period into the Christian era. [The] great break took place in the Migration Period . . . [and] is associated with . . . social and political changes that in an archaeological perspective seem more radical than those at the conversion [to Christianity] in the tenth century."[3]

In a drastic South-Scandinavian religious change, natural settings, especially watery ones, ceased to be the focus of religious exercises by about the sixth century. Votive sacrificing of food, pottery, metal, or persons in bogs and lakes ended. Instead, public religious practice became connected with buildings of a new kind which had begun to appear, in a development spreading from the south, linked with the enlargement of farms and the reorganization of settlements, and indeed the source of a new category of landless persons.[4] Figure 1

---

[3] Ulf Näsman, "The Ethnogenesis of the Danes and the Making of a Danish Kingdom," in *Anglo-Saxon Studies in Archaeology and History* (hereafter *ASSAH*) 10 (1999): 1–10. See also Frands Herschend, "The Origin of the Hall in Southern Scandinavia," *Tor* 25 (1993): 175–99; Ebbe Nyborg, "Church and Cloister," in *Digging into the Past: 25 Years of Archaeology in Denmark*, ed. S. Hvass and B. Storgaard (København, 1993), 242–47; Stefan Brink, "Political and Social Structures in Early Scandinavia," *Tor* 28 (1996): 235–81; Johan Callmer and Erik Rosengren, eds., ". . .Gick Grendel Att Söka Det Höga Huset. . ."—*Arkeologiska källor till aristokratiska miljöer i Skandinavien under yngre järnålder* (Halmstad, 1997); Charlotte Fabech, "Organizing the Landscape: A Matter of Production, Power and Religion," *ASSAH* 10 (1999): 37–47.

[4] Lotte Hedeager, *Iron Age Societies* (Oxford, 1992), 247–48. I would associate some of these changes with the Early Germanic Iron Age rather than the Late Roman, as Hedeager did. A Hodde type leader everywhere appropriating tribute from outside his own village (Hedeager, *Iron Age Societies*, 245) is too early a hypothesis in the Late Roman Iron Age. A survey by Michael Parker Pearson of farmhouse changes in relation to other social events was faulted by John Hines as too restrictive in its database; see Pearson, "Economic and Ideological Change: Cyclical Growth in the Pre-state Societies of Jutland," in *Ideology, Power and Prehistory*, ed. Daniel Miller and Christopher Tilley (Cambridge, 1984), 69–92; Hines, "Ritual Hoarding in Migration-Period Scandinavia: A Review of Recent Interpretations," *Proceedings of the Prehistoric Society* 55 (1989): 193–205, here 195. See now regarding sacrifice locations, Jesper Hansen, "Offertradition og religion i ældre jernalder i Sydskandinavien—med særlig henblik på bebyggelsesofringer," *Kuml* (2006): 117–75.

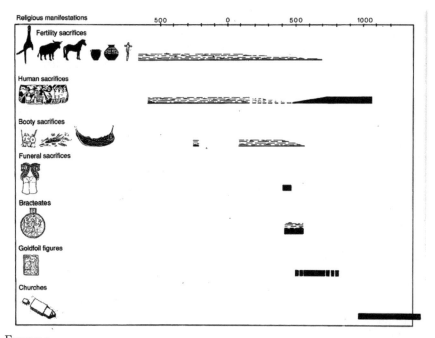

Figure 1.
A chronological diagram of religious manifestations in southern Scandinavia. Sacrifices in wetlands are marked with a water symbol, dry land sacrifices with a black line. After Fabech 1991.

shows bog deposits in relation to dry land religious manifestations.[5] With the types and places of sacrifice changing slowly, the analysis reflects considerable continuity. Holy places in bogs were sometimes marked with heaps of stones, as at Forlev Nymølle in Jutland, where from the third century B.C.E. through the fourth century C.E. offerings were made in an area originally marked by a ten-foot-tall female figure.[6] The bog practice seems to have been the origin of Old Danish *hørg* and Old Norse *horgr* for 'stone heap at a holy place'—on dry land.[7]

---

[5] Fabech, "Samfundorganisation," Fig. 3.

[6] Jørgen Lund, "Forlev Nymølle: En offerplads fra yngre førromersk jernalder," *Kuml* (2002): 143–95.

[7] Forlev Nymølle exhibit, Silkeborg Museum, August 2001—Wijnand van der Sanden and Thorsten Capelle, *Mosens Guder / Immortal Images* (Silkeborg, 2001), 16, 18, 63, 65, Figs. 65, 90; T.L. Markey, "Germanic Terms for Temple and Cult," in *Studies for Einar Haugen*, ed. Evelyn Scherabon Firchow et al. (The Hague, 1972), 367–70, 375; Bente Holmberg, "Om sakrale sted- og personnavne," in *Nordisk Hedendom*, ed. G. Steinsland et al. (Odense, 1991), 149–59.

Figure 2 diagrams first millennium C.E. changes in the way humans and land-scape participated in the sacral.[8]

The buildings which began to replace bogs as the site of rituals were large, and different in design and function from farmhouses.[9] Often they had fewer internal support posts and steeper roofs. Sometimes a seating area was built in. Generally if food was eaten in the structure it had been cooked elsewhere, for these buildings show little evidence of domestic work. What has been recovered at them, however, are remains of luxury articles, especially fancy drinking gear and imported goods. When not serving as religious centers, these were upper-class men's clubs—a potent clue to why *Beowulf*'s Heorot was opposed by Grendel. The halls created new sacral relationships and memorialized the centralization of power which was responsible for them.

This essay is participating in two conversations, and I hope to get them to fit together a little better than they now do. One concerns the cultural landscape and geography of power in South Scandinavia in the mid-first millennium,[10] a discussion which is intensifying since the discovery in 1993 of a Danish kingly hall site at Gudme on Funen.[11] The other conversation, about the meaning of *Beowulf*, is one where, in the light of thoughtful arguments for a late date of composition,[12] the actual situation in South Scandinavia within the time frame of the poem may seem almost irrelevant.

Dating *Beowulf* is not my topic here. But to warrant seeing the poem in close relation to early Scandinavia, I draw attention to an argument of H.M. Chadwick's in support of early composition which has never been answered.

---

[8] Charlotte Fabech, "Reading Society from the Cultural Landscape: South Scandinavia between Sacral and Political Power," in *The Archaeology of Gudme and Lundeborg*, ed. P.O. Nielsen, K. Randsborg, and H. Thrane (København, 1994), Fig. 6.

[9] Herschend, "The Origin of the Hall," 175–99; Brink, "Structures"; idem, "Social Order in the Early Scandinavian Landscape," in *Settlement and Landscape*, ed. Charlotte Fabech and Jytte Ringtved (Aarhus, 1999), 423–39. See also Lotte Hedeager, "Scandinavia," in *The New Cambridge Medieval History*, vol. 1, *c.500–c.700*, ed. Paul Fouracre (Cambridge, 2005), 496–523, here 517–22.

[10] Jytte Ringtved, "The Geography of Power: South Scandinavia before the Danish Kingdom," *ASSAH* 10 (1999): 49–63; Fabech, "Between Sacral and Political Power"; eadem, "Slöinge in Perspective," in ". . .Gick Grendel" —*Arkeologiska källor*, 147–60; eadem, "The Spatial Distribution of Gold Hoards in Southern Scandinavia and the Geography of Power," in *Roman Gold and the Development of the Early Germanic Kingdoms*, KVHAA Konferenser 51, ed. Bente Magnus (Stockholm, 2001), 189–204.

[11] Palle Ø. Sørensen, "Hal På Hal," *Skalk* 6 (1993): 9–12.

[12] Nicholas Jacobs, "Anglo-Danish Relations, Poetic Archaism and the Date of *Beowulf*," *Poetica* 8 (1978): 23–42; Colin Chase, *The Dating of* Beowulf (Toronto, 1981); John D. Niles, *Beowulf: The Poem and Its Tradition* (Cambridge, MA, 1983), 96–117. Proposing early ninth-century composition now is Richard North, *The Origins of Beowulf from Vergil to Wiglaf* (Oxford, 2006).

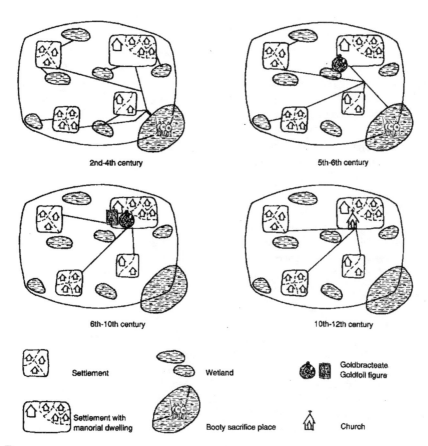

FIGURE 2.
Model of sacral places in relation to settlements in South Scandinavia from the 2nd to 12th centuries.

2nd–4th century: Individual sacrifices are made in all wetland areas. Collective sacrifices are in selected lakes shared among settlements.

5th–6th century: Individual sacrifices almost completely stop in wetlands. The last collective booty sacrifice occurs in late 5th, early 6th century. Dry land and wetland (bracteate) religious manifestations begin to be connected to the manorial settlement.

6th–10th century: Wetlands cease to function as sacrificial places. Religious observances with gold foil figures supplant bracteates.

10th–12th century: the earliest church is built by the nobleman on his property.

After Fabech 1994.

As Patrick Wormald put it, Chadwick "made the quite exceptionally interesting point, to which I have seen no subsequent reference."[13] That is, the names of characters of the poem were recorded of actual persons living in England during the seventh and eighth centuries. Individuals bearing the names of characters of the poem included a Beowulf[14] among six seventh-century persons and a Wiglaf among thirteen from the eighth century, to use only *Liber Vitae* citations. Two other names occur in sources Chadwick judged to be prior to 700 C.E. Such names became less popular in succeeding centuries. It is hard to escape the explanation that these proper names were adopted because a version of the poem was known and admired among Germanic immigrants to England as early as the seventh century.[15]

When and how did two Danish royal halls, at Gudme on Funen and at Lejre on Zealand, come to be?[16] The place where the Angles venerated the goddess *Terra Mater*, 'Mother Earth,' is now generally thought to have been Zealand,[17] the largest Danish island, where wealthy female graves in the Roman period have been seen as evidence of matriliny.[18] The Roman historian Tacitus said the Angles' name for Mother Earth was Nerthus and, despite a valuable recent

[13] H.M. Chadwick, *The Heroic Age* (Cambridge, 1912; repr. 1967), 43; P. Wormald, "Bede, *Beowulf* and the Conversion of the Anglo-Saxon Aristocracy," in *Bede and Anglo-Saxon England*, ed. Robert T. Farrell (Oxford, 1978), 32–95; also idem, "Bede, the *Bretwaldas* and the Origins of the *Gens Anglorum*," in *Ideal and Reality in Frankish and Anglo-Saxon Society*, ed. idem, Donald Bullough, and Roger Collins (London, 1983), 99–129.

[14] This occurrence of the name Beowulf was noted in a 1968 volume, G.N. Garmonsway and Jacqueline Simpson, Beowulf *and Its Analogues* (New York, 1968), 91.

[15] Worth attention here is that names like Hrōðgār, Hrōðulf, Hygelāc, and Scedenīg in *Beowulf*, as linguistic forms, provide presumptive evidence of their existence in England, perhaps in a written version of the poem, early enough to avoid the sound changes which occurred on the continent and affected other instances of these names. They are, as Fulk called them, "authentic [English] inheritances from a much earlier time": R.D. Fulk, "Dating *Beowulf* to the Viking Age," *Philological Quarterly* 61 (1982): 341–59, here 344. Discussion and other references in R. W. Chambers, *Beowulf: An Introduction* (Cambridge, 1967), 103, 323 and Sam Newton, *The Origins of* Beowulf *and the Pre-Viking Kingdom of East Anglia* (Rochester, NY, 1993), 14–16, where the cited pages of Moltke should be 152 and 156.

[16] See *Beowulf and Lejre*, ed. John D. Niles (Tempe, 2007). Tissø a possible royal hall house on Zealand: see Lars Jørgensen, "En storgård fra vikingetid ved Tissø, Sjælland—en foreløbig præsentation," in *Centrala Platser—Centrala Frågor*, ed. Lars Larsson and Birgitta Hårdh, Acta Archæologica Lundensia, Uppåkrastudier 1 (Lund, 1998), 233–48.

[17] See Frank Battaglia, "The Germanic Earth Goddess in *Beowulf*?" *Mankind Quarterly* 31 (1991): 415–46; and *Beowulf and Lejre*, ed. Niles, 210, 273–75, 283, 449.

[18] Hedeager, *Iron Age Societies*, 155; Battaglia, "Germanic Earth Goddess," 419–26. Hedeager suggested some African matrilineal analogues: *Iron Age Societies*, 89.

reexamination of this passage,[19] I believe we should take Tacitus at his word. Gabriel Turville-Petre agreed with Elias Wessén that East-Swedish place-name evidence makes it likely that the gender of the Germanic deity Njorð was originally female.[20]

About a hundred years after Tacitus's account, the largest collection of Roman swords in the world was deposited in a Danish bog. From Illerup (Figure 3) in East Jutland have come more swords than have been found in the entire Roman empire,[21] apparently borne by raiders from middle Sweden or Norway[22] who had themselves been Roman mercenaries or had acquired swords illegally. Indeed, it was forbidden under pain of death to export swords from the empire.[23] After defeating at least several hundred men, the local defenders of Eastern Jutland deposited the weapons of that invading force in a marsh, apparently thanking the power believed to be responsible for their victory. Even if this was a female earth and water deity venerated at such sites for thousands of years, the conceptual system is apt to have been changing as a result of such extraordinary circumstances. Further to the south, male deities, possible precursors of Woden and Tir, are recorded as being thanked for war victory in similar ways.[24] The earlier votive deposit of war booty at Hjortspring in Denmark was accompanied by a sacrifice of animals[25] which, as we shall see, seems to anticipate rituals which would subsequently be dedicated to male gods in Denmark and Sweden. Because other, smaller weapon deposits were made in the bog at Illerup about the year 400 and again about 500, it is accepted that a continuing community occupied the area and cooperated in its defense, under established leadership[26] — a local militia but not a standing army: a point of consequence in assessing the process of Danish political centralization.

In Figure 3, which refers to roughly the first half of the third century, the threat from middle Sweden and/or Norway is represented by the upper arrow.

---

[19] Richard North, *Heathen Gods in Old English Literature* (Cambridge, 1997), 21.

[20] Elias Wessén, "Schwedische Ortsnamen und Altnordische Mythologie," *Acta Philologica Scandinavica* 4 (1929): 97–115; E.O.G. Turville-Petre, "Fertility of Beast and Soil in Old Norse Literature," in *Old Norse Literature and Mythology*, ed. Edgar C. Polomé (Austin, 1969), 244–64.

[21] Ulla Lund Hansen, *Himlingøje — Seeland — Europa* (København, 1995), 388, Fig. 16.3; Jørgen Ilkjær, "The Weapons Sacrifices from Illerup Ådal, Denmark," in *The Birth of Europe*, ed. Klaus Randsborg (Rome, 1989), 54–61.

[22] Ilkjær, "Weapons Sacrifices"; idem, *Illerup Ådal* (Moesgård, 2000), 70–73.

[23] Jørn Lønstrop, "Mosefund af hærudstyr fra jernalderen," in *Jernalderens Stammesamfund*, ed. Peder Mortensen and Birgit M. Rasmussen (Moesgård, 1988), 93–100.

[24] C.D. Fisher, ed., *Cornelii Taciti Annalivm* (Oxford, 1906), 13. 57; Michael Grant, *Tacitus, The Annals of Imperial Rome* (New York, 1971), 312.

[25] Klaus Randsborg, *Hjortspring: Warfare and Sacrifice in Early Europe* (Aarhus, 1995), 36.

[26] Lønstrop, "Mosefund," 97; Fabech, "Samfundsorganisation," 285, 301.

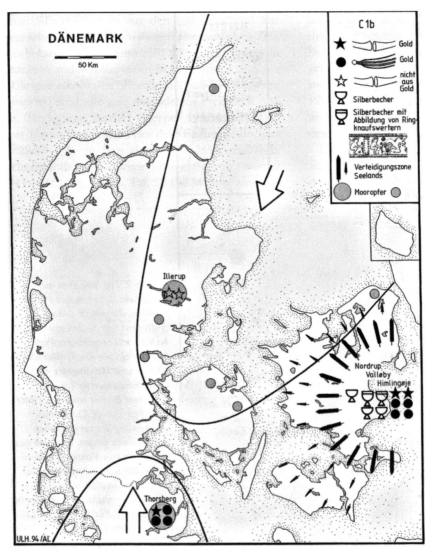

FIGURE 3.
Areas of cultural conflict in Denmark in the early 3rd century (210–250 C.E., Phase C1b). After Lund Hansen 1995.

Earlier attacks had reached the island of Funen, and left a large weapon deposit in the bog at Vimose. The lower arrow, near a similar bog deposit at Thorsberg, reflects encroachment from Germany, between the Elbe and the Rhine.[27]

Pinched by incursions from north and south is an area of influence the hub of which was Himlingøje in East Zealand. There roads were built, defenses organized, and long-distance trade with Rome distributed in gift exchange—notably to an emerging center, Gudme, on Funen. These relationships are diagramed in Figure 4.[28] Interestingly, all the material symbols of power such as gold snake-headed arm rings were worn by women as well as men, except that one male wore an additional gold club-ended arm ring, a sign of highest authority.[29] He has been described as the first king of Zealand, but the leading families apparently shared power.[30] A rich female grave from about 200 C.E. at Himlingøje contained a brooch with the earliest Danish runic inscription.[31]

---

[27] Lønstrop, "Mosefund," 94. For a possible Hedeby gap route, see Randsborg, *Hjortspring*, 66. *Matres* names on Roman inscriptions between the Rhine and the Elbe suggest that the tribes living there had been matrilineal at the point of Roman contact (references in Frank Battaglia, "*Sib* in *Beowulf*," *In Geardagum* 20 [1999]: 27–47, here 27, n. 1). Conquered by Rome after Caesar, these peoples had succeeded in wiping out three legions in 9 C.E., causing Rome to withdraw to the Rhine thereafter; see Maureen Carroll, *Romans, Celts and Germans* (Charleston, SC, 2001), 26–40.

[28] Figure 4 from Ulla Lund Hansen, "Handelszentren der römischen Kaiserzeit und Völkerwanderungszeit in Dänemark," in *Trade and Exchange in Prehistory*, ed. Brigitta Hardh et al. (Lund, 1988), 155–66, here 159, Abb. 2; essays by Eldrid Straume and Lotte Hedeager in that volume consider related gift exchange. For background see T.L. Markey, "Gift, Payment, and Reward Revisited," in *When Worlds Collide: Indo-Europeans and Pre-indo-Europeans*, ed. idem and John Greppin (Ann Arbor, 1990), 345–62, and Marcel Mauss, *The Gift—The Form and Reason for Exchange in Archaic Societies* (New York, 1990).

[29] Lund Hansen, *Himlingøje—Seeland—Europa*, 391; Per Ethelberg, *Skovgårde* (København, 2000), 145–69.

[30] Ethelberg, *Skovgårde*, 161. Possibly parallel is the succession of the Pictish kingship among about thirty individuals, all called Brude, whose full names were paired according to the formula "*Brude X, Brude Ur X*": Marjorie Anderson, *Kings and Kingship in Early Scotland* (Edinburgh, 1973), 81. I have suggested that Pictish kingship was shared between two matrilineal family lines, represented by the two most common Pictish symbols: Frank Battaglia, "The Matriliny of the Picts," *Mankind Quarterly* 31 (1990): 17–43, here n. 5, n. 16, 24, 39. Development from the Neolithic of these societies has also been argued by idem, "Germanic Earth Goddess," 418–26; and idem, "A Common Background to *Lai de Graelent* and *Noínden Ulad*?" *Emania* (Belfast) 11 (1993): 41–48; idem, "Goddess Religion in the Early British Isles," in *Varia on the Indo-European Past: Papers in Memory of Marija Gimbutas*, ed. Miriam Robbins Dexter and Edgar C. Polomé (Washington, DC, 1997), 48–82.

[31] National Museum of Denmark exhibit, August 2001. *Widuhudar*, the runic inscription, apparently named the brooch's maker: see Jørgen Jensen, *Guides to the National*

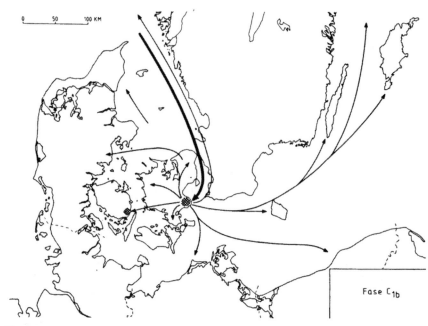

FIGURE 4.
The path of Roman prestige goods into Denmark by gift exchange from 210 to 250
C.E. After Lund Hansen 1988.

After the mid-third century, East Zealand declined in regional influence
while Southeast Funen became more prominent. A trading site on the coast
at Lundeborg operated as a sanctuary, a circumstance known elsewhere in the
North in the late Iron Age.[32] Peacefulness was apparently required of all visitors,
one reason why the seasonal trading activity has been linked to the festival of
Nerthus in which all weapons were put aside.[33] Several districts on Funen with
comparable indicators of wealth, power, and cult have been proposed (Figure
5).[34] The village of Gudme, a few kilometers from the coast, became increasingly
prosperous. It may have been the center of an emerging confederation. The name

---

Museum — The Prehistory of Denmark (Copenhagen, 1993), 98; Erik Moltke, *Runes and
their Origin, Denmark and Elsewhere* (Copenhagen, 1985), 128.

[32] Fabech, "Slöinge"; Ole Crumlin-Petersen, "Maritime Aspects of the Archaeology of Roman and Migration-Period Denmark," in *Aspects of Maritime Scandinavia AD
200–1200*, ed. idem (Roskilde, 1991), 41–54; Henrik Thrane, "Import, Affluence and
Cult – Interdependent Aspects?" in *Trade and Exchange*, ed. Hardh, 187–96.

[33] Crumlin-Petersen, "Roman and Migration-Period Denmark."

[34] Fabech, "Between Sacral and Political Power," Fig. 7.

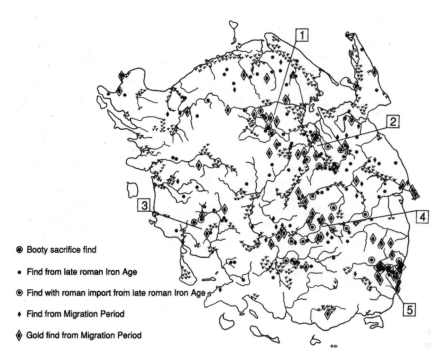

● Booty sacrifice find

• Find from late roman Iron Age

◉ Find with roman import from late roman Iron Age

♦ Find from Migration Period

◈ Gold find from Migration Period

FIGURE 5.
Five areas of Funen show comparable wealth, power and cult during the Late Roman Iron Age and Migration Period as a center developed at Gudme. After Fabech 1994.

Gudme, which also identified ten other locales in Scandinavia, means 'home of the gods.'[35]

The largest building of the Roman period in all of Scandinavia was erected at Gudme in Southeast Funen, perhaps before the third century ended (Figure 6): a huge hall, 47 meters long and over 9 wide.[36] It may have stood through the fifth century.[37] A shard of a pot made in Anglo-Saxon England in the fifth century

[35] John K. Sørensen,"Gudhjem," in *Gudme Problemer*, ed. Henrik Thrane (Odense, 1985), No. 33, 10–17. Repr. as "Gudhem," *Frühmittelalterliche Studien* 19 (1985): 131–38.

[36] Karsten K. Michaelsen and P. Ø. Sørensen, "En kongsgård fra jernalderen," *Årbog for Svendborg og Omegns Museum* 1993 (1994): 24–35; Sørensen, "Hal På Hal"; idem, "Gudmehallerne, Kongeligt byggeri fra jernalderen," with English summary "The Gudme Halls: Royal Buildings from the Iron Age," *Nationalmuseets Arbejdsmark* (København, 1994), 25–39.

[37] K.L. Rasmussen, U. Rahbek, and P.Ø. Sørensen, "Kulstof-14 datering af hus 1 (Kongehallen) ved Gudme," in *Gudme-Lundeborg—metodisk set*, ed. Mogens Bo Henriksen

FIGURE 6.
The Gudme hall was the largest in Scandinavia in the Roman Period. After Michaelsen and Sørensen 1994.

has been recovered there.[38] The Gudme area has yielded the largest amount of gold treasure ever found in Denmark,[39] some of it, in a transitional religious rite, buried in dry land deposits.

Gudme was an early and prolific producer of gold bracteates,[40] one type of which (Figure 7) depicted Othin sacrificing Baldr.[41] This type is called the *Dreigötter*, 'Three-Gods,' bracteate because of the presence of a third figure, Loki

and Karsten Kjer Michaelsen (Odense, 1995), No. 40, 55–58; Ole Stilborg, *Shards of Iron Age Communications* (Lund, 1997), 63.

[38] Stilborg, *Shards*, 62.

[39] Heinrik Thrane, "Gudme—A Focus of Archaeological Research 1833–1987," in *Gudme and Lundeborg*, ed. Nielsen et al., 8–15.

[40] Morten Axboe, "Gudme and the Gold Bracteates," in *Gudme and Lundeborg*, ed. Nielsen et al., 68–77; and Karl Hauck, "Gudme als Kultort und seine Rolle beim Austausch von Bildformularen der Goldbrakteaten," ibid, 78–88.

[41] Figure 7 from Hauck, "Gudme als Kultort," Fig. 5A (Gudme II-B, IK 51,3); a color photograph with discussion in Lars Jørgensen and Peter Vang Petersen, *Guld, Magt og Tro, — Gold, Power and Belief* (København, 1998), 237–39, Fig. 175. Design elements are treated in Karl Hauck, "Motivanalyse eines Doppelbrakteaten: Die Träger der goldenen Götterbildamulette und die Traditionsinstanz der fünischen Brakteatenproduktion," *Frühmittelalterliche Studien* 19 (1985): 139–94.

FIGURE 7.
Bracteates began by imitating Roman coins, but developed into Germanic political and religious art. This design shows Othin on the right with a spear, speaking and overseeing while Baldr in the center is killed by Loki or Höð. After Hauck 1994.

or Höð, in addition to Othin and Baldr.[42] Such bracteates are said by Karl Hauck to be "Bilddokumente des Handelns der Götterversammlung zur Gewinnung des Wohlwollens der Mächte der Anderwelt," 'images of the bargaining of the divine assembly to obtain the favor of the powers of the Otherworld.'[43] In this interpretation, Othin participates in the divine assembly and leads it in invoking a power higher than itself. Othin is first among equals of the (male) gods, who are not the ultimate authority. This mythological power structure seems to show Othin developing a new leadership function while neither he nor the (male) gods have primacy, an ideological pattern which might suit humans who were building a new kind of confederated central authority. Figure 8 shows that three of the known bracteates of Othin sacrificing Baldr were found on Funen,[44] with bracteate number 4 of Figure 8 (pictured above in Figure 7) being found in a posthole

---

[42] Axboe, "Gold Bracteates"; Hauck, "Gudme als Kultort"; Jørgensen and Vang Petersen, *Gold, Power and Belief*, 237–39. Only Roman referentiality is asserted by Gunilla Åkerström-Hougen, "Adventus Travels North," *Acta ad Archaeologiam et Artium Historiam Pertinentia* 15 (2001): 229–44; but see Hauck on the suggested Roman interpretation of the *Dreigötter* bracteates, "the alleged Victoria-amulets," "den angeblichen Victoria-Amuletten": *Die Goldbrakteaten der Völkerwanderungszeit* 1.1 (München, 1985), 139–47.

[43] Hauck, "Gudme als Kultort." I am indebted to Professor Merideth Lee, emerita, University of California, Irvine for advice in translating this passage.

[44] Figure 8 from Axboe, "Gold Bracteates," Fig. 7 and Appendix C. Two coins of unknown provenience are not represented.

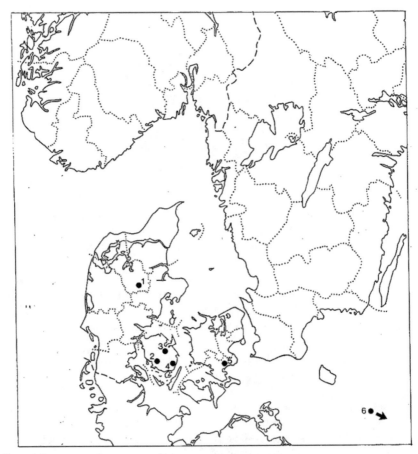

FIGURE 8.
Three of the Dreigötter bracteates were found on Funen, one (Figure 7) at Gudme.
After Axboe 1994.

of a house in Gudme.[45] The *Dreigötter* bracteates are dated to about 500 C.E.,[46]
while activity at Gudme peaked during the late fifth through early sixth century.[47] Joseph Harris has suggested that the theme of the death of Baldr may have

---

[45] Peter Vang Petersen, "Excavations at Sites of Treasure Trove Finds at Gudme," in
Gudme and Lundeborg, ed. Nielsen et al., 30–40.

[46] Jørgensen and Vang Petersen, *Gold, Power and Belief*, 239. On dating of the bracteates, see Morten Axboe, "Amulet Pendants and a Darkened Sun," in *Roman Gold*, ed.
Magnus, 119–36.

[47] Lars Jørgensen, "The Find Material from the Settlement of Gudme II — Composition and Interpretation," in *Gudme and Lundeborg*, ed. Nielsen et al., 53–63.

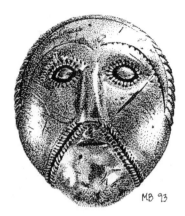

FIGURE 9.
A small silver mask of Othin was found at the Gudme hall. After Michaelsen and Sørensen 1994.

founded the *erfidrápa*, Old Norse funeral elegy.[48] Is it possible that the first songs about the death of Baldr were sung in the great hall at Gudme?

A small silver mask recovered from the building next to the Gudme hall is interpreted as the image of Othin (Figure 9).[49] From the beach at Lundeborg, a few kilometers from Gudme, have been recovered over a hundred *guldgubber,* small gold foil pieces with human figures stamped on them. Most *guldgubber* from Lundeborg represent a man and a woman in close embrace (Figure 10), possibly the god Freyr and the giantess Gerðr.[50] The preponderance of Danish *guldgubber* are from Bornholm,[51] and more commonly represent a single male or female. A solitary male with a staff is regarded as Othin, whereas a well dressed female figure is taken to be Freyja, 'Lady.' In any event, the system of reference of the *guldgubber* appears to have been polytheistic.

---

[48] In "North Sea Elegy and Para-Literary History," his keynote address to the Helsinki ISAS conference, 6 August 2001.

[49] Figure 9 from Michaelsen and Sørensen, "Kongsgård," Fig. 12 (drawing by Michael Banke).

[50] Figure 10 from Per O. Thomsen, "Handelspladsen ved Lundeborg," in *Lundeborg—en handelsplads fra jernalderen*, ed. idem et al. (Svendborg, 1993), 87–91; Jørgensen and Vang Petersen, *Gold, Power and Belief*, 263–68.

[51] Jørgensen and Vang Petersen, *Gold, Power and Belief*, 263–64. Freyr's importance in the symbolic system of the *guldgubber*, especially in light of the subsequent domination by Othin of Danish religion, makes it tempting to conceive of Bornholm as a reference point for the East Danes from whom Ing (intimately linked with Freyr: North, *Heathen Gods*, 32 and passim) has departed in the Anglo-Saxon rune poem: Maureen Halsall, *The Old English* Rune Poem: *A Critical Edition* (Toronto, 1981), 90.

FIGURE 10.
Over 100 small gold foil images were found near Gudme. Many show a man and woman embracing. After Thomsen 1993.

A gap exists between the time when the Gudme hall was taken down and the earliest royal building at Lejre. That village near Roskilde on Zealand has traditionally been regarded as the ancient seat of Danish kings. Excavations in the 1980s uncovered two successive stages of a great hall.[52] Figure 11 represents the newest of these, a Viking period building a little larger than the hall at Gudme.[53] An earlier version stood from the middle of the seventh century. In the late fifth or early sixth century a huge Lejre burial mound, Grydehøj, had marked the death of a princely figure.[54] Because of Scyld's funeral in *Beowulf,* of interest are two fairly complete "ship settings" and two partial ones, with seven others recorded in the eighteenth century. These are monuments of standing stones, each marking the outline of a ship. About 100 meters long, those at Lejre, which are probably no earlier than the late ninth century, are among the largest such structures known.

We have seen indications of political and religious pluralism at Gudme. Danish place names, however, record a hierarchical religious practice in the pre-Christian period, and Kristian Hald said that the sacral place names of Denmark

---

[52] Tom Christensen, "Lejrehallen," *Skalk* 3 (1987): 4–9; "Lejre Beyond Legend—The Archaeological Evidence," *Journal of Danish Archaeology,* 10 (1991): 163–85; repr. as part of Christensen's chapter in *Beowulf and Lejre,* ed. Niles, 21–101; "Lejre's Possible Maritime Connection," in *Aspects of Maritime Scandinavia,* ed. Crumlin-Pedersen, 173–82; "Lejrehallen," in ". . . *Gick Grendel,*" ed. Callmer and Rosengren, 47–54.

[53] Figure 11 from Jesse L. Byock, *The Saga of King Hrolf Kraki* (New York, 1998), xix.

[54] Steen Wulff Andersen, "Lejre—skibssætninger, vikingegrave, Grydehøj," *Aarbøger for Nordisk Oldkyndighed og Historie* 1993 (København, 1995): 7–142; cf. *Beowulf and Lejre,* ed. Niles, 143, 190–96.

FIGURE II.
Inside the ninth century version of the great hall at Lejre. After Byock 1998.

point to an unusually centralized political structure.[55] Thirty-plus ancient Danish place names designate religious sites, whereas well over one hundred are known in Sweden[56] and more than six hundred in Norway. Theophoric toponyms, however, those containing the name of a god, dedicate cult places to virtually only one deity in Denmark, namely Othin. The term *vi* for a religious site in early Denmark corresponds to OE *wīg* or *wēoh*, ON *vé*, OS and OHG *wih*; Goth *weih* is uncertain.[57] In Denmark *vi* was used to designate buildings which were the

[55] Kristian Hald, "The Cult of Othin in Danish Place Names," in *Early English and Norse Studies*, ed. Arthur Brown and Peter Foote (London, 1963), 99–109.

[56] Wessén, "Schwedische Ortsnamen," 97–98; Åke Hyenstrand, "Teofora ortnamn och förkristen organisation," in *Religion och samhälle i det förkristna Norden*, ed. Ulf Drobin (Odense, 1999), 125–38.

[57] Markey, "Terms for Temple and Cult," 373–75; David Wilson, "A Note on OE *hearg* and *wēoh* as Place Name Elements Representing Different Types of Pagan Saxon Worship Sites," *ASSAH* 4 (1985): 179–83; Audrey Meaney, "Pagan English Sanctuaries,

location of ancient public worship. Five -*vi* sites bear the name of a god, and the only deity thus acknowledged is Othin. Other *vi* place names are known which do not identify the deity (or deities) worshipped in those locations.[58]

The exclusive occurrence of one deity name in association with places of community worship suggests that "a single god, Othin, played a completely dominant role in the public cult" and this predominance shows "a concentration of political power" in the aristocratic families of early Denmark.[59]

Close to Lejre are located *Onsved* in Horns Herred and *Winnincgawe* in Tune Herred, respectively one of the five -*vi* names identifying an early Danish temple which incorporates the name Othin, and a -*vi* site not bearing a divine name. Their nearness to Lejre indicates "the close association between the cult of Othin and the royal power in the last pagan centuries."[60] Rituals at these locations may have been the ones Thietmar attributed to Lejre itself, notably the sacrifice every nine years of ninety-nine men. Only human sacrifices would have been devoted to Othin. The accompanying sacrifice of horses, dogs, and cocks thus seems to bear out Thietmar's plural, *diis*, 'to their gods.'[61] That is, other deities were worshipped. A horse, two dogs, and a sheep had been part of the Hjortspring war booty sacrifice, roughly 335 B.C.E.[62]

An offering similar to Lejre's was reported of Uppsala, Sweden, whose name derives from the great hall, *salr*, built there.[63] Nine men at a time were among the living sacrifices at a periodic festival to three gods, with Thor reported to have been the mightiest.

I will close this cultural geography with two questions. Although Gudme continued as an important site, perhaps indeed a royal estate in the second millennium, by the eighth century it had yielded as a regional center on Funen to Odense,[64] another *Othin* + -*vi* site. Likewise in North Jutland, one of the other

---

Place-Names and Hundred Meeting Places," *ASSAH* 8 (1995): 29–42. OE *wīg* or *wēoh* had a somewhat contrasting meaning to that of Danish *vi* in the last half of the first millennium, a topic to which I hope to return.

[58] Hald, "Cult of Othin," 108; Kristian Hald, *De Danske Stednavne Paa –Um* (København, 1942), 37.

[59] Hald, "Cult of Othin," 107–8.

[60] Hald, "Cult of Othin," 108.

[61] Robert Holtzmann, *Die Chronik des Bischofs Thietmar von Merseburg* (Berlin, 1935), 1: 9. See *Beowulf and Lejre*, ed. Niles, 297–99.

[62] C-14 dating of spear shaft and boat rib, Randsborg, *Hjortspring*, 20; animals, 36 (note 25 above); slightly later dating shown in Figure 1.

[63] Brink, "Political and Social Structures"; idem, "Fornskandinavisk religion — förhistoriskt samhälle: En bosättningshistorisk studie av centralorter i Norden," in *Religion och samhälle*, ed. Drobin, 11–55, here 27–30.

[64] Ulf Näsman, "Sea Trade during the Scandinavian Iron Age: Its Character, Commodities, and Routes," in *Aspects of Maritime Scandinavia*, ed. Crumlin-Pedersen, 23–40.

Gudhem, 'home of the gods,' sites, was replaced as a religious center by Vium,[65] whose name indicates a temple though no deity is specified. Is it possible that *Gudhem* sites signal an intermediate confederated stage of religious and political authority in Denmark, and -*vi* sites a later, more hierarchical stage? Can analysis of the story of Baldr bring any light to this discussion?

What implications might these matters have for *Beowulf*? First, since the *flyting* with Unferth includes a taunt that the Danes must learn manliness from the Geats,[66] it is possible that the conflict I have hypothesized between **Gudhem* sites and -*vi* sites has an echo there. Indeed, I am elsewhere suggesting that in an early version of the *Beowulf* poem the hanging of Grendel's arm constituted Othinic ritual, supported among the Danes by the Geats.[67]

Second, and more generally, all of the monsters of the poem are associated with watery places. Even the dragon lives near the sea and is dumped into it in death. All three monsters may be related to the old belief system with its wet sacrifices. Nora Chadwick proposed in 1959 that the monsters may represent a social group early opposed by the Geats, who are implicated by Jørgen Ilkjær's analysis of the origin of the Illerup attackers.[68]

Speaking of Illerup,[69] we note a difference between Scyld's defense of his people and the Illerup militia's. Scyld made his neighbors pay him tribute, by which he maintained a fighting force responsible to him rather than the communities its members came from.

Grendel is explicitly said to mark his bog retreats—*mearcað mōrhopu* (450)[70]—with Beowulf's corpse. It sounds exactly like a ritual activity which the poem is declaring to be forbidden. It sounds a lot like the use of bogs as religious sites. Grendel sometimes appears sub-human, but *mearcað mōrhopu* is one clue that, on his part, an earlier religion was involved. Another is the verb *sendan*,[71] emended by Frederick Klaeber to *snēdan* to avoid "old heathen sacrificial

---

[65] Sørensen, "Gudhjem."

[66] Battaglia, "Germanic Earth Goddess," 427–30.

[67] Frank Battaglia, "Grendel's Arm and the Religion of Woden," Modern Language Association convention paper, New Orleans, December 2001; abstract in *Old English Newsletter*, Fall 2002.

[68] Nora Chadwick, "The Monsters and *Beowulf*," in *The Anglo-Saxons*, ed. Peter Clemoes (London, 1959), 171–203; Ilkjær, "Weapons Sacrifices," note 22 above.

[69] Ulf Näsman believes that the scarcity of excavated Danish weapon graves for the period may be making it hard to see that the raiders at Illerup originated from an area closer than middle Sweden (pers. comm.).

[70] All *Beowulf* references are to Friedrich Klaeber, *Beowulf and The Fight at Finnsburg*, 3rd ed. (Boston, 1950).

[71] Anatoly Lieberman, "Germanic *sendan* 'to make a sacrifice'," *Journal of English and Germanic Philology* 77 (1979): 473–88; Britt-Mari Näsström, "*Blót, sóa* och *senda:* Om offer i fornskandinavisk religion," in *Religion och samhälle*, 157–170.

terminology," which Beowulf complains of in line 600 as something the Danes let Grendel get away with.

The watery site at Forlev Nymølle seems particularly relevant because its more than six-hundred-year period of use overlaps both the nearby Illerup valley weapon offerings and the erection of the Gudme hall.[72] Especially we note that ritually treated human bone was part of a ceremonial concentration there.[73] A piece of human shoulder blade had been defleshed with a knife and perhaps later used as an amulet before its deposit in the bog. Anticipating a larger study,[74] I suggest that: a) the bone came from an ancestor of the person who apparently carried it as an amulet before putting it in the marsh; b) scraping the flesh from the skeleton of an ancestor who had perhaps been excarnated was understood as a ritual of a Danish religious system which included endo-cannibalism ('the eating of relatives') at least in its remote past;[75] c) ancestor worship was an element of the cult. By the *Beowulf* poet's magic, the Scyldings speak for the Danes. Grendel opposes the Scyldings, so he is one of the *untýdras*, the "misbegotten," not even a Dane. Native religious traditions became in *Beowulf* exo-cannibalistic, hardly human.

We would expect that after the shift from bog to hall religious discourse would regularly entail statements of the special relationship between a deity or deities and the ruler. A military elite had taken over religious ritual, moved it to a different place. Subsequent pronouncements of religious sentiment might be expected which explained these changes as a consequence of a ruler's unique favor in the eyes of the deity: the reason why ritual belongs at the building controlled

---

[72] The Silkeborg Museum text (*Mosens Guder* 65, 63) referred to pottery from the last three centuries BC; the 2001 exhibit included pots dated "350 AD." Lund put the date of pottery recovered before the start of supervised excavation at about 400 AD ("Forlev Nymølle," 144). Fertility sacrifices at Bukkerup on Funen ceased at the end of the Early Roman Iron Age, about the time when the first weapons sacrifice was made close to it at Kragehul: Aase Gyldion Andersen, "Frugtbarhedsofringer i Sydvestfyns aeldre jernalder," *Kuml* (1993–1994): 199–210.

[73] Lund, "Forlev Nymølle," 153; for similar sites, Kaul, in *Spoils of Victory*, 40; Charlie Christiansen, "The Sacrificial Bogs of the Iron Age," in *Spoils of Victory*, 346–54, here 352.

[74] A selection from which was presented as "Cannibalism in Denmark and in *Beowulf*," Modern Language Association convention, Old English Division, 27 December 2006.

[75] Flemming Kaul, "Ritualer med menneskeknogler i yngre stenalder," *Kuml* (1991–1992): 7–52. National Museum of Denmark, 2001, *Bøndernes religion 4000–2800 BC*, Exhibit #6, "The sacrificial meal," '*Hellige måltid*,' included these words in English: "Human flesh was sometimes included in the meal." Prehistoric Museum, Moesgård, 2001 Neolithic exhibit on "Man and the unseen" stated: "Many sacrificial sites have evidence of human sacrifice and. . . skeletal remains which can signify cannibalism (*der kunne tyde på kannibalisme*)."

by the elite is that the deity cares especially for the elite. In *Beowulf*, on how many occasions is the deity's special love of the military leader expressed as it is in line 17, *wuldres Wealdend woroldāre forgeaf* 'the Wielder of Wonder conveyed [i.e., thoroughly gave] world honor'? This remark would be especially portentous if the deity formerly honored at watery locations was identified with "giving"—as the Danish chthonic goddess Gefjun was.[76]

The first kings were rulers of peoples, not territories. The hall, however, was an early physical space which belonged to the new order, a first *patria*,[77] which explains its emotional resonance. A whole vocabulary was created in which social identity was expressed by a link with a building—*heorðgenēat*, 'near one of the hearth'; *fletwerod*, 'floor band.' Rosemary Woolf regarded "compounds, of which the second element is *werod* and the first a word for some part of the hall" as the closest Old English comes to having a term for *comitatus*.[78]

Of the terms for the new kind of building used in the poem, the most important are *sele*, *reced*, and *heal*, with *ærn*, *hūs*, and *bold* also being employed on a few occasions. The most frequent word is *sele*, cognate with the *salr* element in the name Uppsala. It occurs eleven times as a simplex and at least thirty-one times in compounds. *Sele* seems to be the word most associated with ceremonies. Three mentions of the "cleansing" of Heorot all refer to the structure as *sele* (826, *bēahsele* 1177, 2352).

In closing, let me draw attention to a recent conference on emerging central places of the late Iron Age in Scandinavia. The conference title was ". . .Gick Grendel Att Söka Det Höga Huset. . ."—'Grendel Sought the High House.'[79] If archaeologists look to past literature for ideas about social relations, language scholars may find something to ground us in the material record. As Rosemary Cramp put it in the first issue of *Medieval Archaeology*: "The picture of Anglo-Saxon society given in *Beowulf* must be fully considered by archaeologists, while on the other hand no critic of the poem can afford to neglect the new material evidence that is constantly being produced."[80]

---

[76] North, *Heathen Gods*, 223; Battaglia, "Germanic Earth Goddess"; idem, "*Gifeðe* as a Word for 'granted by fate' in *Beowulf*," *In Geardagum* 22 (2002): 1–17.

[77] "Halls had a positive value based on their role as . . . centres for early Anglo-Saxon civilization": Kathryn Hume, "The Concept of the Hall in Old English Poetry," *ASE* 3 (1974): 63–74. By the middle Saxon period, "the centre of . . . settlements . . . was the great hall": P.V. Addyman, "The Anglo-Saxon House: A New Review," *ASE* 1 (1972): 273–307.

[78] Rosemary Woolf, "The Ideal of Men Dying with their Lord in the *Germania* and in *The Battle of Maldon*," *ASE* 5 (1976): 63–81, here 69, n. 1; John Lindow, *Comitatus, Individual and Honor* (Berkeley, 1975), 25–27.

[79] A text edited by Callmer and Rosengren with studies from the conference has been cited in notes 3 and 10 above.

[80] Rosemary Cramp, "*Beowulf* and Archaeology," *Medieval Archaeology* 1 (1957): 55–77, here 57. See now *Beowulf and Lejre*, ed. Niles.

Why There Are Three Eddic Meters

Geoffrey Russom

Old English poetry survives to us in just one traditional meter, but three meters are usually distinguished in Norse Eddic poetry: *fornyrðislag*, which is similar to the meter of *Beowulf*; *ljóðaháttr*, characteristically used for gnomic verse; and *málaháttr*, the meter of the Eddic poem *Atlamál*. Metrists have applied Sievers's system of scansion with some success to *fornyrðislag*, but it has proved much more difficult to distinguish *málaháttr* from *fornyrðislag*[1] or to identify constraints on verse rhythm in *ljóðaháttr*.[2]

Our understanding of Eddic meter has been thwarted, I think, in several important ways. First, as Bjarne Fidjestøl points out, scholars of the nineteenth century failed to consider the possibility that strict versecraft might develop without external stimulus in cultures of the ancient Nordic margin, insisting for example that *fornyrðislag* arose by imitation of more civilized Anglo-Saxon poetry.[3] Negative evaluation of Eddic poems with South Germanic legendary content, including *Atlamál*, has been mandated by a theory that they were translated from German originals without concern for the metrical rules obeyed by German poets.[4] Another important obstacle to appreciation of the Eddic poet's art has been Eduard Sievers's analysis of Germanic meter as a system of five verse types.[5] These five types cannot be derived straightforwardly from general

---

[1] E. O. G. Turville-Petre, *Scaldic Poetry* (Oxford, 1976), xiii–xiv.

[2] Kristján Árnason, *The Rhythms of Dróttkvætt and other Old Icelandic Metres* (Reykjavík, 1991), 52.

[3] Bjarne Fidjestøl, *The Dating of Eddic Poetry: A Historical Survey and Methodological Investigation*, ed. Odd Einar Haugen, Bibliotheca Arnamagnæana 41 (Copenhagen, 1999), 29–32.

[4] Hans Kuhn, "Westgermanisches in der altnordischen Verskunst," *Beiträge zur Geschichte der deutschen Sprache und Literatur* 63 (1939): 178–236. Compare Fidjestøl, *Dating*, 157, 321–23; R. D. Fulk, *A History of Old English Meter* (Philadelphia, 1992), 238, n. 3.

[5] Eduard Sievers, *Altgermanische Metrik* (Halle, 1893). Because existing theories make it so awkward to pursue focused research on Eddic meters, the most recent bibliographical survey has practically nothing to report in this area. See Joseph Harris, "Eddic

principles of verse construction, and it was only by keeping the number of types small that Sievers could hope to justify his system. Since Eddic meters employ many additional types, they are necessarily represented by Sievers as permissive.

Within the word-foot theory,[6] which I employ for the analysis presented here, the basic or paradigmatic expression of each verse type is a pair of words. Appreciation of the meter consists in associating variants of types with their two-word paradigms. Thus example 2 below is scanned by associating it with the two-word paradigm represented by example 1, which has a similar stress pattern:

Example[7]	Pattern	Sievers type	Verse number
(1) sēon / sibbe-gedriht	**S/Sxxs**	Db paradigm	Beo 387a
'to see the kindred band'			
(2) secg / weorce gefeh	**S/Sxxs**	Db variant	Beo 1569b
'the man rejoiced in the work'			
(3) on morgen-tīd	**x/Sxs**	B paradigm	Beo 484b
'in the morning-time'			
(4) þæt / mihtig god	**x/Sxs**	B variant	Beo 701a
'that mighty God [ruled]'			

Poetry," in *Old Norse-Icelandic Literature: A Critical Guide*, ed. Carol J. Clover and John Lindow, Islandica 45 (Ithaca, 1985), 68–156.

    [6] Geoffrey Russom, *'Beowulf' and Old Germanic Metre*, Cambridge Studies in Anglo-Saxon England 23 (Cambridge, 1998).

    [7] In word-foot notations, S represents a metrical position normally occupied by a syllable with full stress; s, a position normally occupied by a syllable with subordinate stress; and x, a position normally occupied by a syllable with zero stress. The slash (/) represents a verse-internal boundary between feet. A double slash (//) marks the boundary between a two-foot verse pattern and the additional foot that is added in some extended patterns, such as Old English hypermetrical verses, *dróttkvætt* a-verses, and *ljóðaháttr* c-verses (discussed below). *Beowulf* is cited from Frederick Klaeber, ed., *Beowulf and the Fight at Finnsburg*, 3rd ed. (Lexington, MA, 1950). Eddic poetry is cited from Gustav Neckel, ed., *Edda: Die Lieder des Codex Regius nebst verwandten Denkmälern*, 5th ed. rev. by Hans Kuhn (Heidelberg, 1983). For a description of the native Eddic *fornyrðislag* corpus employed here, see Russom, *Old Germanic Metre*, 8–11. *Haraldskvæði* is cited from Finnur Jónsson, ed., *Fagrskinna: Nóregs Konunga Tal*, Samfund til Utgivelse af Gammel Nordisk Literatur 30 (Copenhagen, 1902–1903), 6–10 (stanzas 1–9) and 16–18 (stanzas 18–25). Stanzas 10–15, which are metrically distinct, are excluded from the analysis. Snorri's example of *málaháttr* is cited from Anthony Faulkes, ed., *Snorri Sturluson, Edda: Háttatal* (Oxford, 1991), 37. Due to the difficulty of the material, *dróttkvætt* examples are cited from Roberta Frank, *Old Norse Court Poetry: The Dróttkvætt Stanza*, Islandica 42 (Ithaca, 1978), which provides full discussion, glosses, and bibliography. The convention for reference to these examples is illustrated by 'F11/3' in example 23 below, which refers to Frank's stanza 11, line 3 (p. 95). If the gloss for an example makes no sense in isolation, I include translated material from adjacent verses, placed within square brackets, as in example 4.

(5) *weorce gefeh   **Sxx/S**   compare to the second foot in (2)
(6) *mihtig god   **Sx/S**   compare to the second foot in (4)

Similarly, example 4 is scanned by associating it with the two-word paradigm represented by example 3. All native words, including unstressed words and compounds, can serve as prototypes for word feet, but no poem employs all possible word pairings as paradigms for verse types. Within a given poem, the types must form a coherent set if the audience is to distinguish feet from verses, an obvious prerequisite for appreciation of verse patterns. Thus in *Beowulf*, verses like example 5 are ruled out because they would look too much like the second foot in verses like example 2. Similarly, verses like example 6 are excluded because they would look too much like the second foot in verses like example 4. In general, the poet avoids overlap of foot patterns and verse patterns.

Just prior to its historical era, the Old Norse language lost unstressed word-internal syllables by syncope and discontinued use of unstressed prefixes, including prefixes internal to compound words. These changes eliminated compounds with the Sxxs stress pattern of OE *sibbe-gedriht*, leaving no linguistic prototypes for a compound foot with two unstressed syllables between the stresses.[8] Verse types employing the Sxxs foot pattern were accordingly abandoned by Norse poets, opening the way for employment of an Sxx/S verse pattern:

(7) kǫlloðo / Karl   **Sxx/S**   new paradigm   Rþ 21/3
    'they called [him] "Karl"'
(8) Freyio at / qvæn   **Sxx/S**   new variant   Þrk 8/8
    'Freyja as a wife'

Example 7 is a two-word paradigm of the new Norse pattern with a dactylic word in the first foot.[9] Example 8 is a variant with a dactylic word group in the first foot. From Sievers's perspective, 7 and 8 are deviant expressions of type E lacking the normal secondary stress on the second metrical position. Within the word-foot framework, these verses are expressions of a new type made possible by language change.

Syncope and loss of internal prefixes eliminated many, though not all, Norse compounds with the stress pattern of OE *morgen-tīd*. The corresponding word foot with one unstressed syllable between the stresses was employed less frequently, and employment of verses with the pattern of example 6 became

---

[8] Russom, *Old Germanic Metre*, 20, 32. Compounds are hyphenated for expository convenience in poetic examples and accompanying discussion.

[9] Stress is assumed on the short medial syllable of preterites like *kǫlloðo* by Sievers (*Altgermanische Metrik*, section 78.5), but this is nothing more than an expedient to protect his two-stress hypothesis from counterexamples. See Geoffrey Russom, "Metrical Evidence for Subordinate Stress in Old English," *Journal of Germanic Linguistics* 13 (2001): 45–47.

somewhat less problematic. In *Rígsþula*, an example of Eddic *fornyrðislag*, the poet found a way to use this pattern while continuing to use type B verses with the pattern of example 3:

(9) grófo / torf   **Sx/S**   short paradigm   Rþ 12/14
     'they dug peat'
(10) við / veiði-mat   **x/Sxs**   B paradigm   Hym 16/7
     'with food from hunting or fishing'
(11) oc / hiorvi brá   **x/Sxs**   B variant   Rþ 37/8
     'and brandished the sword'

In the short type, represented by example 9, the poet normally placed a fully stressed noun or adjective like *torf* on the last metrical position, providing an emphatic realization for the *S* foot that corresponds to a stressed monosyllabic word. In the type B variant represented by example 11, on the other hand, the poet normally placed a word with subordinate stress on the last metrical position, in this case the finite verb *brá*, which has subordinate phrasal stress and provides an appropriate realization for the subordinate *s* constituent of a compound foot. Compare the two-word paradigm of Norse type B in example 10, where the compound *veiði-mat* realizes the compound Sxs foot in the simplest way, with the subordinate constituent *-mat* realizing the *s* position. From Sievers's perspective, *Rígsþula* contravenes a minimum of four metrical positions observed more scrupulously by Old English poets. From the perspective of the word-foot theory, *Rígsþula* maintains coherence in an expanded set of verse types by matching stresses with greater precision than Old English meter would require.

According to E. V. Gordon, loss of unstressed syllables from prehistoric verse established influential precedents for short verse types. "After the syncope of unaccented vowels in the eighth century," he states, "lines originally containing the metrical minimum of syllables were reduced below that minimum, and the reduced lines then came to be regarded as permissible variants and were imitated in later poems."[10] In *fornyrðislag*, these new short types tended to displace the longest older types, represented below by Old English examples:

(12) síde / sæ-næssas   **Sx/Ssx**   expanded Da   Beo 223a
     'large headlands'
(13) frēcne / fen-gelād   **Sx/Sxs**   expanded Db   Beo 1359a
     'dangerous fen-path'
(14) æghwylc // ōðrum / trȳwe   **Sx//Sx/Sx**   hypermetrical a-verse Beo 1165a
     'each true to the other'
(15) þǣr þā // gōdan / twēgen   **xx//Sx/Sx**   hypermetrical b-verse Beo 1163b
     'where the two worthies [sat]'

---

[10] E. V. Gordon, *An Introduction to Old Norse*, 2nd ed. rev. by A. R. Taylor (Oxford, 1957), 315, section 178.

(16) (ge)wāc æt / wīge	**(x)Sx/Sx**	A1 with anacrusis	Beo 2629a
'failed in battle'			
(17) (swā) sǣ be-/būgeð	**(x)Sx/Sx**	nonprefixal anacrusis	Beo 1223b
'as the sea surrounds'			

There was a sharp decline in the frequency of expanded D verses comparable to Old English examples 12 and 13. Hypermetrical verses comparable to Old English examples 14 and 15 were excluded altogether. Extension of verses by anacrusis was also discontinued. In Old English poetry, anacrusis usually consisted of an unstressed prefix added at the beginning of a type A or D verse, as with the parenthesized *ge*-prefix in example 16. After Old Norse lost prefixes, of course, this kind of anacrusis was simply impossible. In Old English poems, nonprefixal anacrusis is largely restricted to variants of type A1 placed in the second half of the alliterative line. Example 17 is typical. Old Norse variants of this kind must have survived in poetry inherited from the prehistoric period, but the developing bias toward shorter, lighter verses made it awkward to incorporate them. Not all of the new short types could readily be accommodated in *fornyrðislag*. Verses like example 18 are vanishingly rare:

(18) Breiðr, / Bóndi	**S/Sx**	short paradigm	Rþ 24/5
'Breiðr and Bóndi'			
(19) sat / berg-búi	**x/Ssx**	C paradigm	Hym 2/1
'there sat the rock-dweller'			
(20) þér / býðr bróðir	**x/Ssx**	C variant	HHII 35/1
'your brother offers you [wealth]'			

Verses like example 18 are problematic because they look too much like the second foot of extremely common verses like example 20, a variant of the type C paradigm represented by example 19. Unlike type B, type C maintained a high frequency in Eddic verse because compounds like *berg-búi* were not subject to syncope. Despite ingenious efforts, then, the need to restrict overlap made it impossible for *fornyrðislag* to incorporate all verse types with traditional precedents. Some types would have to be accommodated otherwise. The solution was to employ two additional meters.

Fornyrðislag resembles West Germanic meters in its free placement of verse types. Constraints on overlap are required because there is no way to anticipate which type will come next. *Ljóðaháttr* seems to arise from the realization that a metrical system could accommodate more verse types if otherwise incompatible types were assigned to different locations in stanzaic structure.

Kristján Árnason provides a useful summary of observations about the *ljóðaháttr* stanza, which consists of two half-stanzas with three verses each.[11] Below is a representative half-stanza (*Hávamál* 42/1–3):

---

[11] Kristján Árnason, *Rhythms of Dróttkvætt*, 161–64.

(21) (a) Vin / sínom   **S/Sx**   short a-verse
          'To one's friend
     (b) scal maðr / vinr vera   **xx/Ssx**   b-verse (type C)
          one must be a friend
     (c) ok / gialda giof // (við) giof   **x/Sxs//(x)S**   c-verse
          and give gift for gift'

I will refer to the three verses of the *ljóðaháttr* half-stanza as the a-verse, the b-verse, and the c-verse, respectively. The a-verse and b-verse are linked by alliteration, like the two verses that constitute a line of *fornyrðislag*. Verses 21a–b above are linked by alliteration on *v*. The unpaired c-verse has its own internal system of alliteration. Verse 21c has internal alliteration on *g*. The a-verse is the normal location for the shortest and lightest types and also for the simplest traditional pattern, type A1. The b-verse is the normal location for types B and C, which pose the greatest problems of overlap with short types. The c-verse is the location for the special *ljóðaháttr* types, which are sometimes called "full lines."[12]

If the audience knows that an a-verse is likely to be short, confusion between short verses and long feet occupied by word groups will be significantly reduced. It is not surprising to find that the variety of short types in the first 79 stanzas of *Hávamál*, widely regarded as a representative sample of *ljóðaháttr*,[13] is far greater than in *fornyrðislag*. Of 159 a-verses in this sample, 61, or 38%, have short patterns that would be unacceptable in *Beowulf*. The comparable figure for *fornyrðislag* is only 2%. Type A1, the most common pattern in *fornyrðislag*, is the only traditional pattern with a high frequency in the *ljóðaháttr* a-verse, with a total of 40 instances out of 159 (25%). In this part of the half-stanza, type B (10 examples) and type C (6 examples) are far outnumbered by shorter and lighter types. There are very few of the heavy D and E variants.[14]

In the b-verses of our 79-stanza sample, type B has about nine times its frequency in the a-verse, with 93 occurrences. About one-third of these end with a light disyllable consisting of a short stressed syllable followed by an unstressed syllable:

(22) oc / illa scapi   **x/Sxs**   Type B with resolved *s* Háv 22/2
     'and ill-disposed'

Here the light disyllable *scapi* is 'resolved' and placed on a single *s* position. Verses like example 22 are acceptable in *Beowulf*, but they are excluded from *fornyrðislag*

---

[12] Turville-Petre, *Scaldic Poetry*, xv.

[13] See David A. H. Evans, *Hávamál* (London, 1986), 6–8.

[14] Two examples would be classified as expanded Da by Sievers (one Sx/Ssx verse and one Sx/Sxx verse). There are two examples of four-position Da (S/Ssx), and six examples of type E (Ssx/S). Three of the type E variants have anacrusis.

by its stricter constraints on resolution.[15] The more predictable location of type B verses in *ljóðaháttr* must have made them significantly easier to scan by intuition, allowing for a wider variety of traditional variants. The frequency of type C verses like 21b also rises sharply in the *ljóðaháttr* b-verse, from 6 to 43 examples. Type A1, the most common a-verse pattern, is reduced from 40 to a mere 8 examples in the b-verse. The heavier patterns of types D and E occur with about the same low frequency as in the a-verse.[16]

A widely recognized characteristic of the *ljóðaháttr* c-verse is a constraint on the verse-final constituent, which is normally a stressed monosyllable (as in 21c) or a light disyllable consisting of a short stressed syllable followed by an unstressed syllable.[17] Occasional exceptions to this rule have not raised doubts about its general validity.[18] There is no comparable constraint in *fornyrðislag*. In *dróttkvætt* court meter, we find a different constraint on the verse-final constituent, which must consist of a long stressed syllable followed by an unstressed syllable, as in the example below:

(23) við / góma sker // glymja   **x/Sxs//Sx** type B + Sx   F11/3
'to resound against the skerries of the gums (= teeth)'

The *dróttkvætt* a-verse is normally derived by addition of a trochaic foot (Sx) to one of the two-foot verse types attested in *fornyrðislag*, in this case type B. The line-final foot of the *ljóðaháttr* c-verse looks like a shorter relative of the line-final *dróttkvætt* foot, suggesting that c-verses might also be derived by addition of a third foot.

Ljóðaháttr retains some traditional freedoms that are severely restricted in *dróttkvætt*, such as addition of extrametrical unstressed words before the foot.[19] If we represent the verse-final constituent of the *ljóðaháttr* c-verse as an *S* foot, which seems correct, the immediately preceding unstressed syllable of example 21c, which is placed between parentheses, will have to be analyzed as extrametrical. Compare example 24 from *Beowulf*, which also has an extrametrical word before a verse-final *S* foot:

---

[15] Russom, *Old Germanic Metre*, 100–7.

[16] There are two examples of expanded Da (Sx/Ssx), two examples of four-position type Da (S/Ssx), and three examples of type E (Ssx/S). All the type E verses have anacrusis, and would not be acceptable in an Old English poem. The percentage of type E with anacrusis is very high in *ljóðaháttr*, too high, I think, to be explained in terms of deficient versecraft or scribal error. I set aside here the question of exactly why such an unusual kind of anacrusis might be easier to accommodate in *ljóðaháttr*. For our present purposes it is sufficient to observe that the total frequency of type E is kept very low in this meter.

[17] Turville-Petre, *Scaldic Poetry*, xv–xvi.

[18] Fidjestøl, *Dating*, 260–65.

[19] Russom, *Old Germanic Metre*, chap. 4.

(24) wergendra / (tō) lȳt   **Ssx/(x)S**   Type E variant   Beo 2882b
     'too few defenders'

Verses like 24 are common variants of type E in Old English poetry and can also be found in *fornyrðislag*.

As it turns out, when we subtract the verse-final *S* foot and any preceding extrametrical words from a *ljóðaháttr* c-verse, what remains, in the vast majority of cases, is a *ljóðaháttr* a-verse. Like the *dróttkvætt* a-verse, the *ljóðaháttr* c-verse is derived from a two-foot verse type by addition of a third foot with a fixed pattern. This structure is clearly marked in a c-verse like 21c, which consists of a familiar type B pattern to which the poet has added an extrametrical unstressed word and a stressed monosyllable. Note the similarity to *dróttkvætt* example 23, which is derived by adding a trochaic word to the same type B pattern. C-verse structure is also readily apparent in examples derived by addition of the verse-final *S* foot to familiar patterns of types A1, A3, and C:

(25) annars / brióstom // í   **Sx/Sx//S**   Type A1 + S (15x)   Háv 8/6
     'in another's breast'
(26) síns um / freista // frama   **xx/Sx//S**   Type A3 + S (41X)   Háv 2/6
     'to try one's luck'
(27) enn sé / of-dryccia // ǫls   **xx/Ssx//S**   Type C + S (6X)   Háv 11/6
     'than is excessive drinking of ale'

Of the Norse verse types that are also used in Old English meter, the one most often employed as the first segment of a *ljóðaháttr* c-verse is the ultralight type A3, with 41 attestations, followed by type A1 (15x), type C (6x) and type B (3x). As we have seen, such a bias toward the lighter types is characteristic of the *ljóðaháttr* a-verse.

A researcher concerned primarily with Old English meter may find it more difficult, at least at first, to appreciate the structure of *ljóðaháttr* c-verses like those below:

(28) um / scoðaz // scyli   **x/S//S**   x/S + S (3x)   Háv 1/3
     'should peer about'
(29) friðr / fimm // daga   **S/S//S**   S/S + S (3x)   Háv 51/3
     'friendship for five days'
(30) oc á / kné // kalinn   **xx/S//S**   xx/S + S (19x)   Háv 3/3
     'and cold in the knees'
(31) í / hófi // hafa   **x/Sx//S**   x/Sx + S (7x)   Háv 64/3
     'maintain in moderation'
(32) oc / víg-diarft // vera   **x/Ss//S**   x/Ss + S (2x)   Háv 15/3
     'and be bold in battle'
(33) ǫl / alda // sonum   **S/Sx//S**   S/Sx + S (7x)   Háv 12/3
     'ale for the sons of men'

(34) sialdan / sút // ala	**Sx/S//S**	Sx/S + S (14x)	Háv 48/3
'(they) seldom nurse anxiety'			
(35) ef hann við / víg // varaz	**xxx/S//S**	xxx/S + S (19x)	Háv 16/3
'if he avoids warfare'			
(36) fé eða / fior // hafa	**Sxx/S//Sx**	Sxx/S + S (11x)	Háv 58/3
'to take wealth or life'			

These c-verses are constructed by adding a stressed monosyllable or light stressed disyllable to the kind of short verse that would be unacceptable in an Old English poem.[20] To summarize: the *ljóðaháttr* c-verse is constructed like the *dróttkvætt* a-verse, except that the c-verse tends to be lighter and shorter in each part and allows for employment of extrametrical unstressed words, as with other Eddic verse patterns.

Before we turn to *málaháttr*, it will be useful to summarize the distributions of verse types in the meters discussed thus far. Table 1 provides these distributions, along with the distributions for *málaháttr*.[21]

---

[20] On employment of an xxx foot in Eddic verses like example 35, see Russom, *Old Germanic Metre*, 33. Example 33 is cited from Evans, *Hávamál*, 41, with an emendation of *sona* to *sonum* that does not change the metrical value and is much easier to translate.

[21] For ease of comparison, verses are scanned in the same way for all poems, though as we shall see the preferred scansion for a particular poem may differ in certain cases. The *Beowulf* verses scanned as xxx/Sx, for example, would have to be analyzed within the Old English metrical system as xx/Sx verses to which an extrametrical syllable has been added. Absence of Norse patterns with an Sxxs foot is due to disappearance of the corresponding compound pattern from the language, as discussed above. Statistics for *málaháttr* include three verses not present in *Fagrskinna* but usually thought to be part of this poem. See *Den norsk-islandske skjaldedigtning*, ed. Finnur Jónsson (Copenhagen, 1908–1915), vol. 1B (rettet tekst), p. 24, stanzas 12–14. Some of the function words in these stanzas, notably definite articles, should probably be emended out as inauthentic, but only two cases would involve a change in verse pattern: 14/5, in which retention of *enn* would allow for scansion as expanded Da rather than as four-position Da; and 14/6, in which normal scansion for this meter requires exclusion of *ena*. Lists of examples for *ljóðaháttr* are provided in Appendix A. Lists for *málaháttr* are provided in Appendix B (*Atlamál*) and Appendix C (*Haraldskvæði*). In Appendix C, examples of a given pattern are cited first from *Fagrskinna*, according to the stanza numbers in Jónsson's edition, then (after a semicolon) from the three stanzas absent in *Fagrskinna*, which are cited according to the stanza numbers in *Skjaldedigtning*.

Table I

no.	example	notation	P	Beo	an	forn	an	Ij / a	an	Am	an	Hrk	an	Sn	an
1	deyr / fé	x/S	2					2							
2	sonr / húss	S/S	2			2		7							
3	þá þat / finnr	xx/S	3					7							
4	glaðr / Eggþér	S/Ss	3			1									
5	oc / Hiordis	x/Ss	3			4		2							
6	dáðraccr / Þórr	Ss/S	3			5		5							
7	Breiðr, / Bóndi	S/Sx	3			8		5							
8	grófo / torf	Sx/S	3			38		24							
9	þá qvað þat / Þórr	xxx/S	4			15		6							
10	ganga / fimtán	xx/Ss	4			26		3							
11	kǫlloðo / Karl	Sxx/S	4			43									
12	swā / ríxode	x/Sxx	4	3		10									
13	verða / flestir	xx/Sx	4	8		130		5							
14	gūðrinc / goldwlanc	Ss/Ss	4	33		12		1							
15	wīges / weorðmynd	Sx/Ss	4	75	5	25		1							
16	swā / giōmormōd	x/Sxs	4	83		114		6				1			
17	hēah / hlīfian	S/Sxx	4	105		65									
18	hār / hilderinc	S/Sxs	4	138	8	23									
19	þrēanȳd / þolað	Ss/Sx	4	245		214		6	2	1	1	3	3		
20	of / feorwegum	x/Ssx	4	260		488		1		6		1			
21	wīs / wēlþungen	S/Ssx	4	356	9	148		2	3	21	4	5	2		
22	wonsǣli / wer	Ssx/S	4	443		96		6	3	3	2				

no.	example	notation	P	Beo	an	forn	an	lj / a	an	Am	an	Hrk	an	Sn	an
23	gomban / gyldan	Sx/Sx	4	1420	17	807		40	2	79	54	22	12	1	1
24	ǫlvaerir / urðo	Ssx/Sx	5							12	1	5	2	1	
25	hvítabiorn / hugðir	Sxs/Sx	5							29	2	1			
26	ne / wintergeweorp	x/Sxxs	5	15											
27	sēon / sibbegedriht	S/Sxxs	5	18											
28	þenden / rēafode	xx/Sxx	5	18		7									
29	kiósattu / Hiorvarð	xxx/Ss	5	23		45									
30	oftost / wīsode	Sx/Sxx	5	28		2		1		5					
31	frēcne / fengelād	Sx/Sxs	5	38	5	2				1					
32	tryddode / tīrfaest	Sxx/Ss	5	51		27									
33	sīde / sǣnaessas	Sx/Ssx	5	151	14	20		1		157	8	29	2	5	
34	eroma / varmar	xxx/Sx	5	285		202		1		9		3			
35	þrēatedon / þearle	Sxx/Sx	5	690	25	255		12	1	256	15	14	2		
36	ofer / eormengrund	xx/Sxs	5	752		110		4		1		1			
37	ofer / hronrāde	xx/Ssx	5	840		241		5		133		16		1	
38	vǫknoðo / velborin	Sxx/Ssx	6							10		9			
39	orðanc / entageweorc	Sx/Sxxs	6	2	1										
40	ǣghwylc / ōðrum / trȳwe	Sx/Sx/Sx	6	5						13	2	4			
41	þǣr þā / gōdan / twēgen	xx/Sx/Sx	6	9						25		7		1	
42	sende / ǣrendgewrit	xx/Sxxs	6	158											
	remainders			112		44		6		3		5			
	total verses			6364		3229		159		764		126		8	

The first column on table 1 provides a row number for each type. The second column provides an Old English or Old Norse example. The third column provides a word-foot notation. The fourth column, headed 'P,' indicates the number of metrical positions. The number of instances for each pattern in *Beowulf* and in relevant Norse poetry is tallied in columns to the right. Each of these columns is followed by a column headed 'an,' which indicates how many of the tallied instances have anacrusis.

We begin by comparing some type counts for *Beowulf*, presented in the column headed 'Beo,' with corresponding type counts for *fornyrðislag*, presented in the column headed 'forn.' In the upper range of these columns it is evident that the Norse meter employs short types unattested in *Beowulf*. In the lower range it is equally evident that types with six metrical positions employed in *Beowulf* are unattested in *fornyrðislag*. A simple expedient for direct comparison with *Beowulf* is to multiply the Norse figures by two, since the Norse sample is about half the size of the Old English poem. In row 33, there is a comparatively small Norse total for the expanded Da pattern Sx/Ssx, which is long, with five metrical positions, and also heavy, with three metrically significant stresses. In row 13, on the other hand, there is a comparatively large Norse total for the A3 pattern xx/Sx, which has four metrical positions and only one metrically significant stress. *Fornyrðislag* is clearly biased toward short, light types.

Our sample of *ljóðaháttr* a-verses is analyzed in the column headed 'lj/a.' An even stronger bias toward short, light types stands out clearly here. Most of the short patterns from which c-verses are constructed can be found in this small sample of a-verses, with two exceptions. The missing patterns are represented by the following verses from outside the sample:

(37) svá / gjǫflan   **x/Sx**   reversible to Sx/S   Háv 39/5
     'so generous'
(38) nýsta ec / niðr   **Sxx/S**   light *fornyrðislag* type   Háv 139/3
     'I peered down'

Absence of verses like 38 from our corpus is surely accidental. This Norse type has significant frequency in *fornyrðislag*, and examples can be found in the later stanzas of *Hávamál* as well as in other *ljóðaháttr* poems. Verses like 37, on the other hand, do not appear in *fornyrðislag* and are not at all easy to find in *ljóðaháttr*. Example 37 is an emendation, perhaps not an acceptable one, and it occurs as a b-verse.[22]

There are good reasons to expect that constraints on two-word patterns in the *ljóðaháttr* a-verse might be slightly stricter than those for the first two feet of the *ljóðaháttr* c-verse. First, it is important to note that reversal of word order

---

[22] This and similar emendations are discussed by Evans, *Hávamál*, 91–92.

in an x/Sx pattern can produce the highly valued pattern Sx/S, as illustrated below.

(39) vági / á   **Sx/S**   short pattern with archaic syntax   Háv 154/5
    'on the sea'

The constituent *á* occurs here as an archaic postposition, acquiring phrase-final stress to produce the metrical pattern Sx/S. With normal word order, *á* would stand first as an unstressed preposition, and *á / vagi* would scan as x/Sx. A glance at the table will show that the pattern Sx/S is the most highly valued short pattern in both *ljóðaháttr* and *fornyrðislag*.[23] Potential x/Sx verses seem to be eliminated through reversal, in some cases at least. As we have observed, the fact that type B (x/Sxs) appears primarily in the *ljóðaháttr* b-verse makes it particularly convenient to place the Sx/S pattern in the *ljóðaháttr* a-verse.

It is also important to observe a comparable freedom in the notoriously strict *dróttkvætt* meter:

(40) Mikla-garðs / fyr // barði   **Sxs/x//Sx**   reversed type B + Sx   F41/6
    '(the roofs) of Constantinople before the prow'
(41) harð-múlaðr / es // Skúli   **Ssx/x/Sx**   reversed type C + Sx   F29/4
    'hard-mouthed [i.e., callous] is Skúli'

Although a *dróttkvætt* a-verse is normally constructed by adding an Sx foot to a *fornyrðislag* pattern, the reversed patterns to the left of the double slash in 40 and 41 do not appear in *fornyrðislag*. In both *dróttkvætt* a-verses and *ljóðaháttr* c-verses, constraints on ordering of the first two feet are slightly relaxed in comparison to constraints on two-foot verses. Apparently, the special environments created within these extended verse patterns allow for experimentation with new two-word patterns as subcomponents.

Researchers who admire *ljóðaháttr* have characterized it as extremely resistant to analysis.[24] This meter has seemed so puzzling, I think, because its short verses are so obviously incompatible with a two-stress, five-types system. Within Sievers's framework, the metrist's first impulse is to dismiss short types as casual imprecisions or historical accidents. The word-foot theory, which represents short verses as legitimate two-foot structures, makes it easier to appreciate their crucial role in *ljóðaháttr*.

Málaháttr has found few admirers, and its very existence is at issue. In her edition of heroic poems from the Edda, Ursula Dronke feels obliged to accept, though with evident reluctance, the common opinion that *Atlamál* is clumsy

---

[23] The special status of Sx/S was noticed by Andreas Heusler in *Deutsche Versgeschichte mit Einschluss des altenglischen und altnordischen Stabreimverses* I, Paul's Grundriss der germanischen Philologie 8 (Berlin, 1925), section 235.

[24] Kristján Árnason, *Rhythms of Dróttkvætt*, 161.

and prosaic—hardly a poem at all.[25] The idea that *málaháttr* is a loose kind of *fornyrðislag* might almost be said to have achieved consensus.[26] A look at table 1 will show that, on the contrary, *málaháttr* is a well-defined verse form with a distinct purpose: to accommodate traditional types and variants excluded by the other Eddic meters. Three poems in *málaháttr* are represented on table 1: first the Eddic *Atlamál* ('Am'); then *Haraldskvæði* ('Hrk'), a skaldic praise poem for Harald Finehair; and finally, a stanza provided by Snorri Sturluson in *Háttatal* ('Sn') to illustrate this meter. Snorri clearly understands that *málaháttr* is the meter for long, heavy verses. He provides only one instance with four metrical positions, tallied in row 23. This has the familiar type A1 pattern (Sx/Sx) and it is extended with nonprefixal anacrusis to compensate for its subnormal length. A glance to the left along row 23 will show that the *málaháttr* poems employ an astonishingly high frequency of anacrusis in type A1 relative to *Beowulf,* which has a norm of four metrical positions. Norse poets are careful to observe the traditional placement of type A1 variants with nonprefixal anacrusis. All 67 examples in the *málaháttr* poems appear in the second half of the line, the preferred location for such variants in Old English poems. The expanded Da pattern (Sx/Ssx), represented in row 33, has three stresses and five metrical positions. This pattern is reiterated most emphatically by Snorri: five times in a total of eight verses. Since expanded Da is long and heavy, there is no need to extend it with anacrusis. A glance along row 33 will show that the *málaháttr* poems have an even *lower* frequency of anacrusis than *Beowulf* for this pattern. In *Beowulf* and *fornyrðislag,* expanded Da is the most common verse type with more than four metrical positions and more than two stresses. For a metrical system designed to accommodate long, heavy patterns, expanded Da provides an excellent norm. Observe the high frequencies for this verse pattern in the other two *málaháttr* poems.

Snorri's stanza includes an example of five-position type C (xx/Ssx, row 37). Within Sievers's system, this cannot be distinguished from four-position type C (x/Ssx). Instances with two unstressed syllables before the first stress are necessarily scanned by Sievers as four-position type C with an extra syllable in the first thesis. Such an analysis is implausible for *málaháttr* due to the extremely low proportion of type C verses with the minimum number of syllables, which comprise just 6 of 139 type C verses in *Atlamál* and just 1 of 17 in *Haraldskvæði.* In *fornyrðislag,* which has a four-position norm, the bias is dramatically reversed, with 488 clear cases of four-position type C and fewer than half that many C verses with two syllables before the first stress (241). Within the word-foot theory, five-position type C can be associated with the two-word paradigm of row 37, as distinct from four-position type C, which is associated with the two-word

---

[25] Ursula Dronke, *The Poetic Edda,* vol. 1: *Heroic Poems* (London, 1969), 106; Gustav Neckel, *Beiträge zur Eddaforschung* (Dortmund, 1908).

[26] Fidjestøl, *Dating,* 295, n. 4.

paradigm of row 20. Poets who value these paradigms differently will have different attitudes toward addition of unstressed words in type C.

The remaining verse type selected as representative by Snorri corresponds to the most common hypermetrical b-verse pattern in Old English poems (xx//Sx/Sx, row 41). This type can be found in the a-verse in some Old English poems, but its ideal location is clearly the b-verse. Among 33 instances in the *málaháttr* poems, 32 are b-verses.

The two long, heavy types represented in rows 24 and 25 occur only in *málaháttr*. These types arise, I think, from two defining characteristics of the meter. The first is the normative status of expanded type Da; the second is a well-known preference for trochaic closure. In *Beowulf*, which has a norm of four metrical positions, the order of feet in four-position type Da (S/Ssx, row 21) can be reversed to create type E (Ssx/S, row 22). The metrical complexity added by unusual placement of a long, heavy foot is acceptable in *Beowulf*, since type E has the normal number of positions for Old English meter. In *málaháttr*, four-position type Da is abnormally short and its reversal is much less acceptable. There are only three examples of type E in the *málaháttr* poems. Relative to a four-position norm, expanded Da is complex, and there are no instances in *Beowulf* of reversed expanded Da (Ssx/Sx, row 24). In *málaháttr*, expanded Da is normative, and its reversal is favored over type E, the reversal of four-position Da. Expanded Db (Sx/Sxs, row 31) is problematic in *málaháttr* because the last two syllables in this type have a rising stress contour. Reversed expanded Db (Sxs/Sx, row 25) is preferred because it combines normative length and weight with trochaic closure, which is highly valued in this meter, as in *dróttkvætt* court meter.[27]

Though concern with literary form may be regarded as elitist or apolitical in certain quarters, attention to formal problems sometimes provides the best way to unsettle hegemonic complacency. Meters of the ancient Nordic margin are not clumsy or prosaic. Domestic *fornyrðislag*, *ljóðaháttr*, and *málaháttr* are indispensable components of a tripartite system that maintains both old and new verse types in a changed linguistic environment. The well-defined character of the system rules out attribution of these Eddic meters to cultural influence from centers of supposed urbanity.

---

[27] Kristján Árnason, *Rhythms of Dróttkvætt*, 52.

Appendix A
Distribution of Verse Patterns in *Ljóðaháttr*

Pattern 1:	76/1, 77/1.
Pattern 2:	22/1, 27/1, 40/1, 52/1, 54/1, 55/1, 56/1.
Pattern 3:	18/1, 23/4, 25/4, 50/4, 62/4, 77/4, 78/4.
Pattern 5:	7/1, 76/4.
Pattern 6:	23/1, 24/1, 25/1, 26/1, 79/1.
Pattern 7:	2/1, 31/1, 42/1, 43/1, 63/4.
Pattern 8:	2/4, 3/1, 4/1, 5/1, 8/1, 9/1, 14/1, 15/4, 16/1, 17/4, 20/1, 27/7, 32/4, 35/1, 35/4, 50/1, 56/4, 59/4, 61/1, 64/1, 67/1, 68/1, 75/1, 78/1.
Pattern 9:	12/1, 22/4, 24/4, 26/4, 27/4, 64/4.
Pattern 10:	9/4, 14/4, 67/4.
Pattern 13:	20/4, 51/4, 54/4, 60/4, 69/4.
Pattern 14:	41/4.
Pattern 15:	44/1.
Pattern 16:	16/4, 21/4, 48/4, 52/4, 53/4, 61/6.
Pattern 19:	11/4, 28/4, 29/4, 34/1, 36/4, 55/4.
Pattern 20:	13/4.
Pattern 21:	70/4, 73/1.
Pattern 22:	1/5, 6/7, 8/4, 19/4, 43/4, 68/4.
Pattern 23:	1/1, 3/4, 4/4, 7/4, 10/1, 10/4, 11/1, 15/1, 18/4, 28/1, 29/1, 30/1, 31/4, 32/1, 33/4, 36/1, 37/1, 38/1, 42/4, 47/4, 48/1, 49/1, 57/1, 57/4, 58/1, 59/1, 60/1, 61/4, 62/1, 63/1, 65/1, 66/1, 66/4, 71/1, 71/4, 72/1, 72/4, 74/1, 74/5, 75/4, 79/4.
Pattern 30:	51/1.
Pattern 33:	17/1.
Pattern 34:	40/4.
Pattern 35:	6/1, 19/1, 21/1, 33/1, 37/4, 41/4, 44/4, 45/4, 47/1, 49/4, 53/1, 79/4.
Pattern 36:	6/4, 12/4, 39/1, 46/1.
Pattern 37:	30/4, 34/4, 39/4, 45/1, 69/1.
Remainders:	5/4, 13/1, 38/4, 46/4, 58/4, 70/1.

Appendix B
Distribution of Verse Patterns in *Atlamál*

Pattern 19:   70/3.

Pattern 20:   4/7, 32/4, 37/2, 60/4, 87/8.

Pattern 21:   1/7, 6/3, 15/3, 17/2, 24/5, 26/6, 35/2, 37/3, 42/5, 44/3, 50/9,
                  53/3, 53/8, 64/4, 75/1, 77/8, 83/11, 90/5, 97/2, 100/3, 100/4.

Pattern 22:   36/5, 50/4, 84/2.

Pattern 23:   3/8, 5/2, 6/6, 7/5, 9/4, 9/6, 11/6, 12/6, 16/2, 19/2, 19/4, 19/7,
                  19/8, 20/5, 22/8, 23/4, 25/6, 27/1, 30/2, 30/6, 31/1, 33/1, 34/1,
                  36/4, 36/6, 38/4, 40/2, 40/8, 42/4, 42/6, 43/3, 43/2, 46/3, 46/6,
                  47/4, 50/3, 50/10, 52/2, 54/4, 55/6, 56/2, 56/3, 56/4, 56/6, 57/5,
                  58/3, 58/4, 59/8, 61/4, 62/5, 63/4, 64/1, 69/2, 70/4, 71/2, 72/8,
                  73/1, 73/2, 74/4, 76/6, 78/1, 83/2, 83/8, 84/5, 87/7, 90/2, 91/6,
                  92/4, 92/8, 94/2, 95/8, 97/6, 97/8, 99/4, 99/6, 100/6, 101/2,
                  103/2, 103/6.

Pattern 24:   3/3, 5/1, 8/5, 10/1, 41/1, 44/6, 53/1, 76/5, 81/3, 91/1, 93/1,
                  97/1.

Pattern 25:   2/3, 4/6, 12/9, 17/3, 33/2, 33/7, 38/2, 44/8, 47/5, 47/6, 48/3,
                  48/6, 49/8, 50/2, 50/6, 53/9, 63/1, 70/1, 79/6, 82/8, 92/10,
                  93/2, 93/4, 94/8, 95/6, 98/2, 98/4, 98/7, 101/3.

Pattern 30:   13/7, 35/5, 35/6, 38/3, 69/8.

Pattern 31:   92/3.

Pattern 33:   1/3, 1/4, 1/5, 2/7, 3/1, 3/2, 4/3, 6/1, 7/3, 8/3, 9/1, 9/2, 9/3,
                  10/3, 11/3, 11/4, 11/8, 13/1, 14/4, 15/5, 16/5, 19/1, 19/5, 22/2,
                  22/4, 25/2, 25/3, 25/5, 26/5, 27/3, 27/5, 27/6, 27/7, 28/5, 29/1,
                  30/7, 31/2, 31/5, 32/2, 32/5, 34/4, 35/3, 38/6, 39/3, 43/1, 44/4,
                  45/1, 45/3, 46/5, 46/7, 46/8, 47/1, 47/3, 49/2, 49/4, 50/1, 50/5,
                  51/3, 51/6, 51/7, 52/4, 53/10, 54/5, 55/2, 55/3, 56/5, 58/5, 58/8,
                  59/1, 59/2, 59/3, 59/4, 59/5, 59/9, 60/3, 60/7, 61/3, 61/6, 62/1,
                  62/3, 62/4, 62/6, 62/8, 63/2, 63/7, 63/8, 65/3, 67/2, 67/3, 67/6,
                  67/7, 68/5, 68/7, 69/1, 69/3, 69/6, 70/2, 70/8, 71/1, 71/3, 72/2,
                  72/4, 72/5, 72/6, 73/4, 73/5, 73/6, 73/7, 73/8, 74/5, 76/1, 76/2,
                  76/3, 76/4, 77/2, 77/4, 77/7, 78/5, 79/2, 79/4, 80/4, 80/7, 81/2,
                  83/3, 83/4, 83/5, 83/7, 84/8, 85/1, 85/2, 85/3, 86/1, 86/2, 86/3,
                  87/2, 88/4, 88/5, 89/2, 89/8, 91/4, 91/5, 92/2, 92/6, 93/3, 94/6,
                  95/3, 95/5, 95/9, 96/2, 96/4, 97/3, 100/2, 100/7, 102/2, 102/3,
                  102/8, 103/3.

Pattern 34:   5/4, 10/6, 16/7, 38/1, 56/1, 57/7, 78/7, 84/3, 99/2.

Pattern 35:   1/6, 2/2, 2/4, 2/6, 3/6, 4/1, 4/2, 4/5, 5/5, 5/7, 5/8, 6/2, 6/4, 6/5,
               7/6, 7/7, 8/2, 9/5, 9/7, 9/8, 10/2, 10/4, 11/2, 11/5, 11/7, 12/1,
               12/7, 13/2, 13/3, 14/1, 14/5, 14/6, 15/1, 15/2, 15/4, 16/3, 16/8,
               17/1, 18/4, 18/5, 19/3, 19/6, 20/3, 21/2, 21/3, 21/4, 21/6, 22/5,
               22/6, 22/7, 23/1, 23/2, 24/3, 24/4, 24/6, 24/8, 25/1, 25/4, 25/8,
               26/1, 26/3, 27/2, 27/4, 27/8, 28/1, 28/2, 28/3, 28/6, 29/4, 30/1,
               30/3, 30/5, 31/3, 32/1, 32/3, 32/6, 33/3, 33/4, 33/5, 33/6, 35/1,
               35/4, 36/1, 36/2, 36/3, 37/1, 37/4, 37/5, 37/6, 37/7, 37/8, 38/5,
               38/8, 39/1, 40/1, 40/3, 40/5, 40/6, 41/5, 41/6, 42/1, 42/3, 44/1,
               44/5, 44/7, 45/2, 45/6, 46/1, 46/2, 46/4, 47/7, 48/1, 48/2, 48/4,
               48/5, 48/7, 48/9, 49/1, 49/9, 50/7, 50/8, 51/1, 51/4, 51/8, 52/1,
               53/2, 53/4, 53/5, 53/7, 54/1, 54/2, 54/3, 54/6, 54/7, 54/9, 55/1,
               55/4, 55/5, 55/7, 56/7, 56/8, 57/1, 57/2, 57/3, 58/1, 58/2, 58/7,
               60/2, 60/5, 60/6, 60/9, 61/1, 61/2, 61/5, 61/7, 61/8, 62/7, 63/3,
               63/5, 64/2, 64/3, 65/1, 65/2, 65/5, 65/6, 66/1, 66/3, 66/6, 66/7,
               67/4, 67/5, 68/1, 68/2, 68/3, 68/6, 69/5, 69/7, 69/9, 70/5, 72/1,
               72/3, 72/7, 74/1, 74/2, 74/3, 74/6, 75/3, 75/4, 75/5, 75/6, 75/7,
               76/7, 77/1, 77/3, 78/2, 78/3, 78/4, 78/6, 78/8, 79/1, 79/3, 79/5,
               80/3, 80/5, 80/8, 81/4, 82/1, 82/4, 82/7, 83/1, 83/12, 84/1,
               84/6, 84/7, 85/4, 87/5, 88/1, 88/2, 89/1, 90/1, 90/3, 90/4, 91/2,
               91/3, 92/5, 92/7, 93/5, 93/6, 94/5, 94/10, 95/1, 95/4, 95/7, 96/1,
               96/3, 96/5, 96/6, 96/7, 97/4, 97/5, 97/7, 98/1, 98/5, 98/8, 99/1,
               99/7, 100/1, 100/5, 101/1, 101/4, 102/1, 102/4, 102/5, 102/6,
               103/1, 103/5.

Pattern 36:   15/8.

Pattern 37:   1/1, 1/8, 2/5, 2/8, 3/4, 3/5, 3/7, 4/4, 5/3, 5/6, 6/7, 6/8, 7/1,
               7/2, 7/4, 7/8, 8/1, 8/4, 8/6, 10/5, 12/2, 12/3, 12/4, 12/5, 13/5,
               13/6, 13/8, 14/3, 14/7, 15/6, 15/7, 16/4, 17/4, 18/3, 18/6, 20/2,
               20/4, 20/6, 21/5, 22/3, 23/3, 24/7, 25/7, 26/2, 26/4, 28/4, 29/2,
               30/4, 30/8, 31/4, 31/6, 33/8, 34/2, 34/3, 35/7, 35/8, 37/9, 38/7,
               39/2, 39/4, 40/4, 41/2, 41/4, 42/2, 43/4, 45/4, 45/5, 47/2, 47/8,
               48/8, 48/10, 49/3, 49/6, 49/7, 49/10, 51/2, 51/5, 52/3, 54/8,
               54/10, 57/8, 58/6, 59/6, 59/7, 59/10, 60/1, 60/8, 60/10, 62/2,
               63/6, 65/8, 66/2, 66/4, 66/5, 66/8, 67/1, 67/8, 68/4, 69/10,
               70/6, 70/7, 71/4, 73/3, 82/6, 83/9, 84/4, 86/4, 87/1, 87/3, 87/4,
               87/6, 88/3, 88/6, 89/7, 90/6, 91/3, 91/4, 92/1, 92/9, 94/1, 94/9,
               95/2, 95/10, 96/8, 98/3, 98/6, 99/3, 100/8, 101/6, 102/7, 103/7,
               103/8.

Pattern 38:   2/1, 16/1, 18/1, 20/1, 24/1, 40/7, 41/3, 49/5, 65/7, 82/5.

Pattern 40:   11/1, 18/2, 21/1, 22/1, 24/2, 29/3, 75/2, 80/1, 80/6, 81/1, 82/3,
               94/7, 99/5.

Pattern 41:   1/2, 4/8, 12/8, 12/10, 13/4, 14/2, 14/8, 16/6, 37/10, 44/2, 53/6, 55/8, 57/6, 65/4, 68/8, 69/4, 75/8, 76/8, 77/6, 80/2, 82/2, 83/6, 83/10, 94/3, 94/4.

Remainders: 57/4, 77/5, 101/5.

Appendix C
Distribution of Verse Patterns in *Haraldskvæði*
(see footnote 21)

Pattern 16:   3/3.

Pattern 19:   2/4, 6/4, 18/8.

Pattern 20:   13/6.

Pattern 21:   3/4, 4/6, 8/2, 8/8; 14/5.

Pattern 23:   2/2, 4/5, 5/5, 5/6, 5/8, 6/6, 6/7, 8/4, 8/6, 9/4, 16/2, 16/6, 16/8, 17/1, 17/2, 17/4, 17/8, 19/6, 20/2; 13/4, 14/2, 14/4.

Pattern 24:   3/5, 3/6, 4/4, 16/7; 13/2.

Pattern 25:   5/4.

Pattern 33:   1/1, 1/3, 1/7, 2/5, 2/7, 4/1, 4/3, 4/7, 5/3, 6/3, 6/8, 7/3, 8/7, 16/1, 16/3, 16/4, 17/3, 18/3, 19/3, 19/5, 19/8, 20/3, 20/4, 20/5, 20/7; 12/3, 13/3, 13/7, 14/3.

Pattern 34:   8/1, 9/1, 9/7.

Pattern 35:   1/5, 3/1, 3/2, 5/7, 8/5, 9/5, 17/6, 18/7, 19/1, 19/2, 19/4, 20/1; 12/1, 13/8.

Pattern 36:   5/2.

Pattern 37:   1/4, 1/6, 1/8, 2/3, 2/6, 3/8, 6/1, 6/2, 7/1, 7/2, 8/3, 18/4, 19/7, 20/6; 13/5, 14/6.

Pattern 38:   2/1, 3/7, 6/5, 17/5, 17/7, 18/1; 12/2, 12/4, 14/1.

Pattern 40:   5/1, 9/3, 16/5; 13/1.

Pattern 41:   4/2, 4/8, 9/2, 9/8, 18/2, 18/6, 20/8.

Remainders: 1/2, 2/8, 7/4, 9/6, 18/5.

ON FINNIC AND ENGLISH
ALLITERATIVE METRES

JONATHAN ROPER

The alliterative metres current in the Germanic languages during the early Middle Ages were not an isolated phenomenon.[1] While discussions of Old English metre often make reference to the other Germanic alliterative metres, they habitually ignore another group of alliterative metres which were current on the eastern shores of the Baltic Sea. These metres flourished in Finland, Estonia, and those neighbouring territories where Karelians, Vadjans, and Ingrians lived. The large amounts of surviving material in these alliterative metres form significant comparanda for Old English alliterative verse. I shall refer to these closely related Baltic-Finnic metres here as 'Finnic alliterative metre'. This term is intended to encompass traditional Finnish (and Ingrian and Karelian) alliterative metres (which are sometimes referred to collectively as 'runo metre', or as 'Kalevala metre' because this is the metre that *The Kalevala* is in), as well as Estonian *regivärss* and Vadjan alliterative verse.[2] My discussion will fall into two parts: first, I shall argue that Finnic alliterative metre forms relevant comparanda for Old English metre, and second, I intend to suggest some of the questions that might be raised regarding the Anglo-Saxon poetic corpus by consideration of the findings of research into the Finnic material.

[1] I should like to thank Jayne Carroll, Peder Gammeltoft, Alaric Hall, Tiiu Jaago, Harold Paddock, Philip Shaw, Ülo Valk, and Ulrika Wolf-Knuts for help and advice received while developing my ideas on this subject. This research was supported by the European Union through the European Regional Development Fund (Centre of Excellence CECT).

[2] Alliterative metre is not universal among the Baltic-Finnic peoples: the Livonians and the Vepsians have either lost or never had this metre. As Matti Kuusi remarks, "Kalevala metre was cultivated in Finland, Karelia, Ingria, by the Votes [i.e. Vadjans] and the Estonians": Matti Kuusi, "Questions of Kalevala Metre," in *Songs Beyond the Kalevala*, ed. Anna-Leena Siikala and Sinikka Vakimo (Helsinki, 1994), 41–55, here 41.

The basis of alliteration — initial syllable stress

The fundamental justification for considering Finnic alliterative metre as forming relevant comparanda for Old English alliterative metre is phonological: initial syllable stress in native words is common to all of the Germanic languages
and all of the Baltic-Finnic languages. This phonological feature is rarely found
outside of these two groupings. For example, in Europe, it can be found only in
the Germanic and Baltic-Finnic languages, or in those languages and dialects
which border them (such as Latvian, Gaelic, and Czech). In no other set of language groups is this feature found so thorough-goingly.

Let us elaborate. In the Baltic group of languages, while Latvian and some
Lithuanian dialects possess initial syllable stress, standard Lithuanian does not.
In the insular Celtic languages, while some of the dialects of Goidelic Celtic
have this feature, none of the Brythonic Celtic languages have adopted this feature. Likewise, while some of the forms of West Slavic found to the immediate
east of the Germanic bloc, Czech, Slovak, Lusatian ('Wendish'), and the southern dialect of Kashubian[3] have initial syllable stress, the other forms of West
Slavic and the other Slavic languages do not. Furthermore, this feature is not to
be found in the Romance,[4] Armenian, Albanian, Hellenic, or Iranian language
groups, nor is it posited to have existed in reconstructed Proto-Indo-European.
If we look elsewhere in Eurasia, while it is well-known that many of the other
Finno-Ugric languages[5] have initial syllable stress in native words, this feature
is not found in the Indo-European languages of Asia, nor is it found in other of
the significant language groups of Eurasia, such as the Sino-Tibetan languages,
the Turkic languages, or the Semitic languages. Neither is it to be found in

---

[3] These languages and dialects also display the results of Germanic influence in various of their grammatical and syntactic features. For example, "a striking feature of the
verbal system [of Kashubian] is the analytical perfect with the verb 'to have' as auxiliary,
as in German: e.g., *ja mom widzel* = German *ich habe gesehen* 'I have seen'": George L.
Campbell, *Compendium of the World's Languages* (London, 1991), 1: 719.

[4] Although none of the modern Romance languages possess initial syllable stress,
various researchers have suggested that Latin (in common with Oscan and Umbrian)
may have had initial syllable stress at a very early stage of its development: e.g., A.G. and
P. Ramat, *The Romance Languages* (London, 1998), 271–72, and R. Beekes, *Comparative
Indo-European Linguistics* (Amsterdam, 1995), 149. On the basis of this, F.H. Whitman
has suggested in *A Comparative Study of Old English Metre* (Toronto, 1993) that the earliest Latin poetry, Saturnian verse, a) had an accentual basis, and b) is interesting comparanda for Germanic accentual verse. But despite his claim that it contains "a surprising
amount of alliteration," Whitman sensibly does not push the analogy too far, noting that
in Saturnian verse "binding alliteration is uncommon . . . alliteration is [often] confined
within the boundary of the half-line . . . [and] alliteration, oddly enough, does not always
coincide with stress" (56–57).

[5] Udmurt, and some dialects of Mansi, however, do not have initial syllable stress.

language-isolates such as Basque, Japanese, or Korean. The only other languages with initial syllable stress on words of native origin in Eurasia are varieties of Mongolian.[6]

That this feature should be essentially limited to those parts of northern Europe where the Germanic and the Baltic-Finnic groups are spoken, or to territories and languages immediately bordering upon them, is a matter that demands investigation in itself. Such studies might argue, for example, that this distribution arises through chance, through contact, or via the influence of a shared northern European linguistic substrate. But this is not a question I shall address here.[7] It is the implications of this phonological feature for poetic metre that are of present interest. This common phonological characteristic enabled there to be a great deal of similarity in the metrical systems which held sway in the Germanic and in the Baltic-Finnic worlds, prior to the successful introduction from the south of rhyme into the vernacular poetry of the Anglo-Saxons and other northern European peoples.[8]

Regular initial syllable stress enables a word-initial phonetic feature, i.e., alliteration, to be perceived clearly enough for it to act as an element of metre. While other languages which possess a regular stress that falls elsewhere than on the initial syllable have also developed alliterative metres, such metres differ fundamentally from those in stichic traditions, where alliteration binds together a single line. (Of course, initial syllable stress is a necessary, but not a sufficient, condition for the existence of a stichic alliterative metre, as the development of complex stanza forms in Old Norse alliterative verse shows.)[9] Examples of

---

[6] Campbell, *Compendium*, 2: 953.

[7] One attempt to explain the route by which the mobile stress of Proto-Indo-European developed into the word-initial stress found in some modern-day Indo-European languages is provided by Morris Halle, "On Stress and Accent in Indo-European," *Language* 73 (1997): 275–313, esp. 298–99. Halle, however, does not touch on the presence of this feature in the neighbouring Baltic-Finnic languages.

[8] In Europe, rhyme is a phenomenon which originates with Latin and after it the Romance languages. See William Harmon, "Rhyme in English Verse: History, Structures, Functions," *Studies in Philology* 84 (1987): 365–93.

[9] Although such forms are found from the (comparatively late) beginnings of the surviving record in Old Norse, I follow Lehmann in believing them to be later developments from an originally stichic Old Germanic tradition: "The evidence against considering the stanzaic form the more original is therefore stronger than that in favour of the form maintained in the south [i.e. in Old English, Old Saxon and Old High German]": Winfred Lehmann, *The Development of Germanic Verse Form* (Austin, 1956), 31. The case of the Goidelic languages is another example of initial stress not being a sufficient condition for this development. Though they developed initial stress comparatively late, these languages could still have gone on to develop a stichic alliterative metre. However, because they had already been sufficiently influenced by southern European models to make use of strophes and of rhymes (and consonance and assonance for that matter), and due

non-stichic alliteration can be found in the Turkic languages, where stress falls on the final syllable, and where alliterative verse is widespread. Such verse is strophic rather than stichic, as, by focussing the attention on the final syllables of lines, alliterating word-final syllables bind lines into strophes. Strophic alliteration should be considered as a variant of line-final rhyme, the classical method of strophe-binding in Europe. Indeed, in stichic alliterative traditions there is a pronounced tendency to avoid alliterating on the final stressed syllable of a line, precisely in order to prevent line-final features drowning out the line-internal binding.[10]

I have stressed the phonological similarities between Baltic-Finnic and Germanic in the account above because there will have been contact, including metrical contact, between the two language groups. In the Baltic Sea area, where these two groups bordered each other, representatives of one language group, e.g., Finns, must have heard the alliterative verse of representatives of the other language group, e.g., Swedes (and, indeed, vice versa).[11] Given this, one tradition *may* have exercised outright influence upon the formation of the other. Writers as diverse as Otto Andersson, Francis Peabody Magoun, and William Entwistle have suggested that this was the case.[12] However, the occurrence of contact does not necessarily imply that the use of alliterative metre by these two neighbouring

---

to metrical conventions which grouped their twenty-odd phonemes into just six classes (meaning that a 't' did not chime only with a 't', but also with a 'p' and a 'k'), these languages developed other, more complex forms of sound-patterning. In this context, alliteration could never play the all-important role it did in stichic verse traditions.

[10] The so-called 'winnowing principle' operating in Finnic alliterative metre, by which longer words appear at the ends of lines, can be understood as a convention devised to reduce the threat of an alliterating word appearing in that fourth and line-final position. In both metres, the lack of alliteration in the fourth position is also key in signalling the line-ending, and thus revealing the speaker's utterance to be in verse.

[11] Some other Germanic groupings in the Baltic area that Finnic peoples may have had contact with include Gepids, Goths, and Vandals.

[12] Otto Andersson pursued the idea that cultural transmission from the (Germanic) west to Finnic areas played a role in the formation of Kalevala metre and performance in articles such as "Kalevalameter—fornydislag" and "Framförandet av Kalevala runorna," now most easily accessible in his *Studier i musik och folklore* (Åbo, 1964), 347–60, 361–72 respectively; Magoun remarks that "in the Viking Age, in which they were active participants, or even earlier, Finns must often have heard Swedish singers and Swedish-speaking Finnish singers of the time may well have picked up and adapted phrases, images and conceivably other techniques of Old-Germanic versification" at the start of his discussion of "Conceptions and Images Common to Anglo-Saxon Poetry and the Kalevala," in *Britannica—Festschrift für Hermann M. Flasdieck*, ed. Wolfgang Iser and Hans Schabram (Heidelberg, 1960), 180–91, esp. 181; William Entwistle suggested that "the hint [that the Baltic Finns should use alliterative metre] may have come originally from the Swedes" in *European Balladry* (Oxford, 1939), 294.

cultural groups is a contact phenomenon. Because of the phonological logic of the languages in question we might have expected alliterative metres to have developed within them, even if these language groups had been far apart geographically. If the ancient Finnic peoples and ancient Germanic peoples had never come into contact, if we were to imagine for the sake of argument that they had lived at opposite sides of the globe, many of the similar metrical characteristics I am about to adumbrate might well have developed anyway, simply because they are inherent in the effective running of a stichic alliterative metre. It should thus come as no surprise that, though they are far from northern Europe, those forms of Mongolian which have initial syllable stress also possess alliterative metre.

Metrical similarities

The Finnic and English alliterative metres cannot be considered to be the same system (as later discussion of some of their differences will show), any more than they can be considered to be monolithically uniform within themselves throughout their spread in space and time. And yet they share a great deal. As might be expected, some of these shared features are those that John Niles has identified as typifying oral and oral-derived traditions:

> a reliance on traditional . . . plots and characters, together with an allusive way of calling these legendary materials to mind; a pleonastic and additive style, coupled with a weakness for all things deictic and gnomic; a peculiar mixture of dialect forms, including many archaisms; a habit of invoking the authority of words heard aloud, rather than read; a blind eye to the timeline of clerical history; and a reliance on stock themes, interlocking systems of formulaic diction, and parallel, chiastic, or echoic patternings that serve or could serve a mnemonic function.[13]

But, over and above such expected features, the two metrical systems share other significant similarities. These include:

(1) the binding of a line internally by alliteration;[14]

(2) a stichic, as opposed to a strophic, organisation;[15]

---

[13] John Niles, *"Beowulf* and the Ballads," *Oral Tradition* 9 (1994): 440–67, esp. 442.

[14] A detailed study of alliteration in Finnic alliterative metre is to be found in Matti Sadeniemi, "Die Metrik des Kalevala-Verses," *Folklore Fellows Communications* 139 (Helsinki, 1951), 79–113.

[15] "A poem consists of an optional number of successive independent lines. Minimal poems in this tradition are one-line proverbs, whereas the longest ones are epic songs of over 400 lines": Pentti Leino, *Language and Metre: Metrics and the Metrical System of Finnish* (Helsinki, 1986), 130.

(3) in the absence of strophes, the deployment of syntactic and semantic parallelism[16] to bind the lines to one another;

(4) the widespread use of poetic synonyms, which in the more extreme cases can be thought of as "kennings";

(5) commonly the presence of four metrically-relevant units in each line.[17]

The *Metrical Charm* for a wen may stand as a suitably brief example illustrating these characteristics in Anglo-Saxon verse:

> Wenne, wenne,   wenchichenne,
> her ne scealt þu timbrien,   ne nenne tun habben,
> ac þu scealt north eonene   to þan nihgan berhge,
> þer þu hauest, ermig,   enne broþer.
> He þe sceal legge   leaf et heafde.
> Under fot wolues,   under ueþer earnes,
> under earnes clea,   a þu geweornie.
> Clinge þu   alswa col on heorþe,
> scring þu   alswa scerne awage,
> and weorne   alswa weter on anbre.
> Swa litel þu gewurþe   alswa linsetcorn,
> and miccli lesse alswa anes handwurmes hupeban,
> and alswa litel þu gewurþe þet þu nawiht gewurþe.[18]

Line-binding alliteration (1) is found throughout, and most richly in the first line. Given (2) the absence of strophes, structure is provided by various forms of (3) parallel syntax throughout the text, most obviously in the three–line section beginning 'Clinge þu . . .'. Although Dobbie sets out the irregular ending of the charm as prose, alliteration and syntactic parallelism are present here too. Along with such parallelism, we find (4) the use of synonyms, such as 'timbrien' and 'tun habben' in the second line. Finally, (5) four metrically relevant stresses are found in each line, and it is no doubt this felt need that gives us the four stresses of 'Wenne, wenne, wenchichenne', rather than a simple 'Wenne, wenne, wenne'.[19]

---

[16] When reading or hearing Finnic alliterative verse, one is often reminded of the applicability to it of Fred Robinson's remark about "the poet's penchant for parallel statements which carry contrasting versions of the same action": Fred C. Robinson, *Beowulf and the Appositive Style* (Knoxville, 1985), 21.

[17] Leino, *Language and Metre*, 130: "The Kalevala metre is trochaic tetrameter. The line thus comprises four successive rise and fall positions."

[18] Elliott van Kirk Dobbie, ed., *The Anglo-Saxon Minor Poems*, ASPR 6 (New York, 1942), 128.

[19] It was the resemblance of 'Wenne, wenne, wenchichenne' to the opening invocations in certain Kalevala metre items, for example 'Lōpe, lōpe, linakene' (*Stop, stop, little*

These five features are also to be found in this example of Finnic alliterative verse:

Suru virret suuhun tuopi	Sorrow brings songs to the mouth
Ikäväinen itkettää	Longing makes us weep
Vieein silmää vettää.	And draws water to the eyes.
Äijä lauloin lapsempana	I sang much when a child
Paljon huusin hullumpanna	I shouted a lot when wilder
Pieksin kieltä pienempännä;	I banged my tongue when smaller:
Silloin lauloin lapsuuttain	Then I sang about childhood
Ja huusin hupeluuttain,	And shouted about folly.
Nyt jo huuvan huolissain	Now I shout amid cares
Poaan pahoissa mielissäin	Set forth in my bad spirits
Poaan päivissä pahoissa.	Set forth amid evil days.[20]

This example is an extract from a woman's lament recorded in late-nineteenth-century Ingria. The lament displays the features delineated above: it possesses (1) line-binding alliteration (here marked in bold), (2) stichic organisation, and (3) parallelism e.g. ll. 4–6. There is (4) a widespread use of synonyms, and (5) there are four metrical units to each line. The units in question are trochaic feet (e.g., line 1 has four disyllabic words, each one of which forms a foot), and the metrically relevant principle here is generally considered to be syllabic quantity (though in performance syllabic quantity usually coincides with stress, which could just as well be considered as the metrically relevant principle).

A very late and somewhat irregular example of Finnic alliterative verse is this charm used for healing snake bites, recorded in the south-east of Estonia:

Haina halas, pää palas.	The grass is crying, the head is burning.
Maa vagil, mõtsa nõgil,	Land-worm, forest-needle,
alt kulo koejaja,	spawn-animal from under the compost,
alt samja sammeldaja,	moss-animal from under the moss,
alt rampe rampeldaja,	weak-animal from under the rotten log,
su kiil kui pähna leht,	your tongue will be like a linden leaf
su miil kui pähna liim.	your mind will be like linden resin.

---

flax, Estonian Literary Museum RKM, Mgn. II 622 c), 'Sirise, sirise, sirbike' (*Ripple, ripple, little sickle*, RKM, Mgn. II 350 e), and 'Kokku, kokku, kooruke' (*Thicken, thicken, little cream*, RKM, Mgn. II 520 j), that first raised the question of analogies between the two traditions in my mind. Although the Estonian examples are morphologically different from the Old English one, they too are at once structurally bipartite (a, Lõpe, lõpe, b, linakene), tripartite (a, Lõpe, b, lõpe, c, linakene) and quadripartite (a, Lõpe, b, lõpe, c, lina d, kene).

[20] *Suomen Kansan Vanhat Runot*, vol. 31, item 410. Recorded in or before 1887 from Larin Paraske, translation adapted from that in Keith Bosley, *Skating on the Sea: Poetry from Finland* (Helsinki, 1997), 138.

luust lihast kadoma halu ja haigus!   Pain and illness be lost from bone,
                                      from flesh![21]

In this second example, the use of poetic synonyms for the same referent is evident at the opening of the charm, especially in the parallel lines 3–5. The term
used to denote the snake in line 2, *mõtsa nõgil* ('forest needle'), deserves to be
recognised as a kenning. Further parallelism is to be found in lines 6 and 7, and,
lastly, we can note that the concluding line is irregularly overlong.

The similarities illustrated above lead me to suggest that Finnic alliterative
verse forms especially relevant comparanda to Old English alliterative verse (and,
to a more limited extent, Middle English alliterative verse).[22] In some metrical
concerns, it is more relevant comparanda than the verse of Old Norse, given that
tradition's strophic metres, despite Norse being the linguistic relative of English
and the geographical neighbour of Finnic. There is one important caveat, however: the comparisons I am making are most especially relevant to verse composed
without enjambment. 'Classical' Old English verse makes great use of run-ons
and caesuras, and rather than being thought of as stichic, it could be defined as
primarily hemistichic.[23] This is not the place to enter in an extended debate as to
whether the *Hakenstil*, which dominates 'classical' Old English verse, is a literary departure from the normal practice of versification, in the same manner that
skaldic verse is a courtly departure from the norms of Eddic verse. But it is perhaps appropriate to mention that such a manner was seemingly not the norm in
Old English verse considered relatively early (such as *Widsith* is sometimes imagined to be), in Middle English alliterative verse (such as *Sir Gawain and the Green
Knight* or various of the *Harley Lyrics*), or in more popular Anglo-Saxon forms
(such as the *Metrical Charms*). In other words, before, during, and after the *Hakenstil*, there seems to have been a different, stichic tradition.

Kemp Malone draws a distinction between the classical style of Old English
verse and the pre-classical style, where "the end-stopped style prevailed: every

---

[21] Recorded in 1995 from Nati Lillestik in Saatse parish, Estonia, by Karin Veskioja
and the present author.

[22] In Middle English compositions, criteria (3), (4), and (5) do not always apply.

[23] It is also worth pointing out that the Kalevala metre cannot be described as
hemistichic, despite the presence in it of some bipartite lines (such as the last three lines
in the Estonian charm quoted above) or even of some lines with internal pauses (such as
the first two lines of the Estonian charm). Indeed it would be difficult to imagine, prior
to literacy, of any tradition where the original unit could be a *half*-line. Given that lines
above a certain length are likely to have sub-divisions, we should not be surprised at the
existence of bipartite lines, as a line with four basic units is most likely to fall into two
(rather than three, four, or more) parts. Indeed, while I have followed the ASPR layout
of the Wen charm here, there really is no reason other than convention to set out non-
Hakenstil verse with mid-line spacing.

line ended with a syntactical pause."[24] More recently, Gay Marie Logsdon in her investigation of 'alternative styles' in Old English verse[25] distinguishes between a classical style (such as is to be found in *Brunanburh*) and an informal style, often, but not necessarily always, dating from an earlier period (as in *Maldon*, an interesting example as in this case it postdates *Brunanburh*). She finds that informal texts are heavily endstopped (i.e., take the verse line as the thought-unit, as in Finnic alliterative metre), and are freer in their use of alliteration (again, as in Finnic alliterative metre). Arguing that "the charms provide the most reliable indication of early style that we have,"[26] she characterises the early pre-classical style as exhibiting "one- and two-line sentences, frequent use of subordinate clauses, endstopped lines, weak caesuras, frequent use of subject pronouns, and extensive use of lighter syllables" as well as "'irregular' metrical contours and alliterative patterns."[27] These are all characteristics shared by Finnic alliterative metre, and more likely to be present in orally-delivered verse, than in what John Knight Bostock, following Andreas Heusler, terms "book-epics."[28]

Some metrical differences

We can note briefly some other differences between these two metres, which can be seen as secondary to the similarities outlined above. First, it is the case that while both metres made widespread use of parallelism, the device was more popular in Finnic alliterative verse, especially in the form of anaphora and epana-

---

[24] Kemp Malone, "The Old English Period (to 1100)," in *A Literary History of England*, ed. Albert Baugh, 2nd ed. (London, 1967), 3–105, esp. 26. See also idem, "Plurilinear Units in Old English Poetry," *Review of English Studies* 19 (1943): 201–4.

[25] Gay Marie Logsdon, "*Maldon, Brunanburh, Finnsburh Fragment*, and *Finnsburh Episode:* An Inquiry into Tradition and Alternative Styles in Old English Poetry" (Ph. D. diss., University of Texas at Austin, 1989).

[26] Logsdon, "*Maldon*," 249. Compare Lehmann, *The Development of Germanic Verse Form*, 32: "We may conclude then, that the form of Germanic verse is better preserved in a few of the oldest pieces in our West Germanic literature than in the northern ballads" (by "northern ballads", Lehmann means here North Germanic alliterative verse in stanzaic form).

[27] Logsdon, "*Maldon*," 272.

[28] J. Knight Bostock describes the *Hakenstil*, i.e. the use of frequent run-ons, a tendency to begin clauses and sentences at the middle rather than the start of a line, the wilful separating of a noun from its adjective or dependent genitive by a line-break, etc., as being typical of "Old English and Old Saxon book-epics" (as opposed to oral tradition), and as having "a lesser claim to antiquity" than the straightforwardly stichic manner: *A Handbook on Old High German Literature* (Oxford, 1976), 318.

phora (i.e., ending lines with the same words).[29] A second difference is that Old English alliterative verse is stricter about the positions where alliterating sounds should occur (always on the third main stress, and on at least one of the first two main stresses), whereas, as Entwistle points out, "there is no fixed pattern in Finnish alliteration"[30] of a similar nature (although the location of metrically-relevant alliteration is limited by the fact that only monosyllables or initial syllables of polysyllabic words, i.e., those syllables receiving stress in normal speech, can carry the alliteration). Although alliteration in Kalevala metre "belongs to the metrical part of grammar,"[31] it is permissible for items in Finnic alliterative metre to have a minority of their lines with no alliteration.[32]

The rules regarding what constitutes alliteration also differ slightly in the two metres. For example, the Germanic rule that any initial vowel can alliterate with any other initial vowel does not apply in Finnic alliterative verse. Furthermore, in Finnic alliteration the consonant and the following vowel often alliterate *together* with another consonant and following vowel. A further difference is to be found in the metrical units present in each system: four quantitative units are considered to have made up the line in Finnic alliterative metre,[33] while the line in Old English metre is considered to have been made up of four stress units.[34] Finally, we can note that Finnic alliterative metre often had stricter limits to the number of possible syllables to a line.

---

[29] Users of alliterative metres will not deploy a great amount of epanaphora, to prevent the focus it puts on line-endings developing, and to suppress the hint of rhyme that it carries.

[30] Entwistle, *European Balladry*, 294.

[31] Alliteration is "a tendency, not a rule; a poem in the Kalevala metre which contains no alliteration, however, is nevertheless an anomaly, . . . [so] the alliteration rule belongs to the metrical part of the grammar": Leino, *Language and Metre*, 134.

[32] As regards the English situation, Skeat claims that the metre makes no compulsory requirement of alliteration: "a line wholly without alliteration was quite admissible *as a variation*, and is not to be rejected as spurious": W.W. Skeat, "An Essay on Alliterative Poetry," in *Bishop Percy's Folio Manuscript, Ballads and Romances*, vol. 3, ed. John Hales and idem (London, 1868), xi-xxxix, here xviii. Examples can be sought in the Old English *Metrical Charms*, which contain a number of lines without alliteration in, e.g., *The Nine Herbs Charm*, *Against a Dwarf*, and *For Theft of Cattle*: see Logsdon, "*Maldon*," 267. Also present in the charms is linked alliteration (i.e. alliteration running over successive lines), a feature also found in Kalevala metric items: Logsdon, "*Maldon*," 270–71.

[33] But as noted before, the fact that syllabic quantity usually coincides with stress complicates the question of whether quantity or stress should be considered as the basis of the metre.

[34] A taste of the debate as to how precisely this metre (which, after all, has been a long time dead) worked is given in the following remark by Thomas Cable: "there is a bewildering array of competing modern theories [of Old English metre]: the stress-based system of Sievers; the measure-based system of Heusler, Pope, and Hieatt; the stress and

But, as mentioned before, the exact details of these metrical differences would appear to be secondary to the analogues between these alliterative metres. A much more significant difference between the two corpora than the exact details of metre is rather the difference in their documentary history. For, although the alliterative metres of the Anglo-Saxons, Finns, and other northerners were all eventually overwhelmed by the spread of rhyme and Romance-influenced prosodies from the south of Europe,[35] this process happened at a much earlier date in the north and north-west of Europe than it did in the Baltic-Finnic north-east. Mikhail Gasparov encapsulates the route by which alliterative metres in the Germanic area were progressively ousted by Romance-based or -influenced metres:

> The direction of disintegration goes from south to north. In Germany, old accentual verse disappears as early as the ninth century, after *Muspilli* and *Heliand*. In Britain, it disappears at the end of the eleventh century, after the Norman Conquest . . ., by the fourteenth century we witness a decline of accentual verse even in Scandinavia.[36]

Thus, while Germanic alliterative verse disappeared early, even before the stave-based notation system for notating music in written form became established in northern Europe that could have been used to document it, Finnic alliterative metre survived into the eras of sound-recording[37] and photography (which was used to document its performance context).[38] While Gasparov underestimates

---

breath group system of Bliss; my own earlier contour-based system; the phrasal-rhythm system of Luecke; the alliterative system of Hoover; the foot system of Russom; the stress and measure system of Obst; and in Chapter One of the present study a sketch of yet another theory, based on the intersecting systems of syllabism and strong stress": *The English Alliterative Tradition* (Philadelphia, 1991), 60.

[35] Perhaps we should be thankful that we have any knowledge of the Germanic alliterative tradition at all, thanks to its survival into the age of literacy—literacy being another element in the process of what might be termed 'the southerning' of northern Europe. Literacy did at least allow people to partially save as marks on paper some elements of a tradition that the same processes eventually destroyed in aural reality.

[36] M.L. Gasparov, *A History of European Versification* (Oxford, 1996), 36–37.

[37] Sound recording, in the form of Edison's phonograph, was invented in 1877, and the earliest surviving recording (that of a performance of Handel at the Crystal Palace) dates from 1888.

[38] There are both photographs and pictures of the performance of Finnic alliterative metre. See Tauno Mustanoja, "The Presentation of Ancient Germanic Poetry—Looking For Parallels," *Neuphilogische Mitteilungen* 60 (1959): 1–11. The content of this article is better described by its subtitle: 'A Note on the Presentation of Finnish Runos', as he presents no original remarks about ancient Germanic poetry in his eleven pages.

the survival of alliterative metre in Britain,[39] that tradition has certainly been extinct for century on century, whereas some relict items of Finnic alliterative verse have been collected during the last quarter of the twentieth century.

Although, as Pentti Leino has remarked, "the prehistory of the Kalevala metre remains unclear,"[40] it was still in use when the first written records of vernacular literature appear in Finland and Estonia, often in the guise of alliterative verbal charms recorded in the proceedings of seventeenth-century witch trials.[41] And from the middle of the nineteenth century onwards, when the alliterative metre was finally reaching the end of its full-blooded period of existence, two massive collection programmes based in Finland and in Estonia were successful in recording a very broad and deep sample of items in this metre.

It may seem to us that the 30,000 or so lines of Old English alliterative verse that survive form a large corpus when compared with the corpora in continental Germanic languages for instance, yet this figure is tiny when compared to the Baltic-Finnic corpus. To give an idea of its scale, the 32,000 lines of alliterative verse collected from a single Ingrian woman[42] outweigh the entire Old English corpus. Or to take another example, while there are twelve Old English metrical charms, there are approximately 25,000 Finnish and 15,000 Estonian metrical charms.[43]

In such a comparative context, not only can it be said that there are few surviving items in Old English alliterative metre, but also that we lack firm evidence as to whether those surviving items are at all representative of the performance tradition. There is no firm evidence, for instance, as to whether any of the texts we have in Old English alliterative metre could truly be considered to represent

---

[39] Pearsall, for one, judges the slightly later date of 1250 as being the rough end point for attestations of "the traditional unrhymed alliterative line itself": D. Pearsall, *Old and Middle English Poetry* (London, 1977), 152. And unrhymed alliterative verse was to (re)appear later, especially "in the period 1350–1380, [w]hen, the main drift, the dominant trend, of vernacular verse was towards alliteration, with tail rhyme a very poor second": J.A.W. Bennett, "Survivals and Revivals of Alliterative Modes," *Leeds Studies in English*, n.s. 14 (1983): 26–43, here 29.

[40] Leino, *Language and Metre*, 140.

[41] If no English, German, or Danish literature had survived from before the seventeenth century, we would have no idea that there ever had been alliterative metres in these countries!

[42] The singer in question is Larin Paraske, a few of whose lines were quoted above. For more details on the amount of verse collected from Paraske, see Senni Timonen, "Thick Corpus and a Singer's Poetics," in *Thick Corpus, Organic Variation and Textuality in Oral Tradition*, ed. Lauri Honko (Helsinki, 2000), 627–59, esp. 633.

[43] These figures are derived from an estimate, based on my familiarity with the relevant archival materials, that approximately half of the 55,000 Finnish and 30,000 Estonian charms in the respective archives will be in alliterative metre.

an accurate ethnographic transcription of a live performance.[44] As far as Finnic alliterative metre is concerned, the records are fuller and more representative, and even include sound recordings.

New ways to interrogate an old corpus

Although I have been concerned with setting forth the similarities between these metres, the relevance of Finnic alliterative verse for students of Old English alliterative verse arises paradoxically from the non-identity of the two corpora. It is the *difference* between the English and the Finnic material which enables the latter to serve as comparanda. In the remainder of the paper, I shall draw upon the work of Finnish and Estonian scholars to touch on four issues regarding alliterative verse. Two of these (performance and genre) will be dealt with rather briefly, the other two (melody and metrical death) at slightly greater length. While not all of the following suggestions, parallels, and questions may be successfully applied to the Anglo-Saxon poetic corpus, they constitute some new ways to interrogate an old corpus.

Genre and Performance

The first topic is that of performance. Are we correct in assuming that the longer Anglo-Saxon metrical items were always sung straight through by one person? Magoun, in his commentary to *Widsith*, interprets the 'Scilling' of lines 103–105

> Ðonne wit Scilling sciran reorde
> for uncrum sigedryhtne song ahofan,
> hlude bi hearpan hleoþor swinsade,

as "a scop who sang with Widsith on at least one occasion like the two minstrels at the court of Attila."[45] Magoun also makes the suggestive remark "one may compare the Finnish custom of reciting by twos."[46] Identification of further ana-

---

[44] "No single exact record of an Old English scopic song as it was sung remains to us. We have only written records, which do not represent performances accurately, and some of which will probably prove, once our methods of discrimination have been refined, to be imitations of scopic song": Frederick Cassidy, "How Free was the Anglo-Saxon Scop," in *Franciplegius: Medieval and Linguistic Studies in Honor of Francis P. Magoun*, ed. Jess Bessinger and Robert Creed (New York, 1965), 75–85, esp. 82.

[45] Kemp Malone, ed., *Widsith* (London, 1936), 184.

[46] Malone, ed., *Widsith*, 184.

logues to this practice in Icelandic tradition[47] has led Peter Dronke to write "that alternate singing was an ancient and wide-spread Germanic practice."[48] Dronke also suggests that the practice in medieval religious music of a second soloist or a second half-choir repeating "each new melodic phrase by singing it alternately" with the lead singer or half-choir may be an adaptation of a prior secular practice.

Some brief details from the extensive ethnographic documentation of the Finnic tradition, where alternate singing was the standard practice, may be suggestive as to the details of this practice elsewhere. Finnic alternate singing was not a match of equals, but decisively dominated by the lead singer, who sang first. At the end of each verse line, the lead singer's words would then be repeated either by another person or by a group of people. In either case, the two alternating voices (or groups of voices) would slightly overlap with one another to produce a continuous web of sound—it was unusual for there to be a common pause for breath at the end of each verse-line. On occasion, there could also be a short one- or two-word refrain at the end of a verse-line, prolonging the melody, and allowing for easier overlap, as, for instance, in the South Estonian tradition of alliterative metre.

The second topic that I shall touch on briefly is that of genre. Almost two millennia ago, Tacitus described the ancient Germanic peoples as possessing "songs of cosmogony, . . . heroic lays, panegyric songs, genealogical poems, magical incantations, songs of victory, and dirges."[49] The surviving corpus of Anglo-Saxon verse does not bear out this description, consisting as it does in large part of written biblical translations. It would appear that the surviving corpus is not a very broad or a very deep sample of Anglo-Saxon verse as it once existed. Some of the other uses alliterative metre may have been put to are suggested by the surviving examples of Old English verse in genres other than book-epic, such as the lyrics, charms (e.g., the *Metrical Charms*), riddles (e.g., the *Exeter Riddles*), and proverbs (e.g., the *Proverb from Winfrið's Time*). In the Finnic comparanda, these genres exist in alliterative form, as do other genres, such as calendric verse for annual feasts and festivities, verse for weddings or other rites of incorporation, and verse for funerals or other rites of separation. The existence of *erfidrápur* in the more closely related Icelandic tradition would tend to confirm this last

---

[47] Stefán Einarsson, "Alternate Recital by Twos in *Widsiþ* (?), *Sturlunga* and *Kalevala*," *Arv* 6 (1951): 59–83. See further idem, "Harp Song, Heroic Poetry (Chadwicks), Greek and Germanic Alternate Singing," *Budkavlen* 42 (1963): 13–28. For a mention of possible dual singing at the court of the East Anglian King Ethelbert, see Hermann Moisl, "Anglo-Saxon Royal Genealogies and Germanic Oral Tradition," *Journal of Medieval History* 7 (1981): 215–48, here 239.

[48] Peter Dronke, *The Medieval Lyric*, 2nd ed. (London, 1978), 23.

[49] As summarised by Dronke, *The Medieval Lyric*, 16.

suggestion. Other documented Finnic genres include communal dance songs,[50] and work songs.

If these internationally common poetic genres existed in the Anglo-Saxon period, as we might think they did, what form did they take? An alliterative one? Were the presumably large number of unrecorded Old English riddles and proverbs in alliterative metre on the whole, as they are in the Baltic-Finnic comparanda? Or, let us take the example of another genre: lullabies. While this genre is undocumented in the surviving material from Anglo-Saxon England, anthropological research suggests that lullabies are a cultural universal. What metre then would the Anglo-Saxon lullabies have been in? If the Old English alliterative metre was not used as widely in its society as the Finnic alliterative metre was in its own (including in the sphere of lullabies, or others of the genres mentioned above), then we must ask what other metre(s) co-existed with Old English alliterative metre and what were the genres it was (or they were) used in? Do we have to imagine a plurality of vernacular metres in the Old English period?[51]

General melodic form

The third topic is that of melody. The melodies used in the performance of Old English verse songs have not survived. Eric Stanley has stated that "the melodic line is lost beyond hope of theoretical reconstruction."[52] This is no doubt correct. But one might consider the recordings made in the twentieth century of songs in Finnic alliterative metre, and the musical transcriptions made of such melodies at an even earlier date,[53] as forming relevant comparanda in attempts to establish the general form of the melodies of Old English verse songs (if not, however, their exact melodic lines).

The general melodic form of Finnic alliterative songs is well documented. The tradition used short tunes which were only one or two verse-lines in length.

---

[50] For example, ring dances: the Estonian name *regivärss* for Finnic alliterative metre is said to derive from a Germanic word for *ring* (and thus means 'ring-verse'), because such verse was sung by people who joined hands in a ring, or circle, and took small steps of movement during the recitation.

[51] Quite what these other metres, if they existed, might have been is anybody's guess. The presence of rhyme, however, in parts of the Old English verse corpus, e.g., in *Elene* 1236–1251, and in the so-called *Rhyming Poem*, may suggest that it had a role in unrecorded verse as well.

[52] Eric G. Stanley, *A Collection of Papers with Emphasis on Old English Literature* (Toronto, 1987), 126.

[53] One could also consider the musicological works on these melodies by such researchers as Tampere and Rüütel: e.g., Herbert Tampere, *Eesti regivärsiliste rahvalaulude muusika liigilised iseärasused ja stiilid* (Tartu, 1960), and Ingrid Rüütel, *Eesti uuema rahvalaulu kujunemine* (Tartu, 1969).

The melodies progressed with narrow intervals (i.e., steps rather than leaps were the norm), and spanned a narrow ambit (often of just a fourth, a fifth, or a sixth). Often the same tune was used for many different songs (rather than following the modern practice of each song having its own tune). They were predominantly performed in a recitative, speech-like manner, the mode of performance being one in which the words were of primary, and the melody was of secondary, importance. The same tune was varied throughout the course of a song largely in accordance with the rhythmic characteristics of a particular line of verse.[54] John Dover Wilson, who heard Finnic metric performance while he was teaching in Finland, described the style very well as "a monotonous chant but not wearying in the slightest."[55]

Recent work by the musicologist Urve Lippus has connected the music that Finnic alliterative verse was performed to with both medieval secular music and with twelfth- and thirteenth-century church music, in terms of its 'linearity'. "I would define *linear music*," she writes:

> as monophonic music produced by a mind which (1) has no concept of harmony or abstract regular metre, and (2) which has never felt the need to match voice[s] in well-tuned harmony, nor to arrive [together] with the other performers on some certain (accented) beats or more important points of the musical expression.[56]

In contrast to later 'multidimensional music', these monophonic melodies contain no implicit harmonies, and there is no role for polyphony. If Old English verse songs belong to the same medieval European song tradition of linear music, then we might expect, if we take the word of Lippus, that to modern ears they would seem to have been sung at a rather slow tempo. In her experience of transcribing recordings of Estonian alliterative songs, Lippus found that "a pair of constituent notes are about 600–1000ms. Faster or remarkably slower tempo seems extraordinary or abnormal. . . From this perspective we can also draw a parallel between early medieval European music and the runo song: tempus = longa = MM80."[57] Furthermore, as with many metrical systems, rhythmic movement was more rapid and less regular at the opening of a line, and more stately at

---

[54] This feature might have been shared not just in the Baltic and North Sea areas, but also elsewhere in Europe, if we credit Johannes de Grocheo's observation made c.1300, about *chanson de geste*: "Idem etiam cantus debet in omnibus versibus reiterari", i.e. "that each line of *chanson de geste* was sung to the same tune": quoted in Cable, *The Metre and Melody of Beowulf*, 101, 109.

[55] Cited in Mustanoja, "The Presentation of Ancient Germanic Poetry—Looking For Parallels," 9.

[56] Urve Lippus, *Linear Musical Thinking: A Theory of Musical Thinking and the Runic Song Tradition of Baltic-Finnish Peoples* (Helsinki, 1995), 13.

[57] Lippus, *Linear Musical Thinking*, 46.

the close, at times even involving the lengthening, or drawing out, of the last one or two syllables.[58] On the whole, however, the characteristic rhythmic pattern was "an even movement consisting only or mostly of short durations."[59]

Maintaining the integrity of the line was important in performance. Investigation of the sound recordings has revealed that in the event of an overlong verse line, the tune would be modified. Singers would then attempt to transfer the melodic contour at the middle of a standard-length line (i.e., the link between the two halves of that line) to the new middle of the line.[60] Significantly, Lippus also found from the study of recordings (rather than from the wishful thinking of a baffled metrist) that metrical exceptions are often compensated for in melodic performance: "In many cases, one can point to a musical component that balances an unusual part of the text line," although "the most important features of verse prosody survive their musical setting."[61]

The descriptions above may well hold true in some measure for the melodies that Old English verse was sung to. At the very least, they provide us with a reminder that Old English verse songs must too have had their own tempi, ambits, dynamics, and melodic variants, etc.

Metrical death

The final topic I wish to discuss here is the process of metrical death. Could our knowledge of the death of English alliterative metre be informed by the well-documented reasons for the ousting of Finnic alliterative metre? Both prosodic systems underwent metrical death when end-rhyme permitted multi-line structures, such as couplets and stanzas, to thrive at the expense of stichic alliterative verse. Ülo Tedre, a specialist on the Finnic alliterative metre, has outlined four factors as being key to its decline in Estonia: a) the loss of audience, b) linguistic change, c) the shift from an orally-based to a written culture, and d) a greater intensity of foreign contacts.[62] If we examine these categories in turn, some parallels with the death of English alliterative metre can be observed.

The first factor he identifies, loss of audience, is easily identifiable in the high cultural sphere, where the dissolution of the Anglo-Saxon monarchy and

---

[58] "A general trend is that, if not equal, then the first half-line is more compressed than the second half. It is standard to begin a melody with a more rapid movement and to slow down at the end": Lippus, *Linear Musical Thinking*, 48.

[59] Lippus, *Linear Musical Thinking*, 61.

[60] Lippus, *Linear Musical Thinking*, 66.

[61] Lippus, *Linear Musical Thinking*, 41.

[62] Ülo Tedre, "The Change in Estonian Folklore in the 19th Century," in *National Movements in the Baltic Countries during the 19th Century*, Acta Universitatis Stockholmensis — Studia Baltica Stockholmensia 2 (Stockholm, 1985), 495–505.

aristocracy clearly meant the destruction of an audience of a particular kind. But
as far as people of lower social status are concerned, it is not clear that the audience for alliterative verse was lost as a direct consequence of the Battle of Hast-
ings, as the existence of Laʒamon's *Brut* and the later upsurge of alliterative verse
in the fourteenth-century 'revival' suggest. It may be the case that longer-term
social and economic changes play a more significant role here. In Estonia, for
example, after the more prosperous and urban population had moved on to new
metres, rural people of lower social class still used the alliterative metre, most
commonly in group-songs sung when employed together on manorial estates in
joint labour. As such forms of economic activity withered, this audience was lost,
and so the role of alliterative verse significantly diminished. It may be that economic and social changes parallel to those Tedre delineates in Estonia[63] diminished the role of alliterative verse among the lower classes in England in the later
Middle Ages in a similar way by reducing the joint audiences for such verse.

The second factor, that of linguistic change, certainly applies to languages
in both groups. Estonian and English, for example, both underwent a series of
radical linguistic changes, including the partial loss of, or reduction in, inflec-
tions, and the introduction of foreign loan-words with different stress-patterns
complicating the phonologies of the native languages.[64] Such phonological and
morphological changes rendered the languages less amenable for use in the traditional alliterative metres.[65]

The third factor, the change from an orally-based culture to a written one
(which Tedre dates as taking place as late as the nineteenth century in Estonia),
is highlighted in Adam Fox's work on orality and literacy in sixteenth- and seventeenth-century England.[66] Fox showed just how deeply mass semi-literacy had
come to affect seemingly oral cultural products both high and low by the close of
the Middle Ages and the opening of the Early Modern age. Both Tedre and Fox
document the ousting of oral transmission by print as the primary source of new

---

[63] Tedre, "The Change in Estonian Folklore in the 19th Century," 498; see also
502–3.

[64] Similarly, Leino in *Language and Metre* describes how the gradual loss of syllabic-
ity in Finnish from the seventeenth century onward "finally destroyed the basis of the syllable structure rules" undergirding alliterative metre (139).

[65] On linguistic change influencing verse form in English, see Lehmann, *The Development of Germanic Verse Form*, 103: "as substantives gradually lost their distinctive stresses, the [English] language with its great increase in number of function words was more
adaptable to rimed than to alliterative verse, and even a strong tradition could not hinder
the gradual adoption of rime." See further Margaret Stobie, "The Influence of Morphol-
ogy on Middle English Alliterative Poetry," *Journal of English and Germanic Philology* 39
(1940): 319–36, which discusses the death of Middle English alliterative verse from the
point of view of linguistic change.

[66] Adam Fox, *Oral and Literate Culture in England, 1500–1700* (Oxford, 2000).

songs.[67] Likewise, Leino's comment that alliterative metre "lost its major function and began to be displaced"[68] with the spread of literacy and by the concomitant replacement of memorized knowledge by the written documents literacy involved, is paralleled by Clanchy's study of the same, but somewhat earlier, shift in communication and thought in England.[69] In a literate context, repetitive and parallelistic works that echo well in the ear may well come to be rejected as reading poorly for the eye.

The fourth factor, a greater intensity of foreign contacts, is also relevant in late medieval England, where the examples of other metres, and other musics, and indeed of other instruments and dances, now came to the fore. Tedre, commenting on the Estonian situation after the introduction of new instruments and songs, remarks that the previous sharp "difference between vocal and instrumental music disappeared. . . . Any normal piece of music was [now] danceable and could also be sung. . . . Such changes in lifestyle could not fail to bring about a new style of song."[70] The example of rhymed verse was more increasingly present through the different spheres of life, whether in the school room, in 'foolish' songs (such as the Estonian *lorilaulud*), or in religious hymns. Songs in the new end-rhymed style were felt to have "more melodious and rhythmic tunes than the old alliterative song."[71] In the end, the last performers of alliterative verse were elderly people unable to master the new style. The four factors that Tedre mentions all took effect in a period of great social change, and left Finnic alliterative metre seeming clumsy, irrelevant, slow, old-fashioned.[72] Is this how English alliterative metre was perceived at the end of its active life?

The foregoing examples serve to indicate the kinds of details of Anglo-Saxon poetic practice that can be imagined or reimagined by following the clues that

---

[67] Tedre documents how the increase in literacy in Estonia led to an increase in publishing small, "slim and cheap book[s] which contained singable songs . . . the first songbook was published in 1852. In the 1850s ten song-books were published . . . in the 1870s forty (reprints not included). All this influenced the stock of songs of the people (many songs of literary origin became popular), the folk-song itself and the spreading of folk-songs": "The Change in Estonian Folklore in the 19th Century," 503–4.

[68] Leino, *Language and Metre*, 149.

[69] M.T. Clanchy, *From Memory to Written Record* (London, 1992).

[70] Tedre, "The Change in Estonian Folklore in the 19th Century," 503.

[71] Ants Viires, "A Great Change in Estonian Folk Culture," in *National Movements in the Baltic Countries during the 19th Century*, 543–56, here 544.

[72] Tedre in "The Change in Estonian Folklore in the 19th Century" describes the alliterative songs as being slow "with their laborious insistence on detail" as against the rhymed songs which "were fast and abounded in vitality" (503). He also, more dubiously, goes on to suggest that Finnic alliterative poetry could not respond to political events in terms of satire or social critique: surely *Piers Plowman* is a counter-argument to this mistaken belief about the uses alliterative metre can be put to.

the well-documented corpus of Finnic alliterative verse can yield up.[73] It may be that the critical works of Lippus, Tampere, Honko, and Peegel,[74] amongst others, can provide the Anglo-Saxonist with much food for future thought.

---

[73] Could it not be possible for the reverse also to be true, namely that researchers into Finnic alliterative metre could find a similar broadening of possibilities by a comparative consideration of English alliterative metre? On this see Jonathan Roper, "Former Metres in Northern Europe," in *Congressus Internationalis Nonus Fenno-Ugristarum, Pars VII*, ed. T. Seilenthal (Tartu, 2001), 204–14.

[74] Peegel in his works has paid especial attention to the use of poetic synonyms in Finnic alliterative verse. See, for instance, Juhan Peegel, *Nimisõna Poeetilised Sünonüümid Eesti Regivärssides* (Tallinn, 2004), and idem, *Kuld on jäänud jälgedesse: Regivarsi keelest ja poeetikast* (Tartu, 1997). The study of the comparative use of poetic synonyms in the two corpora is one of the more obvious and intriguing areas of future research to suggest itself.

THE GHOST OF M.I. STEBLIN-KAMENSKIJ: INTERPRETING OLD ENGLISH LITERATURE THROUGH SAGA THEORY

JONATHAN WILCOX

'Anglo-Saxons and the North' conjures up for the literary scholar the fascinating similarities and differences between Old English literature and Old Norse. A fruitful focus for discussing the interrelationship of those two cultures is the neglected Russian critic of the North, Mikhail Ivanovich Steblin-Kamenskij. In this essay, I will consider how Steblin-Kamenskij's discussions of Old Norse saga literature might be of value for interpreting Old English literature. In the process, I hope both to recuperate the critical writings of one of Russia's greatest medievalists and to provide a usefully provocative grounding for the comparison of Old English and Old Norse literature.

Relations between the North and Anglo-Saxons are nicely exemplified in the exploits in Anglo-Saxon England of the viking-poet, Egil. *Egils saga*, indeed, both hints at the reasons to relate the literatures of the two cultures and the challenges of doing so, challenges answered by the work of Steblin-Kamenskij. *Egils saga* appears to give a more textured sense of life in Anglo-Saxon England than virtually anything written in Old English. In the course of his exploits, Egil moves between Old Norse and Anglo-Saxon society, at one point traveling through Anglo-Saxon England as King Athelstan's hired man, receiving provisional baptism from the king, and winning the battle of Brunanburh for the English, then later returning to York inadvertently through a shipwreck, to the court of his arch-enemy Eirik Blood-Axe, where he saves his grizzled head through the composition of the brilliant poem "head-ransom," before heading back to Athelstan's court.[1]

---

[1] *Egils saga Skalla-Grímssonar*, ed. Sigurður Nordal, Íslenzk Fornrit 2 (Reykjavik, 1933), chaps. 50–55, 59–62; trans. Hermann Pálsson and Paul Edwards, *Egil's Saga* (Harmondsworth, 1976). The battle in the saga is called a great battle at Vinheiðr.

These episodes provide with imaginative specificity a rich picture of daily life in Anglo-Saxon England. This is seen, for example, when Egil becomes Athelstan's man:

> England was a Christian country, and had been so for a long time when these events were taking place. King Athelstan was a staunch Christian, and people called him Athelstan the Faithful. He asked Thorolf and his brother [Egil] to accept preliminary baptism [*láta prímsignask*] as was the custom in those days both for merchants and mercenaries serving Christian rulers, since people who had been given this form of baptism could mix equally with Christian and heathen and were free to hold any belief that suited them. So Thorolf and Egil did what the King wanted and received preliminary baptism. They had three hundred and sixty men under them, all on the King's payroll. (chap. 50)[2]

The process whereby a Norse-speaking, heathen viking comes to serve a devout English king is explained here in detail by the saga writer. The saga puts even the *Anglo-Saxon Chronicle* to shame for its care in casting light on some of the most intriguing practices of Anglo-Saxon England.

Not, of course, that anything in *Egils saga* gives straightforward access to historical facts. *Egils saga* as it survives was composed perhaps around 1220, some three hundred years after the events that it describes, with the earliest surviving manuscript fragments dating from about the middle of the thirteenth century.[3] With such a chronology, the saga is unlikely to offer simple reportage. Indeed, understanding the relationship between sagas and history has long been a major topic of saga criticism. An old debate between free prose and book prose pitted a model of composition that depended on oral stories and so preserved the historically real against a literate method that saw the sagas as historical fiction.[4] This

---

[2] *Egil's Saga*, trans. Pálsson and Edwards, 115. Text from *Egils saga Skalla-Grímssonar*, ed. S. Nordal, 127–28:

England var kristit ok hafði lengi verit, þá er þetta var tíðenda; Aðalsteinn konungr var vel kristinn; hann var kallaðr Aðalsteinn inn trúfasti. Konungr bað Þórólf ok þá brœðr, at þeir skyldi láta prímsignask, því at þat var þá mikill siðr, bæði me kaupmönnum ok þeim mönnum, er á mála gengu me kristnum mönnum, því at þeir menn, er prímsignaðir váru, höfðu þat at átrúnaði, er þeim var skapfelldast. Þeir Þórólfr ok Egill gerðu þat eptir bœn konungs ok létu prímsignask báðir. Þeir höfðu þar þrjú hundruð sinna manna, þeira er mála tóku af konungi.

[3] See, for example, the introduction by Pálsson and Edwards. The work is anonymous, although scholarly arguments for Snorri Sturluson's authorship have been frequently offered in view of the its affinity with Snorri's attested saga of kings, *Heimskringla*.

[4] See Theodore M. Andersson, *The Problem of Icelandic Saga Origins: A Historical Survey* (New Haven, 1964). For an excellent survey of trends in saga scholarship to the

was the nature of the debate at the time Steblin-Kamenskij was writing. Such stark dichotomizing has since broken down, and recent analyses offer a more nuanced sense of sagas' relationship to history, conditioned by 'New Historicism' to see in them a process of historicization in which the writing down of tradition creates as much as it reflects history.[5]

Yet, for all the mediated nature of reality within the sagas, there is something distinctive about their presentation of events which it is tempting to treat as realism. Even though most medievalist critics might blanch at the bold claim of Scholes and Kellogg in *The Nature of Narrative* that the sagas' narrative art is "almost miraculously precocious" in constituting a "new synthesis of myth and mimesis as realistic narrative fiction,"[6] the sagas of Icelanders are in some way special among medieval literature for their presentation of detail in an objective style. "Sagas are terse in style and full of meat: incidents follow in swift succession, many characters appear on the scene," observes Jónas Kristjánson. He continues:

> People often remark on the "objectivity" of sagas. When characters are introduced, the author often spends a few words on a description, both of appearance and temperament. After that they are allowed to reveal themselves by their words and deeds — just like people in real life,[7]

thereby succumbing to the temptation to relate sagas to real life, implicitly comparing them with real life as it is lived today.

Such a temptation rarely faces the critic of Old English literature, by contrast, whose corpus lacks any comparable imaginative, apparently realistic, long-prose form.[8] While saints' lives in some ways hint at features of the sagas in a certain pseudo-objectivity of narrative tone, they lack the development, the consistency, and the length of the sagas, and their necessarily edifying conclusion places them in a different world from the apparently objective recounting of

---

mid-1980s, see Carol J. Clover, "Icelandic Family Sagas (*Íslendingasögur*)," in *Old Norse–Icelandic Literature: A Critical Guide*, ed. eadem and John Lindow, Islandica 45 (Ithaca, 1985), 239–315.

[5] See, for example, Jürg Glauser, "Sagas of the Icelanders (*Íslendinga sögur*) and *Þættir* as the Literary Representation of a New Social Space," in *Old Icelandic Literature and Society*, ed. Margaret Clunies Ross (Cambridge, 2000), 203–20. For a comparable idea in relation to Old English literature, see Nicholas Howe, *Migration and Mythmaking in Anglo-Saxon England* (New Haven, 1989; 2nd ed., Notre Dame, 2001).

[6] Robert Scholes and Robert Kellogg, *The Nature of Narrative* (Oxford, 1966), 43, 45.

[7] Jónas Kristjánson, *Eddas and Sagas: Iceland's Medieval Literature*, trans. Peter Foote (Reykjavik, 1988), 207.

[8] On the latter, see Carol Clover, "The Long Prose Form," *Arkiv for Nordisk Filologi* 101 (1986): 10–39.

saga narrative.[9] The odd survival *Apollonius of Tyre* hints at some aspects of saga narrative, but its fragmentary text follows the conventions of Greek romance in Old English, without the broad and circumstantial development of the sagas.[10] A Latin work like the *Life of Alfred* again does not really achieve saga style, staying closer to hagiographic conventions and, in any case, occupying a different world through its Latinity. And the *Anglo-Saxon Chronicle* includes a single entry often associated with saga form, but obviously different from full sagas in its retention of annalistic form, brevity, and lack of development.[11] An Old English tradition of documentary prose, evident at times in charters or legal documents, can be teased out to give interesting historical details, occasionally hinting at the subject matter of feuds that preoccupied saga-writers, but this does not present anything like the carefully crafted extended narratives of the sagas.[12] Through their concern with details of non-saintly, non-aristocratic Icelanders told in an objective yet extended prose style, the sagas really are different from Old English literature.

In broad terms, the distinction may reflect differences between Iceland and Anglo-Saxon England. England's early experience of state formation centering on a monarchic administration contrasts with the proto-democracy of Icelandic government by *goði* and *þing*, and Christianity was more deep-rooted and evolved in tenth-century England than in thirteenth-century Iceland, when the sagas were being recorded there. Such differences make straightforward comparison of Old Norse sagas and Old English literature difficult. Instead of attempting such a comparison, I will turn to some of the critical sophistication unleashed by saga narrative and consider whether it can be applied usefully to Old English literature. Since the ISAS 2001 conference was hosted, in part, by the University of St. Petersburg, where the second half of the conference took place, I have chosen to focus here on that city's most important saga critic, M.I. Steblin-Kamenskij,

---

[9] For a good introduction to Old English saints' lives, see Michael Lapidge, "The Saintly Life in Anglo-Saxon England," in *The Cambridge Companion to Old English Literature*, ed. Malcolm Godden and idem (Cambridge, 1991), 243–63.

[10] *The Old English Apollonius of Tyre*, ed. Peter Goolden (London, 1958); see further Anita Riedinger, "The Englishing of Arcestrate: Woman in Apollonius of Tyre," in *New Readings on Women in Old English Literature*, ed. Helen Damico and Alexandra Hennessey Olsen (Bloomington, 1990), 292–306.

[11] On the Cynewulf and Cyneheard episode, see, most recently, Thomas A. Bredehoft, *Textual Histories: Readings in the Anglo-Saxon Chronicle* (Toronto, 2001), chap. 2.

[12] Note, for example, Simon Keynes's brilliant analysis of "The Fonthill Letter," in *Words, Texts and Manuscripts: Studies in Anglo-Saxon Culture Presented to Helmut Gneuss on the Occasion of his Sixty-Fifth Birthday*, ed. Michael Korhammer et al. (Munich, 1992), 53–97, which has spawned the further studies by Mechthild Gretsch, "The Language of the Fonthill Letter," *Anglo-Saxon England* 23 (1994): 57–102, and Mark Boynton and Susan Reynolds, "The Author of the Fonthill Letter," *Anglo-Saxon England* 25 (1996): 91–95.

who, along with Aron Gurevich, constitutes one of the two most important Russian medievalist critics accessible to western scholars. [13]

M.I. Steblin-Kamenskij (1903–1981) taught and researched linguistics and literature at the University of Leningrad, where he was chairman of the Department of Romance and Germanic Languages from 1950 and of the newly established independent Scandinavian Department from 1958 until the 1970s. [14] Although he began his scholarly career with a dissertation on Old English poetic style, [15] his writings centered on Old Norse, particularly on the literature of the sagas, and on linguistic philology. It was his works of saga criticism that were translated into English and that will be considered here. His biggest impact came with the publication of *The Saga Mind* in 1973, an English translation of a book originally published as *Mir Sagi*, "the World of the Saga," in Leningrad in 1971. [16] A scattering of his articles also appeared in English, while a second critical book was translated and published posthumously in 1982 as *Myth*. [17] I will concentrate on Steblin-Kamenskij's contribution to medieval literary theory as worked out in relation to the Old Norse sagas, since this seems to me to be his most productive contribution to medieval criticism. [18]

Steblin-Kamenskij saw himself as employing philology in the service of "historical psychology." His most provocative contributions center around ideas of truth, of time, and of authorship in the sagas. *The Saga Mind* looks at the big picture, bucking a trend in saga scholarship (and medieval scholarship generally?) to work at a level of concrete detail. In broadest terms, in what he christens "the non-identity hypothesis," Steblin-Kamenskij insists that personhood was different in the Middle Ages from today:

---

[13] I am discounting Mikhail Bakhtin, despite the obvious importance of *Rabelais and His World*, trans. Hélène Iswolsky (Bloomington, 1984), as not primarily a medievalist. Aron Gurevich's works available in English translation include *Categories of Medieval Culture*, trans. George Campbell (London, 1985); *Medieval Popular Culture: Problems of Belief and Perception*, trans. János M. Bak and Paul A. Hollingsworth (Cambridge, 1988); *Historical Anthropology of the Middle Ages*, ed. Jana Howlett (Chicago, 1992); and *The Origins of European Individualism*, trans. Katharine Judelson (Oxford, 1995).

[14] For his life and a bibliography of his writings, see Anatoly S. Liberman, "Epilogue and Biobibliography," in M.I. Steblin-Kamenskij, *Myth*, trans. Mary P. Coote with the assistance of Frederic Amory, Critical Introduction by Edmund Leach, Epilogue by Anatoly Liberman (Ann Arbor, 1982), 103–50.

[15] An abstract of the initial Candidate of Philology dissertation from 1946 is item 1 in Liberman's bibliography, in *Myth*, 132–33.

[16] M.I. Steblin-Kamenskij, *The Saga Mind*, trans. Kenneth H. Ober (Odense, 1973).

[17] Steblin-Kamenskij, *Myth*, trans. Coote.

[18] Owing to my linguistic limitations, I have considered only Steblin-Kamenskij's works that have been translated into English.

It seems to me that approaches of modern man to medieval literature must
be necessarily based on one of two mutually exclusive hypotheses. One of
them assumes that the psychology of medieval man is not identical with
that of modern man, while the other, on the contrary, assumes that the
psychology of medieval man is identical with that of modern man (and in
the latter case the very necessity of such concepts as "medieval man" and
"modern man" is naturally negated).[19]

The distinction is crucial since from it follows the suggestion that an early medieval conception of time, of authorship, and even of truth will be different from a
modern one, thus rendering askew saga criticism that formulates interpretations
based on the modern concepts of these ideas. In an ironic turn, Steblin-Kamenskij suggests that the urge to fasten onto the identity thesis, to assume that the
past works just like the present, is itself a medieval characteristic.

Steblin-Kamenskij expresses some impatience with existing criticism. He
professes a regard for the old philology, the investigations of manuscripts, texts,
and sources, but adds that the importance of such work

does not preclude the fact that the investigator of an ancient piece of literature often apprehends no more of the work itself and of the spiritual world
expressed in it than a worm gnawing the parchment on which it is set forth.
A research worker may, of course, perfectly understand his thankless role and
possess a sense of humor, something hardly possible in the case of the worm.
Admittedly, it may also be absent in the case of the research worker.[20]

Such investigators' failure to acknowledge the alterity of the early Middle Ages,
he suggests, leads them to ignore the essential spirit of the literature.

Steblin-Kamenskij's ideas about the nature of the saga world are best formulated in relation to the historicity of the sagas. If the truth value of the account of
Egil's life is hard to determine, he suggests that the problem lies in the way the
question is formulated. Modern conceptions of validity, he suggests, can be divided into "historical truth"—"the truth presented in the study of history. . . the
exact report of what has occurred"—or "artistic truth"—that is fiction, "whose
purpose is to evoke a vivid and living idea of the reality of the past, but not to report exact information about it."[21] In the modern world, there is a strong dichotomy between these two. Yet, Steblin-Kamenskij suggests, saga writers and saga
audiences and the whole world of early medieval Europe did not think in these
terms. Instead he coins the term "syncretic truth" for a fundamentally distinct early

[19] M.I. Steblin-Kamenskij, "Some Considerations on Approaches to Medieval Literature," *Medieval Scandinavia* 8 (1975): 187–91, at 187.
[20] *The Saga Mind*, 15.
[21] *The Saga Mind*, 22.

medieval conception of reality: "Whoever reported syncretic truth about the past strove simultaneously for accuracy and for reproduction of reality in all its living fullness."[22] He adds a fourth term, "ecclesiastical truth," to allow for the sense of truth implicit in miracle tales, which he sees as a new form of viewing the world that comes with the recent spread of Christianity in Iceland, and which he is un-apologetically against: "In comparison with the syncretic truth of the sagas, this new truth—which was actually not so much truth as falsification of truth—was a great regression (unless, of course, one considers the perfection of methods of fal-sification of truth also a kind of progress)."[23] It is in his attitude to this fourth term that he most fully reminds us that he is writing in the Soviet era.

I want to suggest that Steblin-Kamenskij's ideas here, particularly his release from the bind of history versus literature, are potentially liberating for Anglo-Saxonists. They would release discussion of a poem like *The Battle of Maldon* from straightforward opposition to a document like the *Anglo-Saxon Chronicle* and al-low both to stand as samples of syncretic truth. While there may be a continuum in what we moderns see as degrees of historicity, the historical psychology of audiences of the time would conceive of the past in different, non-dichotomous terms—that is, accept both accounts as "syncretic truth." Such a conception might also provide a good basis for thinking of *Beowulf*'s historicity,[24] with its appeal to "on geardagum" and its mostly untroubled blend of pagan and Chris-tian worlds in a single syncretic truth.

Steblin-Kamenskij's fourth term, "ecclesiastical truth," plays a bigger role in most Anglo-Saxon literature than in the sagas, reflecting the more fully Chris-tianized state of late Anglo-Saxon England. This is especially apparent, of course, in saints' lives and the homiletic corpus, but also in much of the poetry. It is pos-sible to think of stripping "ecclesiastical truth" of the negative valence given it by Steblin-Kamenskij and instead appropriating it as a neutral term for an element of historical psychology that is particularly important for understanding much of early medieval Europe. Indeed, Karen Jolly's work on syncretism in Anglo-Saxon religious practice[25] suggests that a particularly Anglo-Saxonist interven-tion in the whole discussion of truth might lie in bringing together the ideas of syncretic truth and ecclesiastical truth.

Steblin-Kamenskij's other big claim is about the nature of time. "Greatly generalizing," he says, "it may be said that the difference between the concep-tions of time in the family sagas and our modern ones lies in the greater unity of

---

[22] *The Saga Mind*, 24.

[23] *The Saga Mind*, 46–47.

[24] See M. Osborn, "Legends of Lejre, Home of Kings," in *Beowulf and Lejre*, ed. J.D. Niles (Tempe, 2007), 235–53.

[25] Karen Louise Jolly, *Popular Religion in Late Saxon England: Elf Charms in Context* (Chapel Hill, 1996).

the former—the absence of any split, contradiction, or break;"[26] in other words, there is a continuity with the past and future rather than a preoccupation with the present: "A firm organic bond with the past and a consciousness of one's unity with it."[27] This explains the sagas' continual interest in the past. Although the past of *Beowulf* is more remote than that of the sagas of Icelanders, a similar sense of unity with the past helps explain the motivation for the poem and the easy cohabitation of Christian and pagan worldviews. Steblin-Kamenskij's comments on time and its implications have yet more clear resonance for thinking about the Old English elegies with their implied reiteration from personal history to generalized present and implied future—and, indeed, for the Old English gnomic style generally, which reuses the past through the timelessness of the gnomic wisdom. From this sense of time, Steblin-Kamenskij also detects a distinct attitude towards death, apparent in a certain fatalism, which may also be seen in an Old English work like *Beowulf.*

Another corollary of the idea of syncretic truth for Steblin-Kamenskij is a distinct sense of authorship—or, rather, "the absence of the consciousness of authorship"—which he christens "unconscious authorship."[28] He points to the philological evidence and to the anonymity of saga writers, which he contrasts with the auctorial stance evident in skaldic verse. The broad analogy here serves less well for the Anglo-Saxon model. In the vernacular prose corpus, when Christian writers like Ælfric, and to a lesser extent Byrhtferth and Wulfstan, name themselves, they are appealing to a tradition of patristic authorship and validation.[29] What Steblin-Kamenskij describes seems to me to be another consequence of the shift from orality to literacy that is more or less in process in both Old English and Old Norse cultures. In Old English poetry, the whole idea of authorship is vexed but lacks the distinctions of Norse poetics: Cynewulf is a cipher with a name but he probably anticipates the same auctorial tradition as that claimed by Ælfric rather than that of the skalds. Still, some of the ramifications that Steblin-Kamenskij claims for the idea of unconscious authorship are useful for considering Old English works:

> The absence of conscious authorship implies a less distinct realization of the bounds of the human personality. If the writer was not conscious of his function as an author, he naturally could not separate it from what we call recording, copying, compiling, editing, reworking, and the like.[30]

---

[26] *The Saga Mind*, 123.

[27] *The Saga Mind*, 133.

[28] *The Saga Mind*, 50–53.

[29] On Ælfric as *auctor*, see, for example, Jonathan Wilcox, ed., *Ælfric's Prefaces* (Durham, 1994).

[30] *The Saga Mind*, 56.

Steblin-Kamenskij's idea of "unconscious authorship" can thus help to explain the active role of scribes in the transmission of Old English literature and the whole modern difficulty of differentiating an author, a compiler, a reviser, and a scribe in a culture where those distinctions were not part of, or were only becoming part of, the thought world.[31]

Steblin-Kamenskij's enduring contribution, then, lies in stressing the alterity of the worldview of the early Middle Ages, an idea exploited in vastly differing ways in many of the most interesting recent Anglo-Saxon studies, such as James Earl's *Thinking About Beowulf* (Stanford, 1994), or John Hill's *The Cultural World of Beowulf* (Toronto, 1995), or Allen Frantzen's *Before the Closet* (Chicago, 2000). Steblin-Kamenskij's specific ideas about truth, time, and authorship in the sagas can be transferred in part to Anglo-Saxon material, even though the increased Christianization of late Anglo-Saxon England and the more developed state formation make any simple correspondence difficult.

Perhaps the most fruitful point of comparison is slightly more tangential and can be pointed up through one of Steblin-Kamenskij's occasional essays. After his death, Anatoly Liberman published extracts from Steblin-Kamenskij's personal journal. Here the critic considers his own best work to be not *The Saga Mind*, but an essay called "On the History of Laughter."[32] In this essay Steblin-Kamenskij differs with Bakhtin and suggests that medieval laughter is prevailingly non-directed laughter of mirth, which was subsequently replaced by the directed laughter of ridicule, mockery, or parody. Here I disagree with Steblin-Kamenskij in a number of ways: I don't think this short essay is his best work; he has to indulge in special pleading to view the personalized vilification of *Bandamanna saga* as something other than directed laughter; I find his implied chronological development from undirected to directed laughter improbable; and I think this single dichotomy is too simple a frame for a satisfactory exploration of laughter. Still, his strong claims here combined with his theoretical emphasis on non-identity in his investigation of historical psychology suggest how the gesture of laughter requires careful examination with an underlying assumption that the medieval usage will differ from the modern.

Laughter in Old English has received much attention lately. Hugh Magennis has surveyed the Old English poetic corpus and concluded that laughter

---

[31] See Jonathan Wilcox, "Variant Texts of an Old English Homily: Vercelli X and Stylistic Readers," in *The Preservation and Transmission of Anglo-Saxon Culture*, ed. Paul E. Szarmach and Joel T. Rosenthal (Kalamazoo, 1997), 335–51, and idem, "Transmission of Literature and Learning: Anglo-Saxon Scribal Culture," in *A Companion to Anglo-Saxon Literature*, ed. Phillip Pulsiano and Elaine Treharne (Oxford, 2001), 50–70.

[32] Anatoly Liberman, "The Legacy of M.I. Steblin-Kamenskij," *Scandinavica* 24 (1985): 211–21, here 219.

operates in six distinct ways in Old English, both positive and negative.[33] John
Niles has paused on the laughter of Byrhtnoth at his moment of death in *The
Battle of Maldon* to unpack the ways in which this gesture resonates with meaning in the poem.[34] Tom Shippey has demonstrated how laughter in Old English
heroic and proverbial literature centers on a sardonic quality—a bleak awareness
that laughs at any unreflecting assurance.[35] My own essay on the laughter of Sara
and Abraham picks through the patristic tradition to show how laughter could
be both freighted with and voided of ridicule in the early Middle Ages.[36] All
these studies pursue a careful examination of a single gesture to understand its
overtones in a history that is not assumed to be identical with the present. It may
be that it is in such study of gesture that Steblin-Kamenskij anticipated a useful
theoretical opening for Anglo-Saxonist critics and that Egil can most usefully
reside in England.

Sagas palpably depend on the use of gestures for key effects, punctuating
their apparent quotidian realism with scenes centered on a memorable gesture.
Egil's most famous display is probably that following the Battle of Brunanburh
when he mourns the death of his brother, Thorolf, before he is compensated by
Athelstan. The narrative pauses for a physical description of Egil, tall and pre-
maturely bald, who keeps pulling out and thrusting back his sword in his scab-
bard, while

> one eyebrow sunk down right to the cheek and the other lifting up to the
> roots of the hair. . . . He . . . did nothing but pull his eyebrows up and down,
> now this one, now the other. (chap. 55)[37]

This gesture is notable enough to be illustrated in a seventeenth-century manuscript of the saga.[38] While this particular gesture is familiar in Old Norse as a
sign of Thor's anger, I haven't been able to match it very precisely, although the
enigmatic description of Creation as a creature bald and lacking eyebrows from
Riddle 40 suggests an attentiveness to these expressive shaggy body parts even as

---

[33] Hugh Magennis, "Images of Laughter in Old English Poetry, with Particular
Reference to the 'Hleahtor Wera' of *The Seafarer*," *English Studies* 73 (1992): 193–202.

[34] John D. Niles, "Byrhtnoth's Laughter and the Poetics of Gesture," in *Humour in
Anglo-Saxon Literature*, ed. Jonathan Wilcox (Cambridge, 2000), 11–32.

[35] T.A. Shippey, "'Grim Wordplay': Folly and Wisdom in Anglo-Saxon Humor," in
Humour in Anglo-Saxon Literature, ed. Wilcox, 33–48.

[36] Jonathan Wilcox, "The First Laugh: Laughter in Genesis and the Old English
Tradition," in *The Old English Hexateuch: Aspects and Approaches*, ed. Rebecca Barnhouse
and Benjamin C. Withers (Kalamazoo, 2000), 239–69.

[37] Pálsson and Edwards, 128. "þa hleypði hann annarri brúninni ofan á kinnina, en
annarri upp í hárrœtr. . . ýmsum hleypði hann brúnunum ofan eða upp," ed. S. Nordal,
143–44.

[38] Reproduced most accessibly on the cover of Pálsson and Edwards.

it denies them to the odd figure pictured in the riddle.[39] It certainly differs from the visual code for an expression of grief in Old English—placing one hand before the face, as explicated by C.R. Dodwell in his reading of Old English visual gestures based on Terence—by about as much as Egil's aggressive temperament differs from a Christian acceptance of death.[40] Thinking through any such gestures, it is always useful to relate Old English to Old Norse literature and to pay due attention to Steblin-Kamenskij's non-identity hypothesis.[41]

Perhaps the equivalent for the theoretical critic to this kind of heightened gesture lies in the revelatory dream, as is evident in the case of J.R.R. Tolkien, whose dream of the tower at the end of his famous 1936 essay has been interestingly explicated by Clare Lees,[42] and in the case of James Earl, whose two dreams form the centerpiece of the final essay in *Thinking About Beowulf.* Steblin-Kamenskij ends *The Saga Mind* with an account of his visitation at the Saga Hotel in Reykjavik by a ghost named Þorleifr from the thirteenth century, whose Old Icelandic doesn't quite live up to the recreated rules of philology (". . . it seems that he had various peculiarities in the articulation of the vowels. It is quite possible that these were articulatory peculiarities characteristic of the phonetics of ghosts in general" [142]). Þorleifr laments the lack of a sense of kin in the modern world and obligingly lives out Steblin-Kamenskij's theories of truth, of time, and of authorship. This dream ghost is scathing about the idea of the literary critic. He grapples with the concept:

> maybe, instead of telling a saga, he only says that he is going to tell it, but actually does not? Such a thing did happen to Þorir, Þorleifr's great grandfather. Þorir was visiting a man named Asgrimr (here Þorleifr recounted Asgrimr's family tree). Instead of feeding Þorir, Asgrimr only told him about food. Finally, Þorir killed Asgrimr. Þorleifr was interested in knowing whether the same thing happens to those who tell sagas about sagas. (150)

The very use of a dream to ratify a critical act hints at anxiety about the value of criticism, and such anxiety is certainly apparent in Þorleifr's dismissive attitude here, which establishes literary theorizing as a particularly unfulfilling activity.

---

[39] Riddle 40 translates Aldhelm's Riddle 100 closely, yet line 100 adds the detail of the lacking eyebrows. The Old English riddle is edited (as number 38) by Craig Williamson, *The Old English Riddles of the Exeter Book* (Chapel Hill, 1977), 91–94, who includes the source among the notes at 265–75.

[40] C.R. Dodwell, *Anglo-Saxon Gestures and the Roman Stage* (Cambridge, 2000).

[41] For an attempt to relate key gestural language in Old English and Old Norse, see Jonathan Wilcox, "Famous Last Words: Ælfric's Saints Facing Death," *Essays in Medieval Studies* 10 (1994): 1–13.

[42] Clare A. Lees, "Men and *Beowulf*," in *Medieval Masculinities: Regarding Men in the Middle Ages*, ed. eadem (Minneapolis, 1994), 129–48.

This anxiety might derive from the marginal status of saga scholarship in mid-twentieth-century Soviet society, although Steblin-Kamenskij's position within that society was boosted by one of the ironic and arbitrary acts of a command economy. In 1965 Khrushchev visited Sweden and, infected with an enthusiasm for things Scandinavian, encouraged the establishment of Scandinavian groups by the institutes of the Academy of Sciences. Steblin-Kamenskij must have been one of the very few available choices to head such a group in Leningrad. This scholar of the north cashed in on the newfound centrality of northern studies by negotiating for publication without the impediment of the usual bureaucratic red tape, of a semi-popular book, *The Culture of Iceland* (Leningrad, 1967), which was the precursor of *The Saga Mind*.[43] Northern scholarship suddenly seemed relevant to the Soviet state, and this allowed Steblin-Kamenskij to launch a successful publishing career as a medievalist critic.

As Anglo-Saxon scholars in Europe and America consider their relevance in the contemporary west,[44] it may be worthwhile to reflect upon the ghost of Steblin-Kamenskij and reconsider what we can learn from this Russian theorist of Old Norse literature. The broad view he takes in *The Saga Mind* may yet be of value as an antidote to the painstaking but under-theorized work that generally prevails in Anglo-Saxon studies today. And so Steblin-Kamenskij's story may be worth reviving, even at the risk of being one who tells sagas about those who tell sagas about sagas.

---

[43] The story is told by Liberman, "Epilogue," 104.

[44] See, inter alia, Allen Frantzen, "By the Numbers: Anglo-Saxon Scholarship at the Century's End," and Nicholas Howe, "The New Millennium," in *A Companion to Anglo-Saxon Literature*, ed. Pulsiano and Treharne, 472–95, 496–505 respectively.

The St. Petersburg Bede: Sankt-Peterburg, Publichnaja Biblioteka, MS. lat. Q.v.I.18

George Hardin Brown

The National Library of Russia (formerly the Saltykov-Shchedrin Public Library) in St. Petersburg boasts many lovely manuscripts from early medieval Europe, but for us Anglo-Saxonists there is none as precious as MS. lat. Q.v.I.18, the St. Petersburg copy of Bede's *Historia Ecclesiastica Gentis Anglorum*, which I will refer to by its usual manuscript siglum L (from the former name of the city, Leningrad). Written in the Anglo-Saxon pointed minuscule script developed at Bede's monastery of Wearmouth-Jarrow, the manuscript comprises 162 folios measuring 270 x 190 mm, with the neatly written text on each page occupying 220 x 150 mm. The text is divided throughout into two columns of 27 lines. Each main section is introduced by a *littera notabilior*, a simple decorated capital. After the preface (fols. 1a–2a) and the table of contents for the first chapter (2a–3a), Book I begins with the first word "Brittania" in display script (fol. 26v). Book II begins (fol. 26v) with an historiated initial enclosing a figure identified by a later hand as Augustine, but Gregory the Great may have been originally intended. Books III, IV, and V are introduced by a simple *littera notabilior.* After fol. 159 one folio is missing, which contained Book V, ch. xxiii, lines 55–113. The four scribes who wrote the manuscript did a careful job. As a result of Olof Arngart's publication of a facsimile of the manuscript in 1952, scholars increasingly studied and analysed it, if not always correctly.[1] Some highly respected palaeographers have made some claims about the manuscript that are untenable, but they have discovered much that is right. As much as the manuscript has revealed to investigation, it still has more to tell us, provided we look carefully. Some of its secrets, however, will never be disclosed; but by carefully examining the manuscript and its text

---

[1] Olof Arngart, ed., *The Leningrad Bede*, EEMF 2 (Copenhagen, 1952). Although Arngart's plates are not of the best quality, his introduction is valuable in its historic and textual detail. Summary data are now available in T. Voronova and A. Sterligov, *Western Illuminated Manuscripts in the St. Petersburg Public Library* (Bournemouth and St. Petersburg, 1996), 282, plate 11 (fol. 3v), and 283 (fol. 26v).

while taking into account earlier investigations, we make new discoveries and establish more accurate readings.[2]

Even though bibliographers have been able to discover a good deal about the manuscript's creation and early history, as well as its history from the seventeenth century to its present home in St. Petersburg, much of its provenance through the thousand-year period remains a mystery. During the seventeenth and eighteenth centuries the manuscript belonged to the family De Harlay, of Grosbois near Versailles, and the manuscript is still bound in the leather cover stamped with the arms of Count Achille III de Harlay (1639–1712). He left the volume to his son, who in turn willed all his manuscripts to Germain-Louis de Chauvelin "on condition that after his death they were to go to the library of the Benedictine Abbey of Saint-Germain-des-Prés"; that occurred in 1755.[3] After the suppression of the monastery at the French Revolution, the manuscript turned up with many fine early manuscripts in the collection of the Russian nobleman Peter Dubrowsky of St. Petersburg, as his inscription at the bottom of fols. 1 and 161ᵛ attests. In 1805 he donated the manuscript along with 1065 others to the Russian State. First housed in the Hermitage, it was later transferred to the National Library, where it now resides.

Concerning the other end of its history, there was for a time some doubt. The esteemed palaeographer Olga Dobias-Rozdestvenskaja (Dobiache-Rojdestvensky), to whom we owe so much of our information about the early manuscripts in the St. Petersburg collection, opined that the manuscript may have been written on the Continent at Echternach.[4] However, thanks to the compelling evidence amassed by E. A. Lowe and confirmed by others, we know that it was composed in Bede's own monastery of Wearmouth-Jarrow. Along with the main text in pointed insular minuscule, the manuscript uses forms of uncial, rustic capital, and particularly capitular uncial that were developed at Wearmouth-Jarrow for the biblical Codex Amiatinus, the Stonyhurst Gospels, and related manuscripts; and these were subsequently employed as display scripts in manuscripts whose main text is in insular minuscule. Moreover, the language of the Old English Cædmon's Hymn added on fol. 107 by the fourth scribe is Northumbrian and more consistently so than the other extant versions of the Hymn.[5] So L also has the distinction of presenting the text of Cædmon's Hymn in the poet's own Nor-

---

[2] A splendid example of how much can be discovered and accurately reported about this manuscript is Michael Lapidge's introduction in the Italian edition of Bede's *Ecclesiastical History*, Beda, *Storia degli Inglesi* (Milano, 2008), I: lxxxix–xc, xciv–cxv.

[3] Arngart, *Leningrad Bede*, 32.

[4] Olga A. Dobias-Rozdestvenskaja and Wsevolod W. Bakhtine, *Les anciens manuscrits latins de la bibliothèque publique Saltykov-Scedrin de Leningrad, viiiᵉ–début ixᵉ siècle* (Paris, 1991), 42, "Histoire de manuscrit. Scriptorium: Echternach (?), année 746."

[5] See Malcolm B. Parkes, *The Scriptorium of Wearmouth-Jarrow*, Jarrow lecture 1982, 5 and esp. n. 27, with a linguistic analysis by C.J.E. Ball.

thumbrian dialect.[6] As a culmination of the extensive scholarship that the Hymn has generated among Anglo-Saxonists, Daniel O'Donnell, who examined the text in L shortly after I did in 1998, has produced a book-length edition and study of the Hymn.[7] Since L is a copy only once or twice removed from Bede's draft, Cædmon's Hymn in Old English may have been added by Bede himself as a gloss to his Latin text, for there are other glosses in L that from their content seem authorial.[8]

Of course, the value of L even for Anglo-Saxonists derives not just from this early version of Cædmon's Hymn; the manuscript's greatest value results from its being one of the two earliest copies of the *Historia,* written close to Bede's own lifetime, in his own scriptorium; and in the quality and accuracy of its text, it is second to none. Scholars now universally agree with Elias Lowe that it "is the best text of Bede's greatest work."[9] Other than the occasional confusion of letters, particularly **u** for **a**, which is the result of the open **a** form in the handwriting of the exemplar, the text exhibits few errors. As Malcolm Parkes asserts:

> The quality of Bede's text in the copy is very high indeed. There are thirty-two places where a modern editor would seek to emend. Twenty-six of these errors are in sources quoted by Bede and may well have been in his originals, therefore there are only six errors in the text written by Bede himself. The high quality of the text in this copy suggests that it cannot be very far removed from the author's draft.[10]

In the great editions of the *Historia* by John and his son George Smith in 1723 and by Charles Plummer in 1896, the base text used for the editions was the other of the two earliest versions of the *History,* the Moore manuscript, now Cam-

---

[6] See the plate and bibliography in Elisabeth Okasha's note in *Scriptorium* 22 (1968): 35–37, pl. 1.

[7] Daniel Paul O'Donnell, *Cædmon's Hymn: A Multi-media Study, Edition and Archive* (Woodbridge, 2005).

[8] From Michael Lapidge's communication: "L, for example, reproduces at one point (IV. 4, line 22), an interlinear gloss on *comite,* as follows: .i. Endae de progenie prioris Endi. This is a detail about Irish genealogy in Mayo which only Bede himself could have known; it was in the exemplar, and reproduced by L, but not by M, who was in too much of a hurry to copy interlinear glosses (at this stage, one would have to ask whether Cædmon's hymn, in OE, was added by Bede in his working copy, hence copied in L, but again not in M, until it was supplied later at the end of the MS)."

[9] Elias A. Lowe, "A Key to Bede's Scriptorium: Some Observations on the Leningrad Manuscript of the 'Historia Ecclesiastica Gentis Anglorum'," *Scriptorium* 12 (1958): 182–90, at 182; repr. in idem, *Palaeographical Papers,* ed. Ludwig Bieler (Oxford, 1972), 441–49.

[10] Parkes, *Scriptorium,* 5; and see Bertram Colgrave and R. A. B. Mynors, eds., *Bede's Ecclesiastical History of the English People* (Oxford, 1969), xl–xli and xliv.

bridge, University Library MS. Kk. 5.16. But the Moore Bede was written by a
scribe in haste, "as one pressed for time and space," as Lowe remarks. Though
also close to Bede's original and a sister to L, it is less accurate and careful than
L.[11] Written not in orderly double columns like L but in a crowded block with
narrow margins and without spacing between words, it abbreviates heavily, tele-
scopes biblical texts by giving only the first and last words of a citation, greatly
reduces display scripts (capitular uncial and rustic) found in L, and lacks orna-
mentation.[12] Although the scribe's hand is larger and rounder than the hands
of L, because of the crowding M is 33 folios shorter than L. In his hurry, the
scribe also omitted glosses found in L, and it is possible that Cædmon's Hymn
was added later, since it appears at the end of the manuscript instead of its proper
place, as L has it. Since the script and layout are not that of Wearmouth-Jarrow,
and the manuscript was written in haste, Michael Lapidge suggests that it possibly was done by a visitor from York, who omitted what he considered non-es-
sentials, including occasional glosses.[13] So even though M is very early (probably
from 737, written within two years of Bede's demise) it stands in contrast to the
thoughtfully arranged format of L, a truly worthy example of the Wearmouth-
Jarrow scriptorium.[14] Nonetheless, for all its faults M served Plummer well, since
he also tested its text against the version found in the eighth–century manuscript, British Library MS. Cotton Tiberius A. xiv (his B). Although severely
damaged in the Ashburnham House fire of 1731, this manuscript presents such
a good version of the M-text that Plummer was able to ascertain that M and B
derive from a common original, so that "B has at least an equal claim with M to
be consulted in the settlement of the text."[15]

Indeed, the sad fact is that by the time Plummer edited Bede's History,
scholars had published information about L and Plummer could have known
about it, but, for whatever reason and given the distance and difficulty of travel
at the time, he did not consult it; nor did he consult any other manuscripts on
the Continent except the eighth-century Namur MS., which with unacharac-
teristic but justifiable sharpness he maligned for its "deplorable carelessness."[16]
Nonetheless, even without the benefit of L and other early manuscripts, Plum-

---

[11] Elias A. Lowe, "The Script of the Farewell and Date Formulae in Early Papal
Documents, as Reflected in the Oldest Manuscripts of Bede's Historia Ecclesiastica," *Revue Bénédictine* 69 (1959): 22–31, at 27; repr. in idem, *Palaeographical Papers*, 450–58.

[12] All noted by Mynors in the introduction to the facsimile edition of M in P. Hunt-
er Blair and R. A. B. Mynors, eds., *The Moore Bede*, EEMF 9 (Copenhagen, 1959).

[13] Private communication from Lapidge. See also his remarks in his introduction to
the Italian edition (note 2 above), xci–xcii.

[14] See Parkes, *Scriptorium*.

[15] Charles Plummer, ed., *Venerabilis Baedae opera historica* (Oxford, 1896), 1: xci–
xciii, at xciii.

[16] Plummer, ed., *Opera historica*, lxxxvi–lxxxviii.

mer improved on Smith's already fairly reliable edition and furnished invaluable information in the notes and introduction that have not been surpassed, though augmented by Colgrave in 1969 and Wallace-Hadrill in 1988.[17]

After Arngart's facsimile of L was published in 1952 as only the second volume in the *Early English Manuscripts in Facsimile* series, palaeographers and historians like Elias Lowe, David Wright, Paul Meyvaert, and Malcolm Parkes published studies revealing the significance of L as a very early, accurate text, close to Bede's original, written in his own scriptorium. As textual editor for the Colgrave-Mynors standard edition in 1969 of Bede's *Historia Ecclesiastica*, Mynors added it to the manuscripts used by Plummer. However, a comparison of Mynors' text with that of L indicates that Mynors did not collate L with M fully and systematically. Michael Lapidge's textual editions of the *Historia* are the first to incorporate the results of a thorough collation of L and M. One of the editions is being done for the Fondazione Lorenzo Valla, printed by Mondadori in Milan, and translated into Italian by Paolo Chiesa.[18] From the fullness of its *apparatus criticus* and commentary Lapidge refers to it as 'editio maior'. The other edition, now published in the series Sources Chrétiennes, is translated and commented by André Crépin, with Lapidge's reduced *apparatus criticus*. It is the 'editio minor'.[19] Subsequent editions, such as that proposed for the Corpus Christianorum Series Latina, will no doubt also afford L primacy as a witness, for, as Mynors himself admitted, it is "more accurate" than M, and "there seems no reason why both [M and L] should not have been taken from the author's copy—not to say 'autograph', because Bede's own copy may well have been in the hand of an amanuensis."[20]

Four scribes wrote the text, and a rubricator, whose work has been described in detail by David Wright, wrote the titles, *litterae notabiliores*, chapter numerals, and colophons.[21] He also wrote five passages among the farewell and date formulas in a beautiful capitular uncial, that Lowe noted as unique to the Wearmouth-Jarrow scriptorium. The four scribes responsible for the main text di-

---

[17] J. M. Wallace-Hadrill, *Bede's Ecclesiastical History of the English People: A Historical Commentary* (Oxford, 1988).

[18] See note 2 above. To date only volume one has been published; it includes Lapidge's extensive introduction and Books I–II of the Bede's *Historia*.

[19] Of the two editions Lapidge names one 'editio maior' and the other 'editio minor' because the former presents his complete collation of the three principal MSS with full *apparatus criticus* while the latter only a summary of the former. The latter has now been published in the series Sources Chrétiennes 489, 490, 491 (Paris, 2005). Lapidge's textual introduction is found on pp. 50–65 and 68–72 in tome 1. The 'editio maior' is to appear in the collection Fondazione Lorenzo Valla by Mondadori in Milan.

[20] Colgrave and Mynors, eds., *History*, xliv.

[21] D. H. Wright, "The Date of the Leningrad Bede," *Revue Bénédictine* 71 (1961): 265–73, at 270.

vided their stints as follows: Scribe 1 copied folios 1–32^v, Scribe 2 copied folios 33–63^v (correctly, 64^v, since folio 51 was numbered twice); Scribe 3 copied folios 64 (65)–68 (69), and Scribe 4 did all the rest, by far the greater part, folios 68^v (69^v)–161 (162). Scribes 1, 2, and 3 are so disciplined in the house style that, as Ian Doyle remarked to me, only an expert eye can detect the differences among them. Scribe 4, however, wrote in a less compressed, slightly rounder pointed insular hand; his a's, in contrast to scribes 1–3, are open at the top. The only difference between his a and u is that the former is made by two parallel rounded minims, whereas the latter has a slight tick added to the top left of the first minim. As Arngart and Parkes have noted, the spelling errors in which a is substituted for u and vice versa among scribes 1–3, who write with closed a's, indicate that the open-headed a was used in the exemplar, and the Scribe 4 continued that tradition by writing the open a for the most part.[22]

Since the Scribe 4 "writes a somewhat broad roundish" hand and forms some of his letters differently from the other scribes, and differs in some use of punctuation and abbreviation, Lowe concludes that "it would seem, then, that the scribe of ff. 68v–162 got his training outside of Jarrow." He then says this in a prose uncharacteristically loose and circuitous:

> The general impression made by the script of the first three hands (ff. 1–68^r), one must admit, is saec. VIII^2, if not saec. VIII^{ex}. This view must be modified owing to the impression made by the contemporary hand 4 (ff. 68^v–161) which has all the appearances of being saec. VIII^1. Of course, allowance must be made for the possibility that hand 4 is a survival of an older epoch and that the hands which precede it represent the new, the modern trend, in which case a compromise date of around 750 or a little later might seem acceptable. The type of abbreviations and punctuation seen throughout the manuscript bear out the hypothesis of a date of around 750, a decade or two one way or the other. However, a more definite date, namely 746, is furnished by internal evidence. This date is arrived at by noticing that when the marginal numbers inserted to the left of certain annals—seen on f. 159^{rv}—are added to the numeral years of the events in the annals, the result in most cases comes to precisely 746—presumably the scribe's year.[23]

Lowe gives credit to Olga Dobias-Rozdestvenskaja for calling attention to the meaning of these marginal numerals in her 1928 article.[24]

Malcolm Parkes differs with Lowe, forming another interpretation of the data. He contends that Scribe 4 (D), though an older scribe, was a colleague also

[22] Arngart, *Leningrad Bede*, 25; Parkes, *Scriptorium*, 7.
[23] Lowe, "Bede's Scriptorium," 188–89 and n.25; *Palaeographical Papers*, 2:448 and n.3.
[24] Olga Dobias-Rozdestvenskaja, "Un manuscrit de Bède à Leningrad," *Speculum* 3 (1928): 314–21.

at Wearmouth-Jarrow with the other scribes. He uses the open a form that must have been in the Wearmouth-Jarrow exemplar of the *Historia*. Parkes argues, "Since Bede was a Wearmouth-Jarrow author, and since the quality of the text in this copy shows that it must be close to the author's draft, the exemplar of this Wearmouth-Jarrow copy must itself have been written in Insular Minuscule at Wearmouth-Jarrow in handwriting not unlike that of Scribe D himself."[25] I find that a convincing response to Lowe. However, I have serious doubts about what Parkes says in his note to this statement. It reads:

When Dr Meyvaert discussed an earlier draft of this lecture with me, he remarked that the similarity between the hand of Scribe D and that of the exemplar for the other scribes, when considered in conjunction with the quality of the text in this stint, and the absence of the author's name from the original colophon, could imply that Scribe D may have been Bede himself. Bede states that he had to act as his own 'dictator simul notarius et librarius' (quoted by Plummer p. xx, note 3). However, at this stage, we would both prefer to leave the question open.

We must reject the tentative theory that Scribe 4 (D) was Bede himself. If Scribe 4 were Bede, how explain the errors in the text that the corrector emended and Bede as author would never have made? Despite his general proficiency, Scribe 4 wrote, for instance, *ueniens* for *iuuenis*, *ianuarium* for *iuniarum*, *more* for *moueri*, *sibi* for *siue* and *siue* for *sibi*, *ducibus* for *duabus*, *montibus* for *motibus*, *prauitati* for *priuati*. Since such errors are not misspellings but actual substitutions of words, making nonsense of the text, they cannot be considered simple authorial slips. Moreover, even though Scribe 4 employed the old-fashioned open a form, even he confused a and u in some words, for example: *particulum* for *particulam*, *regendum* for *regendam*, *stadio* for *studio*, and *resolationis* for *resolutionis*.[26]

Perhaps it was the same desire to find the *manum ipsam Bedae* in his works that led Lowe to believe that the signature in the colophon on fol. 161, "Beda famulus Xpti indignus," was genuine that also led Meyvaert and Parkes to toy with the idea of Bede's being the fourth scribe who wrote the greater part of L.

If Lowe had been right about the signature as genuinely Bede's, it would of course have made L contemporaneous with the author and indisputably authoritative. But that hypothesis was demolished by Wright[27] and by Meyvaert, who did careful examinations of the fake signature,[28] so Ludwig Bieler as editor discreetly removed Lowe's 1958 article, "An Autograph of the Venerable Bede?"

---

[25] Parkes, *Scriptorium*, 7.
[26] For a complete list of errors in the manuscript, their types, and location, see Arngart, *Leningrad Bede*, 24–26.
[27] Wright, "The Date of the Leningrad Bede."
[28] P. Meyvaert, "The Bede 'Signature' in the Leningrad Colophon," *Revue Bénédictine* 71 (1961): 274–86.

from the two-volume collected *Palaeographical Papers* of Lowe. However, Parkes tried another way to make the larger part of L earlier than 746. He argued that since the hand of scribe 4 looks earlier than those of the other scribes, the stint of 4 was finished considerably earlier than those of 1 and 2. "A close examination of the stints of Scribes A [1] and B [2] indicates that they were supplying eight quires to the beginning of a pre-existing manuscript (up to and including Book III, cap. xix)." But what about Scribe 3? Parkes admits that "Scribe C [3] must be contemporary with Scribe D [4], since D [4] takes over on the verso of fol. 69 in the middle of a sentence begun by C [3] on the recto."[29] Then we must object, if Scribe 3's writing is virtually indistinguishable from Scribes 1 and 2, making it contemporary with those Wearmouth-Jarrow newly trained hands, how can it be contemporary with a late hand 4? The answer must be not that 3 and 4 composed a pre-existing manuscript that 1 and 2 completed, but that, as Lowe suggested as a possibility above, 4 "is a survival of an older epoch and that the hands which precede it represent the new, the modern trend."

These attempts to link L even with Bede himself have failed but they in no way undermine the authority and quality of L as a witness to Bede's own text. My preliminary examination of the text in L and the even more thorough and careful collation of L and M that Lapidge has done for his new editions of the text have resulted in some interesting confirmations. In a private communication to me Lapidge states, "There is abundant evidence that these two MSS were copied from the one exemplar, insofar as they both carefully reproduce corrections and lacunae which they must have found in that exemplar." In his Italian "editio maior" Lapidge notes that in the *Praefatio*, line 49 (after the phrase "Orientalium Anglorum atque") both L and M leave a space of six letters, which indicates there was a lacuna here, waiting for an insertion, in their exemplar. In I.27, lines 379–80 both MSS have a substantial lacuna (caused obviously by eyeskip); I.27, line 416, both MSS have the nonsensical "si mens," where Plummer convincingly conjectured "semen"; II. 8, line 21, both MSS have "signare" (where Plummer rightly conjectured "resignare"); II. 8, lines 43–4, L and M have "imperauimus" (nonsensically) where again Plummer conjectured "impertiuimus"; IV.8, line 7, both MSS read "meditari" where what is meant is "medicari"; V.i, line 34, L and M have "depraedecessori," where Plummer conjectured "praedecessori," and Mynors "prodecessori"; and then there is V. 13, line 49, the case of the missing "uomeres": as the note in Colgrave and Mynors, p. 501, points out, "uomeres" is missing in both L and M but is added by the correctors, and "all our authorities omit the word, but the Cottonian MS. has *cultra* before *in manibus* (perhaps by conjecture or from an earlier draft)."[30] The last is an apt conjecture because Lapidge thinks the Cottonian MS. version of the *Historia* may be from

---

[29] Parkes, *Scriptorium*, 6.

[30] For a complete analysis see Lapidge, "Introduzione," "Relazioni fra I manoscritti," xciv–cxv.

the draft sent by Bede to Albinus, before he did the revisions to the *Historia* resulting in the M version.[31] In any case, this lacuna in L and M may indicate that Bede had not found the *mot juste* and left a space which the correctors dutifully if doubtfully supplied. Lapidge concludes, "L and M were copied from an exemplar which was faulty in various ways, and they reproduced these faults faultlessly." It is probably impossible to determine exactly how close the exemplar was to Bede's autograph, but the clarity and general lack of serious errors in L indicate it was not far removed.

While L is not the earliest manuscript of Bede's *Historia,* it stands with the earliest, M, as a copy of an exemplar close to Bede's original, perhaps an idiograph (that is, a copy made under the author's supervision). Because of the care with which Bede's successors at Wearmouth-Jarrow executed L, it is the best and most accurate of all the manuscript witnesses. It is worthy of the *magister* himself. Every Anglo-Saxonist and every Anglo-Latin historian must give thanks to those four scribes in the Wearmouth-Jarrow scriptorium.

---

[31] Michael Wallace-Hadrill's students Judith McClure and Roger Collins in the paperback edition of Bede's *HE* for the Oxford World's Classics series (Oxford, 1999), call in question the genuinity of the Letter to Albinus (CPL 1374, PL 94: 655–657): "The supposed letter from Bede to Albinus, printed by Plummer (i.3), was first published by Mabillon in his *Vetera Analecta* (Paris, 1723), 398, from a manuscript, apparently since lost, which he had not seen; it is unlikely to be genuine." Michael Gorman informs me that the letter was [first] printed in 1675 by Mabillon, *Vetera analecta* (Paris, 1675), 1: 9–10, from a codex Mettensis S. Arnulfi. Joshua Westgard has now discovered two further manuscript copies of the Letter to Albinus, which he will shortly report on in a publication. The letter is completely in Bede's style. As Paul Meyvaert has called to my attention, the phrase "sedulus intercedere memineris" is typical of Bede, whose fondness for the word "sedulus" is exceptional. (Bede uses the word 49 times, and the Brepols database CLCLT records the word's use only 128 times in all medieval works.) Brief as Bede's letter is, it contains a convincing reference to his *De Templo,* and ends with his characteristic request for prayers.

The 'Old North' from the Saxon South in Nineteenth-Century Britain

Barbara Yorke

The Victorian fascination with all things Scandinavian is an undoubted fact that has been magnificently brought to life in Andrew Wawn's recent study.[1] Even if it did not quite invent the name 'Viking', Victorian Britain did much to popularise the term together with the stereotype of the horn-helmeted warrior leaping from his long ship to rape and pillage the local population.[2] Wawn has shown how a positive image might be adopted in which the drive and skills that had taken Scandinavian settlers to the shores of North America were seen as commendable qualities worthy of imitation in the present day, and, indeed, both a forerunner and an inspiration for the achievements of the British empire. Some of the Victorian appropriations of the Vikings are surprising, not least Charles Kingsley's recruitment of them to support the cause of his favoured brand of "muscular" Christianity:

> I say that the Church of England is wonderfully and mystically fitted for the souls of the free Norse-Saxon race: for men whose ancestors fought by the side of Odin, over whom a descendant of Odin now rules.[3]

But what one could describe as positive manifestations of interest in which the Scandinavians took centre stage are not the whole story. For there was an alternative tradition in which the Vikings were not so much the acclaimed ancestors of the Victorian world, but rather the archetypes of the enemies with which nineteenth-century Britain had to contend. It is this facet of Viking identity and its ramifications with which this paper is concerned.

---

[1] Andrew Wawn, *The Vikings and the Victorians: Inventing the Old North in Nineteenth-Century Britain* (Cambridge, 2000).

[2] See D.M. Wilson, *Vikings and Gods in European Art* (Århus, 1997) for a selection of paintings on such topics.

[3] *Charles Kingsley: His Letters, and Memoirs of his Life*, ed. F. Kingsley, 2 vols. (London, 1877), 1: 203.

The Vikings came to stand for the enemies of the British empire because they had been the enemies of King Alfred, "the king to whom the Empire owes so much in many various ways" as the prospectus to advertise his commemoration in 1901 put it.[4] Alfred's rise to become the ruler who prefigured the greatness of the British empire can be traced back to the eighteenth century "Patriots" whose aim had been originally to embarrass the prime minister Robert Walpole by unfavourable comparisons with true patriots of the past who had protected the country's interests.[5] Alfred was valued highly as a comparative figure on a number of accounts, not least because of his success in defending his country by land and sea, for one of the Patriot criticisms of Walpole was for what was seen as his failure to support the navy adequately in war with Spain in the 1730s. The particular attributes of the Vikings as enemies were not the subject of significant interest at this point; it was enough that they were a threat that had to be defeated by land and sea. One of the most famous literary works of the Patriot movement, Thomas Arne's masque *Alfred*, which included the anthem "Rule Britannia", is set on the Isle of Athelney in the build-up to the battle of Edington, but no Viking appears on stage at all.[6] As Britain's numerous and changing enemies in the eighteenth century mostly had to be fought at sea, there was a continuing appetite for masques, operas, ballets, and plays which celebrated previous naval successes, above all in the 1790s and the first decades of the nineteenth century when the threat was of French invasion.[7] *Alfred* was revised on numerous occasions, and "Rule Britannia" became a patriotic anthem in the modern sense, that is, as a rousing declaration of support for king and country.[8]

In the interests of improving the dramatic content of plays concerning Alfred, it was only a matter of time before the Vikings too appeared on the stage,[9]

---

[4] National Committee for the King Alfred Millenary, *The Thousandth Anniversary of King Alfred the Great 1901* (London, 1899). A version is printed as an appendix to *Alfred the Great: Chapters on his Life and Times*, ed. A. Bowker (London, 1899). In some of the earlier versions of the circular the word 'Kingdom' is found instead of 'Empire'.

[5] C. Gerrard, *The Patriot Opposition to Walpole: Politics, Poetry and National Myth 1725–1742* (Oxford, 1994).

[6] *Alfred: A Masque Written by David Mallett and James Thomson, Set to Music by Thomas Augustine Arne*, ed. A. Scott, Musica Britannica 47 (London, 1981). However, there is no standard version, as the work was recast on several occasions.

[7] For Alfred and his foes in poetry see L. Pratt, "Anglo-Saxon Attitudes: Alfred the Great and the Romantic National Epic," in *Literary Appropriations of the Anglo-Saxons from the Thirteenth to the Twentieth Century*, ed. D. Scragg and C. Weinberg (Cambridge, 2000), 138–56. For a thorough examination of the cult of King Alfred see S. Keynes, "The Cult of King Alfred the Great," *Anglo-Saxon England* 28 (1999): 225–356.

[8] L. Colley, *Britons: Forging the Nation 1707–1837* (New Haven and London, 1992), 11–46.

[9] For reviews of the evidence see L.W. Miles, *King Alfred in Literature* (Baltimore, 1902) and E.G. Stanley, "The Glorification of Alfred King of Wessex (from the

something that became all the easier once more was discovered about them as part of the literary movements and Romantic discovery of the early medieval past which Andrew Wawn describes. Most plays were set between the attempt to capture Alfred at Chippenham and the battle of Edington which gave scope for inclusion of both the cake-burning in Athelney and Alfred's visit to Guthrum's camp disguised as a minstrel, favourite scenes that allowed for a certain amount of humour and burlesque in the less serious productions. In the anonymous "Alfred the Great: Deliverer of his Country" of 1753, for instance, Alfred went in disguise as a poor Welsh harper and is made to speak in a comical Welsh dialect.[10] Most productions found it necessary to add to dramatic interest by inclusion of one or more pairs of young lovers separated by the exigencies of war, and the capture of Alfred's wife with a threat to her virtue from a lascivious Viking leader was also a common addition to the plot. The dramatic potential of the plays was further enhanced by references to Viking paganism with the "Raven Banner", pagan ceremonies and the threat of human sacrifice being very much to the fore.[11] All these themes were also taken up in an early historical novel dealing with Alfred and the Vikings, Anne Fuller's *The Son of Ethelwolf*, published in 1789.[12] Although due credit is paid to Alfred's good judgement and respect for God's and man's laws, in short to his impeccable eighteenth-century sensibility, the plot involves several pairs of star-crossed lovers including the Anglo-Saxon Harold and the Danish Gunilda whose happiness is threatened by the machinations of the chief priest of Odin and his desire for a human sacrifice. On hearing of this Alfred is made to denounce the evils caused by the Vikings' paganism:

> O fanaticism . . . thou pest, and scourge of the human race, how long shalt thou continue to impose on man with thy delusions?—when shall heaven-born reason regain the dominion which thou hast usurped?—when shall she dissipate the errors with which thou has enveloped humankind; when chase from their imaginations the idea of a being, which thou hast depicted as delighting in the miseries of man, thirsty of gore, and authorizing the commission of barbarous deeds, under the specious name of holy zeal.[13]

---

publication of Sir John Spelman's Life 1678 and 1709, to the publication of Reinhold Pauli's, 1851)," *Poetica* 12 (1981): 103–33.

[10] Miles, *King Alfred in Literature*, 63.

[11] The devices these authors were reduced to using in order to make their subject matter more palatable to a wider audience are also those adopted in Clive Donner's 1968 film *Alfred the Great* which included pagan rituals in the Viking camp and a romance between Guthrum and Ealhswith when she became a hostage of the Danes.

[12] Anne Fuller, *The Son of Ethelwolf: An Historical Tale*, 2 vols. (London, 1789); see Stanley, "Glorification of King Alfred," 120–24.

[13] Fuller, *Son of Ethelwolf*, 1: 82–83; Stanley, "Glorification of King Alfred," 121.

Many of these works were undoubtedly written with little purpose but to en-
tertain and to cash in on the popularity of patriotic plays. Alexander Bicknell
had rushed out his *The Patriot King* in 1778 when England was under threat of
invasion from France and Spain, and "its effect, had it then been brought on
the stage, must have been greater than at any other period."[14] The play dwells
on the horrors of occupation by a foreign army, and "shows what can be done
by a few brave men firmly united in a common cause."[15] The "otherness" of the
Vikings is repeatedly stressed within the plays, the dark side of the Germanic
world on which Alfred had turned his back through his espousal of Christian
principles and responsible government. The savagery of the Vikings is attributed
to their paganism which is shown to lack any moral dimension. The Viking leaders (names vary) are prey to bouts of sudden temper and contradictory behaviour,
which contrast with Alfred's calm and judicious conduct. This is brought out
particularly well in the portrayal of Guthrum in what is perhaps the best of the
Alfred plays, *Alfred the Great* by James Sheridan Knowles, which was staged very
successfully with Macready playing Alfred.[16] Knowles, like many of his predecessors, presents the clash of Alfred and the Vikings as prefiguring other military
threats to Britain, but in his dedication to King William IV seems to also accord
them a symbolic role standing for a wider range of evils with which the modern
state had to contend:

> A Patriot Monarch, destined with the blessing of God, to restore the di-
> lapidated fabric of the country's prosperity; and to rescue a devoted people
> from the ravages of the worst of invaders—CORRUPTION.

The Vikings' paganism differentiated them from the most significant of the
European enemies faced by the British in the eighteenth and early nineteenth
centuries, though contemporary portrayal of Roman Catholicism could almost
suggest that it was more suspect as a form of religion than Viking heathenism
had been,[17] and possibly the use of instruments of torture and sacrificial fires
by the Vikings of the plays may have been influenced by popular perceptions
of the Inquisition. But as the British empire grew, so did its involvement with
non-Christian peoples, and this affected approaches to the topic of the Scandinavians as British enemies. Thomas Hughes, in his biography of King Alfred first
published in 1869, reflected on similarities between the followers of Wodan and

---

[14] "Preface," in A. Bicknell, *The Patriot King: or Alfred and Elvida. An Historical
Tragedy* (London; privately printed, 1788). Theatre managers seem rightly to have felt
that the play was unperformable.

[15] Bicknell, *Patriot King*, 67.

[16] J.S. Knowles, *Alfred the Great: or the Patriot King, an Historical Play* (London,
1831).

[17] Colley, *Britons*, passim.

those of Mahomet, for both inspired religions with the "power of consecrating valour, and inspiring men with contempt of pain and death."[18] George Alfred Henty suggested that if his young readers wanted to envisage how Danish raiders treated the Anglo-Saxons they should recollect the fate of English in India at the time of the Mutiny.[19] Knowledge gained as a result of British imperial interests in the East seems to inform Daniel Maclise's celebrated painting of "Alfred the Saxon King disguised as a minstrel in the tent of Guthrum the Dane" completed in 1852.[20] A Christ-like Alfred with his harp looks uneasy in the decadent court of Guthrum, which is kitted out with distinctly oriental accoutrements and armour. Guthrum lounges in his tent with a harem of dark-eyed houris while his men drink themselves insensible or gamble. Although it may have been that Maclise saw an opportunity to recycle some of the fittings and central images that he had used in a previous painting of King Cophetua and the Beggar Maid, it also seems likely that he is projecting the prejudices against the supposed decadence of the Orient on to an earlier non-Christian people.[21] Echoes of such an approach are found in those commentators who commended Alfred for being free of "the bad effects of ease and leisure . . . ruinous destroyers of most people unfortunate enough to possess them,"[22] for among those unfortunates, according to nineteenth-century Orientalist views, were rulers from the East. As the nineteenth century progressed there was greater emphasis on Alfred's war against the Vikings being a religious war whose satisfactory outcome was the conversion of Guthrum and other Danes.[23] The justification for Alfred's wars therefore echoed one of the justifications for the expansion of the British empire — that it was a means of bringing Christianity and all the civilising benefits associated with it to peoples who had lacked its advantages.[24] The Christian Literature Society for India produced a pamphlet on King Alfred in which that point is made, and its Indian audience is invited to reflect on the fact that the English were able to treat

---

[18] T. Hughes, *Alfred the Great* (London, 1869), 58.

[19] G.A. Henty, *The Dragon and the Raven; or the Days of King Alfred* (London, 1886).

[20] The painting is on display in the Laing Art Gallery, Newcastle-on-Tyne. See Wilson, *Vikings and Gods in European Art*, 58–59, 95.

[21] E. Said, *Orientalism* (New York, 1978), and for its implications for interest in the Anglo-Saxons see A.J. Frantzen, *Desire for Origins: New Language, Old English, and Teaching the Tradition* (New Brunswick, NJ, 1990), 27–61.

[22] M. Burrows, *King Alfred the Great* (London, 1898), 23–24.

[23] For instance, the Bishop of Bristol, "King Alfred as Religious Man and Educationalist," in *Alfred the Great: Chapters on His Life and Times*, ed. Bowker, 82–99. Knowles, *Alfred the Great* had ended with the conversion of Guthrum and his transformation into a loyal follower of Alfred, whereas the eighteenth-century plays had preferred to end with all the Danish leaders dead.

[24] For a clear statement of this view see C.W. Stubbs, *King Alfred Patron Saint of England* (Winchester, 1901), 15.

the Danes amongst whom they lived with greater respect once they had been converted to Christianity.[25] Alfred in his statue in Winchester erected in 1901 holds his sword aloft so that the hilt could be seen as forming a cross, a symbol of the greater Cross in whose interests he fought and which guided all his actions.[26]

It was at the time of the celebrations of the millenary of Alfred's death in 1901 that the emphasis on Alfred as the pre-figurer of the British empire became most strident and the parallels drawn between the Vikings and a specific enemy of the empire became most marked. The ceremonies surrounding the unveiling of the statue in Winchester and the long preparations leading up to them coincided with the South African Wars that had begun in 1898. There were reminders of the war at several points on 20 September 1901 when the statue was unveiled. The procession included contingents from several different army regiments and the naval brigade while others lined the route down the High Street.[27] After the statue was unveiled, cannons were fired from a nearby hill and medals presented to men of the Imperial Yeomanry and the Hampshire Volunteers.[28] Indeed, it was precisely because it was felt necessary to make a show of imperial solidarity and strength at a time when fortunes in South Africa were mixed and many were coming to doubt the wisdom of the wars that the King Alfred millenary had received such high-level support.[29] The War Office had felt it imperative to release men from active duty to attend, and the unveiling of the statue was performed by the former prime minister, Lord Rosebery, an ardent Liberal imperialist. Prominent American involvement can be explained by the political manoeuvrings attendant on the war. The British government were keen for tacit American support for their policies in Africa, while a dominant political group in America believed foreign policy should follow shared interests with Britain rather than

[25] J. Abbott, *Alfred the Great* (London and Madras, 1898). Indians are also urged to emulate Alfred by publishing Christian works in their vernacular, and Hindus are recommended to imitate Alfred by treating lower orders with greater respect and abolishing the caste system.

[26] A feature much remarked upon in the press at the time; see B.A.E. Yorke, *The King Alfred Millenary in Winchester, 1901*, Hampshire Papers 17 (Winchester, 1999), 11–12.

[27] A. Bowker, *The King Alfred Millenary* (London and New York, 1902), 105–6.

[28] Bowker, *King Alfred Millenary*, 112–13.

[29] For mixed attitudes towards the empire at this time see B. Porter, *Britannia's Burden: The Political Evolution of Modern Britain 1851–1904* (London, 1994), 119–33, and D. Judd, *Empire: The British Imperial Experience, from 1765 to the Present* (London, 1996), 130–70.

with "alien" racial groups.[30] The American ambassador was therefore instructed to support the celebrations, which were underpinned by American money.[31]

Parallels drawn between the Vikings and the Boers therefore became a means of exploring the British conduct of the war in South Africa. Analyses of the Vikings' methods of fighting on land suggested parallels with the Boers,[32] even though they lacked the most conspicuous feature that the Vikings had shared with many enemies of Britain to date, namely the use of ships.[33] Montague Burrows described the Vikings as "savage and unscrupulous heathen with a remarkably precocious instinct for war,"[34] a description, leaving aside the heathenism, which many felt applied to the Boers as well. Charles Plummer considered "the chief difficulties of our forefathers under Alfred, as of us, their descendants, in South Africa at the present day, arose from the extreme mobility of the enemy, and the way in which they used . . . horses."[35] Parallels between Alfred's Viking opponents and the contemporary Boers gave others the opportunity to comment unfavourably on the conduct of the South African campaigns and the treatment of the enemy. The Reverend C. Lloyd Engström, for instance, pointed out both that Alfred had been rather more successful against the Vikings than the British were against the Boers (which he was inclined to put down to better leadership) and that he had made peace at the right juncture and with the wisest conditions.[36] Charles Stubbs, the Dean of Ely, when invited to preach in Winchester in 1901, was even more outspoken in his condemnation of current policies:

> It is not possible for a nation to be both imperial and Christian if its statesmen should forget that the Royal Supremacy of Christ . . . requires the ultimate social good of the peoples they propose to govern . . . Any imperial

---

[30] S. Anderson, *Race and Rapprochement: Anglo-Saxonism and Anglo-American Relations, 1895–1904* (East Brunswick, NJ, 1981).

[31] B.A.E. Yorke, "Alfredism: The Use and Abuse of King Alfred's Reputation in Later Centuries," in *Alfred the Great: Papers from the Eleventh-Centenary Conferences*, ed. T. Reuter (Aldershot, 2003), 361–80, at 376–77.

[32] Among works which appear to have been influential, in that they are cited by others, were J.R. Green, *The Conquest of England* (London, 1883), 88–90, and Burrows, *King Alfred the Great*.

[33] The British navy, however, was involved in the transportation of troops and suffered its own losses (though due to accidents at sea rather than enemy action), as the Earl of Selborne, First Lord of the Admiralty, reminded the audience in his speech at the millenary luncheon, the day after one such loss; Bowker, *King Alfred Millenary*, 121–22.

[34] Burrows, *King Alfred the Great*, 5.

[35] C. Plummer, *The Life and Times of Alfred the Great* (Oxford, 1902), 106.

[36] C. Lloyd Engström, *The Millenary of Alfred the Great, Warrior and Saint, Scholar and King* (London, 1901)—the work was in origin a sermon preached in London.

enterprise must be condemned which is prompted by insolence of pride, or by passion of vengeance, or by lust of gold.[37]

His conclusion was that King Alfred was not only of a standard far in advance of his own time "but in advance of much of our statesmanship today."[38] Dugald MacFadyen, who had served as an army doctor during the South African Wars, also felt that Alfred had reconciled war and Christian principles rather more successfully than current British military leaders.[39] These commentators were hardly radicals. The Dean of Ely's sermon is full of loyal references to the royal house and the concept of the British empire. Their comments express a widespread unease about why the war was being fought and at the high British death toll, but also show concern at the inhuman treatment of the Boers, such as internment in an early form of concentration camp, not least because they were in origin a northern European people like the British, and, of course, like the Vikings, which is why this comparison of the Vikings as imperial enemy proved so resonant.

In fact, there was much common ground between the impulses which led to the enthusiastic embracing of both Anglo-Saxon and Viking origins in nineteenth-century Britain. In reality there was not a great difference in attitude between Wawn's enthusiastic supporters of the Viking past and those who celebrated the achievements of Alfred, even if the latter meant casting the Vikings as enemy and often dwelling on their negative characteristics in order to make Alfred's positive attributes shine all the more brightly. Both groups were indulging in the cult of medievalism through projecting their own ideals on to the past, and drew endorsement from the association. Whether one was an Anglo-Saxon or a Viking supporter could be a matter of temperament. Those of an artistic nature were drawn to the vividness of Icelandic sagas and other Old Norse literature, and might have a strong interest in King Arthur and chivalry as well. William Morris is an excellent example of someone whose interests spanned both these potentially "romantic" areas of the medieval past, and used both as a retreat from his many personal problems and as a stimulus for his own literary and artistic productions.[40] The supposed democracy of the Norse world was also congenial to him, and may have fed his Socialism, though the Vikings, like King Arthur, could appeal to people of all political persuasions. It has to be admitted that,

[37] Stubbs, *King Alfred Patron Saint*, 16. These sentiments are only to be found in the full printed edition of the text and have been omitted from Alfred Bowker's summary of it, *King Alfred Millenary*, 33–34.

[38] Stubbs, *King Alfred Patron Saint*, 13.

[39] D. MacFadyen, *Alfred the West Saxon King of the English* (London and New York, 1901), 163.

[40] F. MacCarthy, *William Morris: A Life for Our Time* (London, 1994); Wawn, *Vikings and Victorians*, 245–79.

for all his worthiness, accounts of Alfred's life were somewhat lacking in dramatic and literary detail, as the long trail of unsuccessful plays which had tried to dramatise his life testified. The rediscovery of the Old North was part of the Gothick and early Romantic movements and was fed by the apparent recovery of its "authentic" medieval verse, while in the same period the Saxons were valued for their contributions to the constitution. The route to the Old North was through medieval literature, whereas that to the Saxon South was more likely to lie through the more sober chronicles of the past, particularly as interpreted by professional historians such as E.A. Freeman and J.R. Green, whose works found a large middlebrow audience in the third quarter of the nineteenth century.[41] As we have seen, loyalty and love of empire, particularly in the latter part of the nineteenth century, could equate with a love of the Saxons, but those most active in their cause and particularly in the promotion of King Alfred's millenary were most likely to be Liberals who also admired Oliver Cromwell.[42] Conservatives on the whole preferred the "Merrie England" of medieval Arthurian chivalry and the Tudors.[43]

While interest in the Old North or the Saxon South could, of course, be simply a matter of temperament or politics, it was particularly likely to be a matter of geography — or rather historical geography. Those who were interested in the Vikings tended to live in areas that had been settled by Scandinavians. This was only to be expected in somewhere like the Shetlands where the Norse heritage was still apparent in the nineteenth century and to which attention had been drawn by Sir Walter Scott in his novel *The Pirate*.[44] But it might also be a feature of people from other areas of England which had experienced Scandinavian settlement, including the Lake District, the home of W.G. Collingwood who set some of his Viking novels there,[45] and the Danelaw of eastern England whose Viking spirit was celebrated by Charles Kingsley's *Hereward the Wake*, which was inspired in part by his childhood in the fens.[46] Dr George Auden, whose interest in all things Norse led him to inquire whether his surname might derive from

---

[41] E.A. Freeman, *The History of the Norman Conquest of England*, 6 vols. (Oxford, 1867–1879); Green, *The Conquest of England*; see J.W. Burrow, *A Liberal Descent: Victorian Historians and the English Past* (Cambridge, 1981), esp. 155–228, and C. Simmons, *Reversing the Conquest: History and Myth in Nineteenth-Century British Literature* (New Brunswick, NJ, 1990), 45–73.

[42] R. Quinault, "The Cult of the Centenary, 1789–1914," *Historical Research* 71 (1998): 303–23.

[43] R. Chapman, *The Sense of the Past in Victorian Literature* (Beckenham, 1986).

[44] W. Scott, *The Pirate* (Edinburgh, 1822; repr. Lerwick, 1996); Wawn, *Vikings and Victorians*, 65–88.

[45] Wawn, *Vikings and Victorians*, 335–40.

[46] A. Wawn, "Hereward, the Danelaw and the Victorians," in *Vikings and the Danelaw: Select Papers from the Proceedings of the Thirteenth Viking Congress*, ed. J. Graham-Campbell, R. Hall, J. Jesch, and D.N. Parsons (Oxford, 2001), 357–68.

"Odin,"[47] had probably had his enthusiasm fired by his family's association with Repton (Derbyshire) where a large mound in the vicarage garden was believed to have housed part of the Danish army who occupied the site in 873–874.[48] On the other hand, the areas most involved in the celebration of the life of King Alfred were those parts of Wessex with which he was believed to have a direct association. In addition to the recorded places of his birth and death, Wantage and Winchester, where statues to him were erected, there were many other West Saxon towns and villages which demonstrated a personal connection. There was a long-standing interest in him in the West Country, and in Somerset in particular. The millenary of the "Treaty of Wedmore" was celebrated in Wedmore (Somerset) in 1878 in some style, with the usual lectures, luncheon, and loyal toasts,[49] and a commemorative brass was unveiled in the church on the occasion of the millenary.[50] The third and least known of the Wessex statues was erected in Pewsey (Wiltshire) in 1913, celebrating Alfred as "once a chief landowner in the Vale," presumably because Pewsey was one of the estates mentioned in King Alfred's will.[51]

The desire to celebrate the *genius loci* and the history of one's local patch goes very deep into the British psyche and is still a powerful force today.[52] The nineteenth-century local historians avidly searching for traces of the early medieval past in their local districts are the successors of earlier antiquarians who just as enthusiastically recorded the antiquities of their districts and misidentified the sites of battles and the burial places of slaughtered Danes. Francis Wise in 1738 argued, apparently on the basis of no evidence at all other than the fact that the battle of Ashdown had occurred in the vicinity, that the White Horse of Uffington was carved by Alfred to celebrate his victory over the Danes in 871, that the nearby prehistoric burial mound of Wayland's Smithy had been built as a burial place for the Danish king killed in the battle, while his "counts" were interred in

---

[47] Wawn, "Hereward," 357.

[48] The supposition seems to be supported by recent work; see M. Biddle and B. Kjølbye-Biddle, "Repton and the 'great heathen army,' 873–4," in *Vikings and the Danelaw*, 45–96. Dr Auden's interest in Repton is also shown by the fact that he named his youngest son (the poet W.H.) after its patron saint Wigstan (Wystan).

[49] "An Account of the Celebration of the Thousandth Anniversary of the 'Peace of Wedmore', Signed by Alfred and Guthrum," *Wells Journal*, 15 August 1878; Keynes, "Cult of Alfred," 347.

[50] Bowker, *King Alfred Millenary*, 152–53.

[51] The words come from the inscription on the statue which still stands at the junction of the main streets in Pewsey; the statue was erected to celebrate the accession of King George V and seems to be the last attempt to couple respect for Alfred with a compliment to a later British king.

[52] S. Piggott, *Ruins in a Landscape: Essays in Antiquarianism* (Edinburgh, 1996).

the Seven Barrows nearby.[53] The misattributions were subsequently repeated in many publications and only completely unravelled a couple of centuries later.[54] Although motives for this interest in past landscapes could be mixed—Francis Wise hoped to raise his stature as a scholar so that he would be appointed librarian of the Radcliffe in Oxford[55]—the strong identity with a particular locality, whether in Saxon or Danish areas of Britain, was an essential underpinning to national patriotism through an enhanced personal identity with the country's history.

In the course of the nineteenth century people came to believe that their association with their country's past was a matter not just of sentiment, but of actual biological descent as the theories of Darwinism became better known and more widely accepted.[56] The early Middle Ages was a period of prime importance because this was the time from which the recorded histories of different peoples could be traced. More than biological descent was at stake here, for national characteristics were believed to have been passed down through the ages as well, which is why it was deemed important to demonstrate that King Alfred displayed so many of the features which characterised the ideal Victorian Englishman. Many definitions of that ideal existed, but the selection of characteristics named by Bishop Creighton of London sums up their general character:

> Alfred was a man who displayed all the characteristics which were most true of Englishmen. He drove back the invader by his persistency; he watched over the development of his people in every way; he was great as an administrator, great as a practical diplomatist, great as a legislator, and, best of all, great as a modest Christian man, as one who was most interested in developing the highest and best energies of his people, who was, in every way, in fact, a father of his country.[57]

The bishop could almost be sketching a job description for a colonial administrator.

Those whose ancestors were of Scandinavian descent could claim many of these characteristics as well, for, in the system for designating races that had found favour in England and America, the northern European type represented the highest form of development.[58] There was thus a basic kinship between Saxon and Dane, which helps to explain why there were limits to how far the Vikings could be equated with those enemies of the empire who belonged to the so-called

---

[53] F. Wise, *A Letter to Dr Mead Concerning Some Antiquities in Berkshire* (London, 1738).

[54] L.V. Grinsell, *White Horse Hill* (London, 1939).

[55] S. Gibson, "Francis Wise, B.D.," *Oxoniensia* 1 (1936): 173–95.

[56] R. Horsman, *Race and Manifest Destiny: The Origins of American Racial Anglo-Saxonism* (Cambridge, MA, 1981), esp. 25–61.

[57] Bowker, *King Alfred Millenary*, 13.

[58] Horsman, *Race and Manifest Destiny*, 43–61.

"inferior" races, and why they could be used more easily to explore issues concerned with the treatment of the Boers. The major "problem" of the Scandinavians in their Viking incarnation was that they were not Christian, for that religious association was fundamental for the identification of Alfred with the ideal Englishman of the British empire. However, once converted, the Anglo-Danes were fully qualified to contribute to the top nationhood of the embryonic English state.[59] A pagan past was actually seen by some writers as an advantage and one of the characteristics that helped to define the supposed superiority of the Germanic peoples.[60] This topic provided common ground for Anglo-Saxon and Viking supporters in the latter part of the nineteenth century.

Sir Walter Besant, who was one of the major supporters of the Alfred Millenary in its preliminary stages and saw it as an opportunity to teach the people "the meaning of our Empire; not only what it is, but how it came,"[61] was prepared to admit that there had been strengths in the old religion that could be harnessed to the cause of Christianity, for even as pagans the Anglo-Saxons had been a profoundly religious people:

> The Anglo-Saxon was not only afraid of the unknown, which caused him to invent malignant deities, but in his mind the God of Creation was stronger than the god of destruction. There is hope for a people while that belief survives. Long after he became a Christian the Saxon continued to retain his old beliefs under other names . . . the natural tenacity of the Saxon was doubled by his belief that he was fighting the battles of the Lord.[62]

This was Charles Kingsley's opinion too, for he was of the firm belief that Anglo-Saxons and Vikings made the best sort of Christians because of their shared pre-Christian heritage and the general health and vitality that was part of their genetic inheritance. This inheritance was celebrated in his novel *Hereward the Wake: Last of the English*, published in 1866, where Hereward's inherited Viking characteristics are found to be those inculcated into the future governors of the empire by the public school system:

---

[59] For instance, MacFadyen, *Alfred the West Saxon King*, 365 argued that the Danes were absorbed into England and contributed a passion for the sea and a keen commercial interest.

[60] For instance, by Thomas Carlyle; see Horsman, *Race and Manifest Destiny*, 63–65.

[61] Bowker, *King Alfred Millenary*, 8–9.

[62] W. Besant, *The Story of King Alfred* (London, New York, and Toronto, 1902), 130–31.

> Hard knocks in good humour, strict rules, fair play and equal justice for high and low; this was the old outlaw spirit, which has descended to this day, the life and marrow of an English public school.[63]

To Kingsley the real danger in both the early Middle Ages and the nineteenth century came from "southern decadence" as represented above all by the Roman Catholic church. In *Hereward* the real villains are the lying and deceitful monks. Kingsley as a Viking apologist argued that the renewal of the "Teutonic" bloodstock and reinjection of the spirit of Odin was necessary to offset a dangerous ennui that was the result of too much influence from Rome and from which Alfred had had to rally his men. These ideas were summed up in the alarming metaphor of the female Anglo-Saxon race needing to be impregnated by "the great male race" of the Vikings.[64]

Kingsley's views were founded on an uncompromising racialism that was fully expressed in the lectures he gave as Professor of Modern History at Cambridge that were published as *The Roman and the Teuton*.[65] In these the fall of the Roman Empire and much of early medieval history was to be explained as a clash between the decadent southern nations and the energetic Teutons from the northern forests who in their earliest forms might be compared to an English sailor or navvy— "a great simple, honest, baby—full of power and fun, very coarse and plain spoken at times."[66] Their genetic inheritance had programmed the Teutons for ultimate success:

> It was not the mere muscle of the Teuton which enabled him to crush the decrepit and debauched slave-nations, Gaul and Briton, Iberian and African, as the ox crushes frogs of the marsh . . . [but] a calm and steady brain, and a free and loyal heart; the energy which springs from health; the self-respect which comes from self-restraint.[67]

As has already been observed, Kingsley's views were widespread in Victorian Britain and subscribed to by many others who wrote on the early medieval past, including Freeman[68] and Carlyle, who believed that Lowland Scots like himself

---

[63] C. Kingsley, *Hereward the Wake: Last of the English* (London, 1866), 432. See Wawn, *Vikings and Victorians*, 318–19.

[64] Kingsley, ed., *Charles Kingsley: Letters and Memoirs*, 1: 201.

[65] C. Kingsley, *The Roman and the Teuton: A Series of Lectures Delivered before the University of Cambridge* (Cambridge and London, 1864). The lectures were controversial in their own day, but rather because of Kingsley's limited qualifications as a historian than because of the views he expressed.

[66] Kingsley, *Roman and Teuton*, 6.

[67] Kingsley, *Roman and Teuton*, 46.

[68] On Freeman's racist views, see Simmons, *Reversing the Conquest*, 193–97.

were descended from Norse settlers and that the common inheritance of Anglo-Saxon and Viking was more significant than differences in religion.[69] Although Anglo-Saxons and Vikings were kin as they were both of Germanic descent, the Celts, that is, the prehistoric inhabitants of the British Isles and what were construed as their modern descendants in Wales, Gaelic Scotland and Ireland, were held to be racially inferior.[70] The defeat of the British at the hands first of the Romans and then the Saxons could be seen as proof of this inferiority. This meant that "British" had rather different connotations at the end of the nineteenth century from those it had carried at the beginning. In the latter part of the eighteenth century and in the early nineteenth century, as Linda Colley has argued, there was a great attempt to promote a common British identity based on shared values such as Protestantism, the constitution, and loyalty to the Crown.[71] The union was even symbolised in some of the Alfred plays. In *The Battle of Edington; or, British Liberty* by John Penn, the grandson of William Penn, first produced in 1792, the Scots and Welsh are anachronistically shown joining forces with Alfred to defeat the pagan Danes.[72] At the end of the century any reference to a British contribution to Alfred's England is extremely muted, and even those who knew that there must have been a degree of Romano-British survival within England itself argued for the predominance of Teutonic characteristics.[73] The term "British" was not used as often as it had been, and where it might be expected 'English' was often to be found instead.

It would appear that people from other parts of the British Isles were supposed to subsume themselves in an English identity, and there were some surprising transformations. King Arthur, for instance, seems to have been mutated into a Saxon leader of Celtic knights (which explained the ultimate failure of the Round Table, as he could be seen as working with inferior stock).[74] Tennyson noted that Arthur was "fair beyond the race of Britons and of men,"[75] and has him arrive as a baby in a mysterious dragon ship that seems to recall Scyld Scefing's origins as described in *Beowulf.* Vikings had the potential, as fellow

[69] Horsman, *Race and Manifest Destiny*, 63–64.

[70] S. Smiles, *The Image of Antiquity: Ancient Britain and the Romantic Imagination* (New Haven, 1994), esp. 113–28. This was felt also to be demonstrated by their very different physical characteristics; see, for instance, W.H. Hudson, *Hampshire Days* (London and Toronto, 1923), 220–41.

[71] Colley, *Britons*, passim.

[72] Miles, *King Alfred in Literature*, 73–74.

[73] For instance, Green, *Conquest of England*, 2–4, and see Hudson, *Hampshire Days*, 220–41 for physical signs of mixed-blood unions.

[74] S.L. Barczewski, *Myth and National Identity in Nineteenth-Century Britain: The Legends of King Arthur and Robin Hood* (Oxford, 2000), 144–61; Maike Oergel, "Saxon or Celt? King Alfred and King Arthur as English National Heroes in the Nineteenth Century," unpublished lecture, University of London, 31 January 2001.

[75] *Idylls of the King*, ed. J.M. Gray (New Haven and London, 1983), II, 329–30.

Teutons, to become Englishmen, in the way that the British apparently did not. In the tenth century the Scandinavian settlers of the Danelaw had become English formally when they surrendered to Alfred's descendants; hence Kingsley's subtitle for Hereward as "the Last of the English." Americans could also claim to be of Anglo-Saxon descent, and such claims were much to the fore at the time of the Alfred Millenary. General Rockwell, replying at the mayoral luncheon to the toast "The Anglo-Saxon Race and the Memory of Alfred," claimed that "he was our king just as much as yours" and, after evoking English settlement in North America, claimed that "the Anglo-Saxons will be, if they are not already, the dominant race of the world!"[76] The Anglo-Saxon legacy was demonstrated by the Meeting of Learned Societies which preceded the unveiling of the statue in Winchester and consisted of delegates from universities from all over the English-speaking world, that is, from disparate parts of the Commonwealth and America.

The celebration of King Alfred as embodiment of empire in 1901 was a national celebration, but one which had its location and most enthusiastic support in southern England. Alfred's links with London were much emphasized,[77] but what message did the celebrations send to other areas of the British Isles? The event embodies very well the mixed messages at the end of the nineteenth century about the nature of "English" and "British" identity. The uneasiness likely to have been aroused by the fact that large areas of England, let alone the rest of Britain, might not readily identify themselves with Alfred's Wessex is reflected in various novels produced for children around the time of the millenary.[78] J.F. Hodgetts' *Kormak the Viking* and C.W. Whistler's *King Alfred's Viking* both have as their hero a Viking who becomes a loyal follower of King Alfred, a reminder that Scandinavians could also be part of Alfred's England.[79] *Alfred the Great* by William Gordon-Stables makes a rather broader plea for inclusiveness.[80] Its central conceit involves a Scottish doctor (apparently based on the author himself) and an Irish major, both of whom have been forced by illness to retire from the

---

[76] Bowker, *King Alfred Millenary*, 119–21; see also Horsman, *Race and Manifest Destiny*, 82–97.

[77] Bowker, *King Alfred Millenary*, 23, 122–24. Recent archaeological work has provided support for the idea of Alfred's revival of the City as was illustrated by the Museum of London's exhibition in 1999 on "Alfred the Great: London's Forgotten King."

[78] For the didactic uses of children's novels concerning the Anglo-Saxon past see V. Bourgeois Richmond, "Historical Novels to Teach Anglo-Saxonism," in *Anglo-Saxonism and the Construction of Social Identity*, ed. A.J. Frantzen and J.D. Niles (Gainesville, 1997), 173–201, esp. 183–87.

[79] J.F. Hodgetts, *Kormak the Viking* (London, 1902); C.W. Whistler, *King Alfred's Viking: A Story of the First English Fleet* (London, 1899). For Whistler see Richmond, "Historical Novels," 187–92.

[80] W. Gordon-Stables, *Alfred the Great: or Twixt Daydawn and Light* (London, 1898).

British Army, discovering the early medieval legends and history of the British Isles with the aid of an Icelandic professor. The work served as a reminder not to forget the contribution that all the peoples of Britain had made, and continued to make, to the British empire and suggested that interest in Celtic and Scandinavian pasts was compatible with admiration for Anglo-Saxon achievements — that all belonged to rather similar worlds. It has long been a complaint by other areas of Britain that London and the South tend to assume they stand for the whole nation, and at least some of the interest in the Scandinavian past in parts of Scotland and eastern England can be seen as an assertion both of their separate regional identities and of their contribution to "this island's story."[81]

The shared English language was identified as a feature that bound the British Isles together, and was seen as conclusive evidence in some quarters for the dominance of the Anglo-Saxons over the other peoples of Britain. In the King Alfred Millenary it was race together with the speaking of English which defined which nations were the true heirs of Alfred and were invited to be represented in the celebrations. It allowed the inclusion of America, but excluded any role for Scandinavia and the Old North, in spite of the fact that Britain now had in Queen Alexandra a Danish queen.[82] The only Scandinavian to be mentioned with any regularity in the writings and activities connected with the millenary was Alfred's Norwegian visitor Ottar, but any references were to credit Alfred's interest in the world around him, which could be seen as anticipating later British voyages of exploration. In the hands of Sir Clements Markham, Alfred seems to anticipate his own views on the importance of Arctic exploration:

> It is certain that [Ottar's voyage] received the cordial approval of our great king, and that its motives had the sympathy and appreciation of one who, in regenerating the navy of England, knew well that such training was of vital importance to a naval power. The welcome he extended to his Arctic visitor, and the care with which he elicited his information and recorded it, leave no

---

[81] H.E. Marshall, *Our Island Story: A History of Britain for Boys and Girls* (London, 1905) can stand for many such works that tended to equate British with English. However, a movement was already underway to stress the role of the native British, not least because it provided a means of linking with the Roman Empire; see R. Hingley, *Roman Officers and English Gentlemen: The Imperial Origins of Roman Archaeology* (London and New York, 2000).

[82] Kingsley had included a genealogy celebrating Alexandra's descent from King Harald Bluetooth (see Wawn, *Vikings and Victorians*, 320), but it was not something which otherwise seems to have been much celebrated in England. When as Princess of Wales she accompanied her husband to unveil the statue to Alfred in Wantage in 1877, one of the welcoming banners proclaimed:
'Honour to the ancient king who drove the Danes away.
Welcome to our noble prince who brings one here today.'

doubt of what Alfred's feelings were upon the subject . . . it ought not to be
forgotten how highly he [Alfred] valued the work of Arctic exploration.[83]

Sir Clements was later to throw his full support behind Robert Falcon Scott's attempt to be first to the South Pole, but this was also to be a Norwegian, not an
English, achievement.

"Little Englander" tendencies can also help to explain what can otherwise
seem a surprising omission from Victorian Britain's study of the early medieval
past, that is, the relative lack of interest in the poem *Beowulf*, a failure that was
made apparent in the recent collection of studies of the poem edited by Shippey
and Haarder.[84] The poem fell between the two stools of interest in the Germanic
past in nineteenth-century Britain. Although the action of the poem could be
said to have been set in the original northern homelands of the Anglo-Saxons,
this was not part of the early medieval heritage to which supporters of the Saxon
South were interested in laying claim. The poem appeared to belong to a distant
pre-Christian past, and its assumed pagan associations, which were very much
to the fore in nineteenth-century discussions,[85] also damned it as belonging to a
primitive time, for, as we have seen, it was Christian Anglo-Saxons from whom
imperial nineteenth-century Britain wanted to trace its descent. The Victorian
English were not interested in foregrounding their possible common descent
with modern Danes or Germans.[86] Although willing to recognise that all were
Teutons, the English also felt themselves to be a race apart—the people who had
had the initiative to move from their original homelands and, within the British
Isles under the influence of Christianity, had formed their own distinctive characteristics while uniquely preserving the best of their Germanic constitutional
heritage that had eventually given birth to the British parliamentary system. The
Schleswig-Holstein dispute, which generated so much interest in the physical
location of the poem and the origins of Old English,[87] was not a matter that
much concerned the British Foreign Office, any more than the poem itself spoke
to English antiquaries with their interest grounded in local topography. One exception here was the Reverend Daniel Haigh, who believed that all the poem's
locations and central characters could be identified in eastern England through

---

[83] C. Markham, "Alfred as Geographer," in *Alfred the Great*, ed. Bowker, 149–68,
at 162–63.

[84] T.A. Shippey and A. Haarder, *Beowulf: The Critical Heritage* (London, 1998).

[85] E.G. Stanley, *The Search for Anglo-Saxon Paganism* (Cambridge, 1975).

[86] There were of course, notable exceptions such as J.M. Kemble, *The Saxons in England: A History of the English Commonwealth till the Period of the Norman Conquest*, 2 vols.
(London, 1849).

[87] Shippey and Haarder, *Beowulf*, 16–22, 38–39, 123–31; see also R.E. Bjork, "Nineteenth-Century Scandinavia and the Birth of Anglo-Saxon Studies," in *Anglo-Saxonism
and the Construction of Social Identity*, ed. Frantzen and Niles, 111–32.

a mixture of subjective reading of place-names and indiscriminate annexation of archaeological sites that was typical of the English antiquarian approach of men like Francis Wise.[88] Thus Hartlepool was said to derive its name from *Heorot*, and further proof for the identification was claimed from a hundred and fifty-one skeletons unearthed there in 1851 that were interpreted as the bodies of those killed in the fight consequent to the wedding of Ingeld and Freawaru.[89] The poem was also the wrong date and the wrong language to be of interest to most British lovers of the Old North, and so it failed to be claimed as part of either the Anglo-Saxon or the Anglo-Scandinavian heritage in Victorian Britain.[90] On the whole, it seems to have been the legacy from Old English prose rather than po-etry which was considered most significant, not least because a direct line of de-scent could be traced from Alfred, "the real founder of English prose literature" to Shakespeare and Jane Austen.[91]

There was undoubtedly much interest in the early medieval past in Victorian Britain which can be seen, on the one hand, as part of a burgeoning middle-class involvement with the history of localities, but also as part of a wider concern by European nations (including, of course, those of Scandinavia) to claim that their origins and their borders could be traced back to the early Middle Ages.[92] For Victorian Britain this meant finding the seeds of imperial greatness in its Ger-manic past, and to many King Alfred seemed to embody in his ambitions and personal standards of behaviour the paternalistic and Christian ideals that justi-fied the empire and characterised the best of its modern servants. This choice of Alfred affected portrayal of the men of the Old North in two main ways. On the one hand, they filled a long-standing role as the enemies of Britain and might have various characteristics of these foisted upon them. On the other, Alfred's accommodation with the Danes and the eventual incorporation of the Danelaw into England by his descendants meant that there were also positive ways in which a Scandinavian contribution could be made to the achievements of Eng-land before the Norman Conquest, and writers from outside Alfred's Wessex were particularly keen to make this point. But although one can trace an "offi-cial" line symbolised by the support given by all political parties and main reli-gious groups to the Alfred millenary,[93] opinions on empire and support for the

---

[88] Shippey and Haarder, *Beowulf*, 44–45, 317–20; Wawn, "Hereward," 359–60.

[89] The bodies in fact seem to have come from a cemetery associated with Hartle-pool's Anglo-Saxon nunnery.

[90] However, for children's novels influenced by Beowulf, see Richmond, "Histori-cal Novels," 188–89.

[91] Part of the toast to "Alfred and the Learning and Literature of the English-speaking Race" at the millenary luncheon; Bowker, *Alfred Millenary*, 115, 124.

[92] P. Geary, *The Myth of Nations* (Princeton, 2002).

[93] Seen, for instance, in the careful selection of representatives from all such parties on the National Committee. The Subscription List was opened by the leaders of the two

empire were not unanimous, and exploration of the early medieval past was one of the ways through which anxieties could be expressed. Alfred's dealings with his foes, the Vikings, could provide a way of exploring the empire's treatment of its enemies, while consideration of the early history of the British Isles as a whole could serve as a protest against what could seem to other parts of Britain as a construct of an empire that was too southern English in its orientation. Eastern and northern parts of Britain were proud of their Scandinavian heritage, but the view of the "Old North" from the Saxon South was decidedly restricted and Anglocentric. Overall, the image of the Vikings formed in nineteenth-century Britain was the modern popular one, and was much the same whether Vikings were being evoked as enemies of the English or as standing for admirable features of the Old North that injected vitality into the Anglo-Saxon bloodstock. No such popular images exist for the Anglo-Saxons, perhaps because they were too effectively annexed to embody Victorian values and imperial ideals.[94] In this respect it could be said that it has done the Viking reputation no harm in the longer term to be identified with the enemies of empire rather than with its upholders. The Vikings are instantly recognisable today and known to every British schoolchild, while the Anglo-Saxons have to many become dim and distant figures, and even Alfred's burnt cakes have been reduced to ashes.

---

main political parties who donated identical amounts: Bowker, *King Alfred Millenary*, 10–17.

[94] T. Shippey, "The Undeveloped Image: Anglo-Saxon in Popular Consciousness from Turner to Tolkien," in *Literary Appropriations of the Anglo-Saxons from the Thirteenth to the Twentieth Century*, ed. Scragg and Weinberg, 215–36.

Ships and their Terminology between England and the North

Katrin Thier

The Problem

A number of technical terms in Anglo-Saxon seafaring have close parallels in the Old Norse language. Some of these terms are cognates and reflect parallel and closely related developments in England and Scandinavia; others are loans from one language into the other. These terms include names for ship types as well as many for important parts of ships, including the main propulsion engines, oar and sail. A very straightforward example is OE *stefn* 'stem' and ON *stafn*; these words can be readily accepted to be cognates. Similarly, the words for 'anchor' appear to be borrowed from Latin into all North and West Germanic languages. For the names of ship types, the picture is more complicated, and many derivations remain open to debate. As regards oar and sail, even the history of these technologies is uncertain, and the origin of the words might provide vital clues for further research. In the following, I will examine the relationship of each term to its Scandinavian parallel and consider the possible cultural implications.

A number of terms are not difficult to trace. The generic *scip* has parallels in all Germanic languages including Gothic, but only a very tentative etymology beyond Germanic.[1] This might suggest that the word was a loan from a pre-Germanic language of the North and had come into Germanic by the time of the Gothic migrations south (from the second century AD).[2] OE *scip* can thus safely be assumed to be of common origin with ON *skip*.

Some words are almost certainly loans from Old Norse into Old English: OE *scegð* was borrowed from ON *skeið*, OE *barda* from ON *barði*, OE *cnear* probably

---

[1] Pokorny believes that *scip* goes back to a form of IE **skei* 'cut': J. Pokorny, *Indogermanisches Etymologisches Wörterbuch* (Bern, 1959), 922.

[2] The absence of other terms from Gothic is not significant due to the nature of the Gothic material (almost exclusively from the New Testament).

from ON *knǫrr* and OE *floege* from ON *fley*. ON *skeið* denotes a warship, often a large one. OE *scegð* occurs in glossaries translating Latin terms for 'warship' (e.g., *trieris* : *scægð*)[3] and in the will of Bishop Ælfwold of Crediton (Devon) of *c.* 1010, where a ship is described as *ænne scegð .lxiiii.-ære* 'a *scegð* with 64 oars', i.e., more than 30 m long, assuming roughly one metre per rower per side.[4] Coming as it does from the southwest of England, this last reference also shows that the word had transgressed the geographical boundaries of Scandinavian political control. The Old English word preserves the Scandinavian diphthong /ei/ in the spelling <eg>. In the Scandinavian word, this diphthong is attested in a runic inscription from Tryggevælde, Denmark, from the ninth century (spelt <skaiþ>): *raknhiltr sustiʀ ulfs sati stain / þunsi auk karþi hauk þǫnsi auft / auk skaiþ þaisi / kunulf . . .* 'Ragnhild, Ulf's sister, set up this stone and made this memorial and this skeið in memory of Kunulf. . .'.[5]

OE *barð* and *barda/barþa* also gloss terms for 'warship': *rostrata navis i. barda*;[6] *dromo*: *æsc* uel *barð*;[7] *rostrata navis quam demonem* [sic] *vocamus aereum rostrum habet* : *barþa* ('a ram-ship, which we call *dromon*, has an iron ram: *barþa*').[8] They are related to OE *beard* 'beard'. The final /ð/ in *barð*, however, is a Scandinavian feature, which should not occur in its West Germanic cognate, where /d/ would be expected. In Old Norse, *barð* is used for the stem of a ship (*skegg* is used for 'beard'), and *barði* is formed on *barð* as a term for a warship, originally probably 'ship with a special stem'. The Old English forms with the single vowel spelling (outwith the Anglian dialect area) and, in one case, North Germanic /ð/ must be borrowed from this. The implicit reference to a special stem seems to have specialized within Old English to refer to the *rostrum* (ram or ram-like stem) of a Mediterranean ship.

ON *knǫrr* (stem *knarr-*) is well attested as a type of Norse trading vessel in the saga period (thirteenth century onwards). In skaldic verse of the preceding Viking Period, it is also used as a term for a warship.[9] In Old English in the same

---

[3] Brussels Glossary: T. Wright and R. P. Wülcker, eds., *Anglo-Saxon and Old English Vocabularies* (London, 1884), 289, l. 13.

[4] A.S. Napier and W.H. Stevenson, eds., *The Crawford Collection of Early Charters and Documents Now in the Bodleian Library*, Anecdota Oxoniensia, Medieval and Modern Series 7 (Oxford, 1895), 128, no. 10.

[5] L. Jacobsen and E. Moltke, *Danmarks Runeindskrifter*, vol. 1: Text (Copenhagen, 1942), 284, no. 230.

[6] Brussels Glossary, 289, l. 12.

[7] Antwerp Glossary: A. Kindschi, ed., "The Latin-Old English Glossaries in Plantin-Moretus MS 32 and BM MS Add. 32, 246" (Ph.D. diss., Stanford University, 1955), 230, l. 5.

[8] Antwerp Glossary, 187, l. 1.

[9] R. Malmros, "Leding og Skjaldekvad," *Årbøger for Norsk Oldkyndighed og Historie* 1985 (1986): 89–139, here 103.

period, *cnear* only designates a warship, and in the only textual context *cnear* is explicitly used to refer to Scandinavian ships: *cread cnear on flod*;[10] *Gewitan him þa Norþmenn nægledcnearrum.*[11] The other reference is a gloss referring to Roman warships: *navibus actuariis* : *cnearrum.*[12] Formally, the two words could be of common origin, but as Björkman points out, the Old English word could also have attracted the diphthong by analogy with similar words in pronunciation or spelling.[13] ON *knǫrr* has been linked to *knǫttr* 'knot'.[14] There are also a number of other Germanic words in /kn/ referring to knots, knobs etc. Few of these have /a/ as their root vowel, and if so, only in Old Norse. This, together with the very specific reference to Scandinavian ships, suggests that *cnear* is indeed a loan.

Finally, OE *floege* is a *hapax legomenon* only found in two interdependent gospel glosses to John 6: 22: *nauicula* : *floege vel lyttel scipp* (Lindisfarne Gospels), *nauicula* : *floege* (Rushworth Gospels).[15] It is marked out as a Scandinavian loan by the preservation of the diphthong /øi/, which was otherwise alien to Old English, but common in Old Norse. This is spelt <ey> in Scandinavia, and the English loanword transcribes it as <oeg>.

In contrast, one loan from Old English into Old Norse is nearly certain, namely the OE generic *bāt*, ON *bátr*. This word has no known etymology, but it may be connected to ON *beita*, OE *bætan* 'to tack'. There is also a rare Old Norse *beit* 'boat', which supports this theory (attested only in Eddic and skaldic poetry).[16] ON *beit* and OE *bāt* could formally be cognates, with both the Norse and the English displaying regular reflexes of common Germanic /ai/. The Norse form *bátr* with its long /a:/, however, cannot formally go back to a common root with the Old English word. These two can only be related if OE *bāt* was borrowed into Norse, where it subsequently replaced the native *beit*.

---

[10] The Battle of Brunanburh, Anglo-Saxon Chronicle anno 937, cited after MS A: Janet M. Bately, ed., *MS A: A Semi-diplomatic Edition with Introduction and Indices*, The Anglo-Saxon Chronicle: A Collaborative Edition 3 (Cambridge, 1986), l. 35.

[11] Battle of Brunanburh, l. 53.

[12] Gloss in British Library MS. Cotton Tiberius C ii, 7v on Bede *Historia Ecclesiastica* I.ii: H.D. Meritt, ed., *Old English Glosses: A Collection* (London, 1945), 7, l. 20.

[13] E. Björkman, *Scandinavian Loanwords in Middle English*, Studien zur englischen Philologie 7 (Halle/Saale, 1900–1902), 215.

[14] W. Sayers, "The Etymology and Semantics of Old Norse *knǫrr* 'cargo ship'"— The Irish and English Evidence," *Scandinavian Studies* 68 (1996): 279–90, at 283.

[15] Thanks to S. Pons-Sanz for bringing this to my attention. For a detailed discussion cf. A.S.C. Ross, "Four Examples of Norse Influence in the Old English Gloss on the Lindisfarne Gospels," *Transactions of the Philological Society* (1940): 39–52. Examples are taken from W. W. Skeat, ed., *The Holy Gospels in Anglo-Saxon, Northumbrian and Old Mercian Versions* (Cambridge, 1871–1887).

[16] Cf. OGNS, s.v. *beit*; J. Jesch, *Ships and Men in the Early Viking Age* (Woodbridge, 2001), 135.

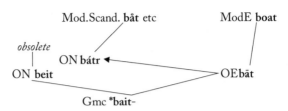

FIGURE I

The development of *bat*. Lines mark developments, arrows mark loans, and broken lines indicate uncertainty.

The situation is complicated by three terms, which appear to go back much further in time and are not restricted to England and Scandinavia. In the case of OE *snacc* / ON *snekkja* and OE *æsc* / ON *askr*, the evidence at first seems to point to a Viking connection, whereas OE *cēol* / ON *kjóll* is mainly associated with England.

OE *snacc* is only attested in two Old English passages in the Anglo-Saxon Chronicle, both referring to ships in the fleet of the eleventh-century English kings Edward and Harold.[17] It is paralleled by the common ON *snekkja*, but cannot formally be a direct loan, since the Norse word shows umlaut, whereas the English one does not. Since *i*-umlaut happened in both languages long before the Viking Age, a common origin has to be assumed. The word is also attested in Old High German in the oblique form *snacgun* and in Low German *snik*. An underlying word for 'snake' can be excluded, as in the Old Norse form *snáca* this displays a long vowel and thus cannot account for the short vowel in *snekkja*. Also, ON *snáca* only shows evidence of a single /k/. Holthausen suggests a relationship between the ship term and the Westphalian Low German *snack* 'slender, swift'.[18] What is significant is that the double consonant appears not only in Old Norse, but also in Old English; at least that is one thing the spelling <cc> could represent. A common origin for OE *snacc* and ON *snekkja* could thus be reconstructed as **snakk-ja*. In Old English, /a/ resists *i*-umlaut if followed by the geminate /kk/. This makes the equation possible and is another hint that we really are dealing with a geminate consonant here. **Snakkja* could then be seen as a nominal derivation of an adjective **snakk* 'slender, swift', which survives in the modern *snak*. LG *snik* does not pose further difficulty; it could equally be descended from **snakkja* or borrowed from ON *snekkja*. In this case, the single <k> is insignificant; Low German shed the distinction between long and short

    [17] G. P. Cubbin, ed., *MS D: A Semi-diplomatic Edition with Introduction and Indices*, The Anglo-Saxon Chronicle: A Collaborative Edition 6 (Cambridge, 1996), anno 1052, anno 1066.

    [18] F. Holthausen, *Altenglisches Etymologisches Wörterbuch* (Heidelberg, 1934), s.v. *snacc*; cf. F. Woeste, *Wörterbuch der westfälischen Mundart* (Leipzig, 1882), s.v. *snack*.

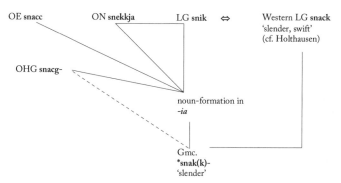

FIGURE 2

The development of *snacc*. Lines mark developments, arrows mark loans, and broken lines indicate uncertainty.

consonants before the advent of literacy. OHG *snacg-* cannot be put into this pattern with absolute certainty. It is recorded in a manuscript of the Middle High German period and displays a spelling <cg> for /k/ after a general loss of gemination in the language. The vowel is the main problem. If the word is from a Southern High German dialect (*oberdeutsch*), it would have resisted umlaut and appeared regularly as /a/ (cf. the problem of ModHG *Asch* and *Esche* below). If it is from any other dialect, it can only be explained if the OHG noun developed directly from the adjective without the {ja}-derivation.

In several passages, Old English *æsc* is used to denote Viking ships, and it is widely believed to have passed from Norse into English. It has also been associated with the tree-name, which has a well-attested Indo-European etymology and seems to always have denoted the ash tree in those areas where it was native.[19] Formally, OE *æsc* is very difficult to assess, as it is indeed indistinguishable from the tree-name 'ash'. The same is true of its ON cognate *askr*, and it seems not unreasonable to suppose that the word moved from one language into the other by means of loan-translation rather than borrowing. The suggestion has been that the word *æsc* denoted ships made at least partly of this type of wood, such as Skuldelev 5 (with some ashen planks) and Hedeby 1 (with ash framing).[20] However, ash wood is not ideal for shipbuilding, and the named examples come from Viking Age Denmark (extending further south than today), which suffered

---

[19] For a list of cognates and their meanings cf. Pokorny, *Indogermanisches Etymologisches Wörterbuch*, 782.

[20] O. Crumlin-Pedersen, "Gensyn med Skuldelev 5—et ledingsskib," in *Festskrift til Olaf Olsen*, ed. A. Andersen et al. (Copenhagen, 1988), 137–56, at 142; idem, *Viking-Age Ships and Shipbuilding in Hedeby/Haithabu and Schleswig*, Ships and Boats of the North 2 (Roskilde, 1997), 87.

from oak shortages in the tenth century and later.[21] In addition, Hofmann points
out that *askr* is only very rarely used in Old Norse.[22] The first attestation of OE
æsc, however, is from the eighth-century Épinal and Erfurt glossaries, which are
thought to go back to a late seventh-century exemplar: *cercylus : aesc uel nauis*.[23]
This is before both the appearance of Vikings in Britain and the Danish oak
shortage. An explanation of the term must thus be sought elsewhere. Among
the few records of continental West Germanic in the Anglo-Saxon period, several instances of a ship term **ask-* can be found. Best known of these is Adam
of Bremen's eleventh-century note on *[classis] pyratarum, quos nostri Ascoman-
nos vocant*.[24] It is uncertain if Adam here refers to speakers of Low German (in
Hamburg–Bremen) or High German (his mother tongue), but thus Latinised,
the difference would have been minimal. In an OHG glossary of the same period, *pirata* is glossed as *ascmann*.[25] Much earlier, however, are two notes in the
Latin context of the Frankish Lex Salica, which first appears in manuscripts of
the eighth century, but is thought to go back to the sixth.[26] These passages appear
in all manuscripts and can thus be regarded as original, and they involve a type
of boat named *ascus: si quis asco deintro clauem furauerit . . ., sol. XLV culp. iudic.*
'if anyone were to steal a lock from within an *ascus*, he would be liable to a fine
of 45 solidi'.[27] The type of ship is not specified. From these, an original (High?)
German **asc-* can be reconstructed, which survives in the Modern High German
name *Asch* for a type of working boat in the Danube area.[28] This differs from the
tree name Modern High German *Esche*; the difference may, however, be a dialect feature. Norse *askr* on its own cannot be used to determine the origin of the
word, as it is not phonologically marked and only attested during and after the
Viking Age. The German, English, and Norse terms between them can be used
to reconstruct an underlying Germanic root **ask-*, which is still homonymous
with the tree name. Swanton therefore believes that the word is derived from a
term for an ash-built boat, in this case not a complex Viking ship but a logboat

---

[21] Crumlin-Pedersen, *Hedeby/Haithabu*, 182.

[22] D. Hofmann, *Nordisch-englische Lehnbeziehungen der Wikingerzeit* (Copenhagen, 1955), 163.

[23] J. D. Pheifer, ed., *English Glosses in the Épinal-Erfurt Glossary* (Oxford, 1987), 11, l. 180. For a discussion of the date see Introduction, lxxxix.

[24] B. Schmeidler, ed., *Adam von Bremen: Hamburgische Kirchengeschichte*, Monumen-ta Germaniae Historica: Scriptores Rerum Germanicarum ad usum scholarum separa-tim editi 2 (Hannover and Leipzig, 1917), 2.31.

[25] E. Steinmeyer and E. Sievers, eds., *Die Althochdeutschen Glossen*, vol. 2: *Glossen zu nichtbiblischen Schriften* (Dublin, 1969), 366, 27.

[26] R. Schmidt-Wiegand, "Lex Salica," *Lexikon des Mittelalters* 5 (München and Zürich, 1987): 1931–1932.

[27] K.A. Eckhardt, ed., *Lex Salica*, Monumenta Germaniae Historica: Leges Na-tionum Germanicarum, 1:4.2 (Hannover, 1969), law 21, §§ 3–4.

[28] J. A. Schmeller, *Bayerisches Wörterbuch* (München, 1872–1877), s.v. *Asch, Hallasch*.

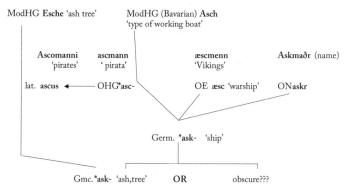

FIGURE 3

The development of *æsc*. Lines mark developments, arrows mark loans, and broken lines indicate uncertainty.

or similar.[29] The disadvantages of ash wood in shipbuilding remain a problem, but they are not insurmountable, so this interpretation may well be correct. Some doubt does remain, and an alternative, but obscure origin for the ship-term **ask-* cannot be ruled out. This idea is supported by my own observation that many technical terms for ships in the North cannot be convincingly traced back beyond the level of "Common Germanic".

OE *cēol* appears in Britain as early as the sixth century, when it is quoted by a Latin author in the form *cyulis* (abl. pl.): *tribus, ut lingua eius exprimitur, cyulis, nostra longis navibus*, 'with three, as expressed in their language, **cyulae*, in ours [=Latin], *naves longae*'.[30] The word also appears in Old Saxon and Old High German as *kiol* and *chiol* respectively. The equivalent Old Norse *kjóll* is rare and as a general term is only used in Eddic poetry.[31] In prose it denotes specifically English merchant ships.[32] It cannot be reliably traced back beyond Germanic, but it has often been suggested to have been borrowed into Finnish as *keula* 'bow',[33]

[29] M. J. Swanton, "King Alfred's Ships: Text and Context," *Anglo-Saxon England* 28 (1999): 1–22, at 16.

[30] M. Winterbottom, ed. and tr., *Gildas: The Ruin of Britain and other Documents*, Arthurian Period Sources 7 (Chichester, 1978), chap. 23, 3.

[31] Cf. Jesch, *Ships and Men*, 136.

[32] G. Vigfusson, ed., *Orkneyinga Saga and Magnus Saga, with Appendices*, Icelandic Sagas 1, Rerum Britannicarum Medii Aevi Scriptores 88 (London, 1964 [1887]), chap. 115.

[33] Cf. J. de Vries, *Altnordisches Etymologisches Wörterbuch* (Leiden, 1957–1961), s.v. *kjóll*. An alternative etymology for Finnish *keula* has been suggested by Koivulehto, who compares it to Old Norse *skjól* 'covering, shelter' (< Germanic **skeula-*). See J. Koivulehto, "Germanisch-Finnische Lehnbeziehungen III: Wörter des Seewesens," *Neuphilologische Mitteilungen* 74 (1973): 561–609, at 564–74. I am grateful to M. Kilpiö for drawing my

which would suggest that it was present in Scandinavia at an early stage.[34] However, the word gained prominence only in England, where it became one of the most common ship terms and was successfully borrowed into local Medieval Latin as *ciula*; e.g., *ciula* : *cēol*.[35] It survives into modern English as the name of a ship type, *keel*. This is unrelated to the homonymous modern word for the bottom plank of a ship, which derives from ON *kjǫlr*, with a different vowel and single /l/.[36] Formally, *kjóll* must be of Scandinavian descent, as the final <ll> cannot be explained otherwise. All other languages have single <l>, although early Germanic languages distinguished between /l/ and /ll/ and usually made the distinction clear in spelling. Most importantly, Finnish, which makes the distinction to this day, has borrowed the word with a simple /l/. Within Scandinavian, final /ll/ can be a assimilation of /lr/, with a stem-final /l/ and the nominative ending /-r/.[37] Although the word seems to have survived within Old Norse, it seems to have been identified with the English word at a later period, presumably through recognition of the common etymology, and applied to denote a specifically English object. The meaning of *cēol* in Old English developed through the centuries from 'warship' to 'merchant vessel'; the latter meaning is first attested in the eleventh century: *Ad Billingsgate* [. . .] *si adueniat ceol uel hulcus et ibi iaceat, quatuor d. ad teloneum*, 'at Billingsgate, if a *ceol* or a *hulcus* arrives and lies there, 4 shillings as a toll'.[38] The Norse use of *kjóll* for English merchant ships thus suggests that the word, though previously known, gained a new significance through contact with England during the later Viking Age or after. It is thus not a true loan-word, but nevertheless an indicator of semantic movement from England to Scandinavia. The *cēol* is one of the ship types which archaeologists have attempted to identify in the material record, partly because it is the one specific name for a ship type mentioned during the period of Anglo-Saxon expansion. On both sides of the North Sea, the ship finds from Nydam (Jutland) and Sutton Hoo (East Anglia) have been linked to the Anglo-Saxon settlement in Britain. The Nydam ship dates from the early fourth century and was designed for rowing, while the Sutton Hoo ship comes from the seventh century and may have been

---

attention to this. It does not, however, invalidate the conclusions reached about Germanic **keula* and its descendants.

[34] The ON diphthong /eu/ changed to /jo:/ over a longer period between ca. 600 and 900: A. Noreen, *Altisländische und altnorwegische Grammatik* (Halle/Saale, 1923), § 56.

[35] R. T. Oliphant, ed., *The Harley Latin-Old English Glossary, edited from the BM MS Harley 3379* (Den Haag, 1966), gloss C1037; *Historia Brittonum*, in variation with *navis*: J. Morris, ed. and tr., *Nennius: British History* and *The Welsh Annals*, Arthurian Period Sources 8 (Chichester, 1980), passim.

[36] B. Sandahl, *Middle English Sea Terms* 1 (Uppsala, 1958), 65, s.v. *kele*.

[37] Noreen, *Grammatik*, § 277.

[38] F. Liebermann, ed. and trans., *Gesetze der Angelsachsen*, vol. 1 (Halle/Saale, 1903), *law* IV, Atr. 2.

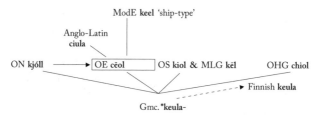

FIGURE 4

The development of *ceol*. Lines mark developments, arrows mark loans, and broken lines indicate uncertainty.

sailed, but both are very evidently from the same indigenous shipbuilding tradition, which was eventually to lead to the development of the Viking ships.[39]

To assess the history of sailing and rowing in Northern Europe, one has to look even further back in time and into the Roman Imperial period. Both technologies have specifically North European words associated with them, and both first appear in the Germanic world at about the time of the Roman expansion northwards. A major advantage here is the presence of at least some archaeological evidence, which can be linked to the words.

It seems interesting that the word *sail* and its cognates occur only in Germanic and Celtic languages. Their exact relationship has been much debated; the most probable explanation in my view is a root **siglo-*, which is common to both Celtic and Germanic, and which can explain all extant forms.[40] In both Welsh and Irish, the /g/ is lost and the /i/ lowered and—by compensatory lengthening—lengthened into /e:/. In Welsh, this long /e:/ is later broken into /ui/ (now spelt <wy>), and initial /s/ is later changed to /h/, giving the present form *hwyl*. The Irish word acquires an additional vowel by irregular processes too complex to detail here,[41] giving Old Irish *séol* (Modern Irish *seól*). The developments in the West Germanic languages are less dramatic. The vowel is regularly lowered and the /g/ turned first into a fricative and then a semivowel (but still spelt <g>), leading to OE *segl*, *segel* (English *sail*). In Old High German, the final cluster developed into a second syllable (OHG *segal*, German *Segel*).

The earliest evidence from Old English comes again from the eighth-century Épinal Glossary, which may derive from a seventh-century exemplar (see above). Here it occurs only in the compound *segilgaerd* 'sail-yard' (glossing Latin *antemna*), but the compound presupposes the existence of the word 'sail', and a term for

---

[39] Cf. O. Crumlin-Pedersen, "Boats and Ships of the Angles and Jutes," in *Maritime Celts, Frisians and Saxons*, ed. S. McGrail, CBA Research Report 71 (London, 1990), 98–116.

[40] P. Schrijver, *Studies in British Celtic Historical Phonology* (Amsterdam, 1995), 357.

[41] For a discussion of the problem, see R. Thurneysen, *A Grammar of Old Irish* (Dublin, 1946), 574.

a part of the rigging presupposes the existence of rigs. Since 'sail-yard' remains the recognised technical term to the present, it is unlikely that it was used in the glossary merely to translate a Latin word for an unfamiliar object. As a simplex, the word *segl* then occurs in the Alfredian translation of Boethius[42] and in the Wulfstan Episode prefixed to Orosius.[43] No evidence from any other Germanic language predates these Old English examples; sails are not mentioned in the texts surviving in Gothic. The earliest Celtic evidence is of comparable date: the first written Irish forms date from around 800,[44] and some use in poetry can be dated back through metrics into the seventh century.[45]

The reconstructed form cannot be traced back beyond Celtic and Germanic, but given that the archaeological evidence of sail from Celtic contexts is quite early, it is conceivable that the word passed from Celtic into Germanic before the forms differentiated. Since the Rhine was a boundary as well as a highway for both Germanic- and Celtic-speaking peoples, the Rhine valley may have been the area where both word and technology were borrowed. What happened then is less clear. Evidence of the use of sail is completely missing from the Germanic world after the Roman withdrawal. On the other hand, there is not much good evidence of ships from this area and time at all. Sail must have been known to all Germanic peoples who were in direct contact with the Roman Empire; this includes the Germanic *foederati* who served in the Roman army in Britain. When the Roman army left the island, it was heavily Romanized, and so was the adjacent Continent. Large parts of Britain were subsequently settled from areas of continental Europe which had been further away from the Empire. In the mid-seventh century, a large ship was buried at Sutton Hoo, which has been shown to have had some sailing capabilities.[46] Not much later, the first evidence of the word *sail* in English appears in the Épinal Glossary (see above). If one assumes that these are not each the very first of their kind seen in the country, the gap left between the end of the Romano-British period and the earliest evidence of sail in England remains quite small, and from this period no relevant evidence of any kind survives, either for or against. It looks fairly likely that there was a certain continuity in the use of sail in Britain. Scandinavia, on the other hand, was

---

[42] W.J. Sedgefield, ed., *King Alfred's Old English Version of Boethius* (Oxford, 1899), chap. 41.3.

[43] Janet M. Bately, ed., *The Old English Orosius*, EETS s.s. 6 (Oxford, 1980), chap. I. i., 16.

[44] A gloss in the Book of Armagh: W. Stokes and J. Strachan, eds., *Thesaurus Palaeohibernicus* (Cambridge, 1901), 1: 498, l. 32.

[45] Cf. Beccán, *Fo réir Choluimb*: T. Clancy and G. Márkus, eds., *Iona — The Earliest Poetry* (Edinburgh, 1995), 138.

[46] E. Gifford and J. Gifford, "The Sailing Performance of Anglo-Saxon Ships as Derived from the Building and Trials of Half-Scale Models of the Sutton Hoo and Graveney Ship Finds," *Mariners Mirror* 82 (1996): 131–53, at 152.

further removed from both the Celtic speakers of the Rhine and the Roman Empire, so that circumstantial evidence of the knowledge of sail is as absent as the related archaeology. A fourth-century ship from Nydam in Denmark was probably built to be rowed only. The first well-preserved ship that might have been a sailing ship comes from Kvalsund in Norway and is dated around 700. At a similar time, sailing ships begin to be depicted on stones in Gotland, although these are often difficult to date.[47] The ON word *segl* is first recorded in skaldic poetry of the late Viking Age. It is therefore not certain whether sailing in Scandinavia was an extension of the Continental tradition or a later and somewhat independent development. The original **siglo-* would have regularly evolved into *segl*, but a later loan from West Germanic would have remained unchanged and thus have given the same result. Interestingly though, while the word *segl* is shared by West and North Germanic, some other key terms for rigging are not: the mast is known as *mæst* in Old English, but *viða* in Old Norse, and the yard, which holds the sail in place, is called *seglgerd* in Old English and *(siglu)-rá* in Old Norse. In both cases, other West Germanic evidence parallels the English use, while Old Norse uses a more unusual term.[48]

Rowing was brought to the Germanic peoples by the Romans,[49] and there is firm evidence that it spread to Scandinavia during the time of the Empire. The earliest rowlocks, from Mangersnes in southern Norway, date from the third century at the latest,[50] but there is no evidence prior to that. The Old High German word *riemo, riomo* 'oar' is a direct loan from Latin *rēmus*; other Continental West Germanic words are similar. In this case, however, Norse is not the only odd one out; Old English, too, has an unusual term: OE *ár* / ON *ár* are unparalleled in any other Germanic language and with their similar forms provide an intriguing link between England and Scandinavia. A long /a:/ in Old English would be expected to correspond to /ei/ in Old Norse. However, this may have been monophthongized to /a:/ before /r/, thus explaining the parallel forms. From this, a Germanic root **airo* can be reconstructed, which exactly matches the Finnish word for oar, *airo*. Pokorny suggested that the Germanic root is in turn derived from an Indo-European **oi-sa-*, which also yields Greek οἴαξ 'helm'. If this were true, the consonant of the surviving Germanic word could only be explained by Verner's Law, supposing stress on the second syllable (**oi-sá-*); in this case the common Germanic would have been **aizo*. This form is difficult

---

[47] E. Nylén, *Bildstenar* (Visby, 1978), 42–43, 166.

[48] K. Thier, "Sails in the North—New Perspectives on an Old Problem," *International Journal of Nautical Archaeology* 32 (2003): 182–90, at 188.

[49] Celtic peoples seem to have had oars at the time, but it is impossible to assess their part in the transmission. The surviving Celtic words for oar (Old Irish *rám*, Welsh *rhwyf*) suggest that the word was very similar to the Latin and might also have been a loan.

[50] A. E. Christensen, "Boat Fragments from Mangersnes," in *Shipshape: Essays for Ole Crumlin-Pedersen,* ed. O. Olsen et al. (Roskilde, 1995), 73–80, at 75.

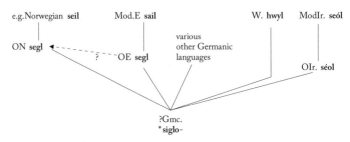

FIGURE 5
The development of *segl*. Lines mark developments, arrows mark loans, and broken lines indicate uncertainty.

to reconcile with the surviving Finnish word, and it would not have developed into Old Norse *ár*, as only inherited /r/, and not /ʀ/ < /z/ could cause monophthongization. Like most words discussed above, OE *ār* / ON *ár* cannot be traced beyond Germanic.

The evidence for the word *ār* in Old English is from eleventh-century glosses and from some poetry in the tenth-century Exeter Book (e.g., *Maxims I*).[51] Only if an eighth-century date for *Maxims I* can be accepted does the English evidence predate examples in Viking Age skaldic poetry.[52] It is therefore not entirely certain if *ār* was a term used in pre-Viking England.

The Indo-European root for rowing also has reflexes in the Germanic languages. The verb *to row* and its cognates are attested in several Germanic languages, including OE *rōwan*, MHG *roien*, and ON *róa*, all in the same sense. This verb gave rise to an instrumental derivative at an early stage, yielding OE *rōðor*, OHG *ruodar*, and ON *róðr*. The senses of these are somewhat more complex. The two West Germanic words are used to denote oars and possibly also the rudder, while the Old Norse word designates the act of rowing. The equivalent Old Norse term for oar is *ræði*, a different instrumental derivative from the same root. Old English *rōðor* significantly predates any evidence of *ār* and in its earliest attestations unambiguously denotes the oar (e.g., glossing Latin *tonsa* in Épinal). It seems strange that several major early Germanic languages have pairs of terms with the sense 'oar' (OHG *riemo/ruodar*, OE *ār/rōðor* and ON *ár/ræði*), if rowing was at the time a relatively recent introduction from abroad. Furthermore, in all cases one of these is a native derivative from an Indo-European root for *to row*, which also survives as a verb in all these languages, and the ON *ár* / OE *ār* also appears to be of non-Roman origin. While rowing was apparently new to the Germanic world in the Roman period, paddling is well attested in archaeology in finds like the warship from Hjortspring (Alsen, off Jutland) from

---

[51] Cf. *Maxims* I, lines 185f: G. P. Krapp and E. Dobbie, eds., *The Exeter Book*, ASPR 3 (New York, 1936).

[52] On the dating of the skaldic corpus see Jesch, *Ships and Men*, 15–33.

the third century B.C. Incidentally, this also shows the use of especially broad paddles for steering.[53] Half a millennium later, a Samian sherd from Trier shows a rather large paddled "barbarian" vessel, presumably Germanic.[54] This postdates the find of rowlocks from Mangersnes mentioned above. Rowing and paddling are closely related techniques, for an oar is essentially a paddle pulled against a fixed pivot. It is therefore not unlikely that rowing was adopted as an extension of paddling, and that existing terminology continued to be used in areas further removed from the linguistic influence of the Roman Empire, while it was replaced with the Latin word on the Continent.[55] In this scenario the verb descending from the Indo-European root would have been used to mean 'to paddle', while *ár* appears to mean only 'oar'. When rowing became popular, the sense of the verb would have been extended to embrace both. It is not possible to trace exactly the semantic development of the derivatives. Perhaps both OE *róðor* and OHG *ruodar* originally had the same sense as ON *róðr* 'act of rowing' (or originally, of paddling), and the sense 'oar' was a secondary development, or the terms actually formed separately in West and North Germanic, and the use of specific suffixes for specific senses was independent. In the latter case, this development would be relatively late, probably postdating the formation of a separate North Germanic group of languages. Either way, all languages involved developed a derivative meaning 'oar' besides the existing term, possibly to emphasize the difference between an oar and a paddle. When paddling became unimportant, the terms fell together to become synonyms, and one set survived by a new semantic split: the instrumental derivative in each of these languages later develops to mean 'rudder, steering mechanism'. As early rudders developed from oars or paddles laid over the side of a boat (as seen in Hjortspring, cf. above), a further semantic shift from 'oar' via 'steering oar' to 'rudder' makes sense. The earliest indisputable evidence for the modern sense in Middle English dates from the mid-fourteenth century.[56]

While *róðor* is attested in Old English from very early on, it is not certain when the word *ár* entered the language. Formally the word could be an old

---

[53] G. Rosenberg, *Hjortspringfundet*, Nordiske Forntidsminder 3.1 (Copenhagen, 1937), 86–89.

[54] D. Ellmers, "Die ersten bildlichen Darstellungen zu Schifffahrender Sachsen aus dem römischen Trier," *Die Kunde* N.F. 24 (1977–1978): 23–62.

[55] K. Thier, "Das Paddel—eine Minikulturgeschichte," in *Itinera Archaeologica: Festschrift T. Capelle*, ed. H. Eilbracht et al. (Rahden/Westf., 2005), 281–94, at 288–89. K. Thier fthc., "Paddling, Rowing and Steering in Word and Deed" in *Between the Seas*, ed. R. Bockins (Oxford). Modern English *paddle* is of uncertain origin; the nautical sense is first attested in the 17th century: Cf. *OED Online: New Edition* s.v. *paddle* n.[1](Oxford, 2008), (state of January 2009): <http://dictionary.oed.com/cgi/entry/50169090>

[56] *MED*, s.v. *rother* n (1) (*Middle English Dictionary*, ed. H. Kurath and R. Lewis [Ann Arbor, 1954–2001]).

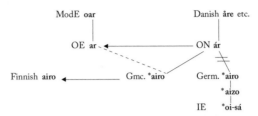

FIGURE 6

The development of *ar*. Lines mark developments, arrows mark loans, and broken lines indicate uncertainty.

cognate of the Old Norse term and could thus have been brought to England in the course of the migration or subsequent contacts. This view is supported by the occurrence of the term in the Exeter Book (e.g., *Maxims I*), but since the date of the poems cannot be certain beyond the date of the manuscript, it is not conclusive proof. On the other hand, the consistent use of the word *rōðor* in early sources may indicate that this had been the recognised term, and that *ār* was a later introduction. It is possible that *ār* was borrowed from Norse as late as the Viking invasion of England and its aftermath.

With the exception of *row/rudder*, the terms discussed above have one thing in common: they cannot be traced beyond the level of early Germanic in time and the northern part of Europe in space. *Sail* is unique in having a non-Germanic parallel which is not a loan; indeed the term may derive from Celtic. Beyond this, however, the picture remains as dark as it is for the rest. This Celtic connection suggests that the term was present in Germanic in the Rhine area; to spread to other areas, it must have moved from there to the coastal areas of the North Sea. *Æsc* appears to have spread along similar routes, considering that its earliest manifestations are from a similar area; later it is mostly attested in England and only rarely in the North. These two contrast with a small set of words which were apparently present in the Baltic Sea area at an early date; at least one was borrowed into Finnish in a pre-Nordic form. Both *ār* and *cēol* belong to this group, and both also appear in Great Britain; indeed, *cēol* became especially associated with that part of the world. Spanning both the North Sea and the Baltic Sea areas, it is likely that the term was present (and perhaps even originated) in Jutland in this period. *Snacc* appears to be an old Germanic word which mainly flourished in Scandinavia, but was also known on the continent and in Britain. Finally, loans from and into Old Norse in the historical period finally show continuing contacts across the North Sea, one of which was the Viking conquest of large parts of England in the ninth century. At the other end of the record, however, the picture is less clear, and the ultimate cultural and linguistic origin of these words will remain an intriguing puzzle for future investigation.

RACE AND TILLAGE: SCANDINAVIAN INFLUENCE ON ANGLO-SAXON AGRICULTURE?

DEBBY BANHAM

Spring came early that year, and the men were already busy sowing their grain.
Njál's Saga, chap. 110[1]

The purpose of this paper is to assess the evidence for Scandinavian influence on Anglo-Saxon agriculture during the period of Viking settlement in England. My main focus will therefore be on similarities between the two cultures in this period, but I should like to start by looking at a contrast. It is a literary contrast, and on the Scandinavian side the material involved is mainly of twelfth-century date, but nevertheless it is possible that a social contrast, at least having its origins in our period, lies behind the literary one. Old Norse poetry, especially the sagas, is full of details about everyday life and farming. In Old English literature, on the other hand, one can search for days without coming across a single reference to agriculture, and when one does, it will probably be biblical, reflecting an interest in religion and scholarship, rather than food-production.[2] A similar picture is presented by the laws: whereas Scandinavian provincial law-codes contain numerous detailed provisions relating to farming, in Anglo-Saxon law there are very few.[3] Again, apart from the celebrated clauses in Ine's laws, the exceptions are mainly biblical, such as Alfred's reference to vineyards in the preface to

---

[1] This is the translation of Carl F. Bayerschmidt and Lee M. Hollander, *Njál's Saga* (London, 1956), 226.

[2] Such as Ælfric's description of olive trees in his homily for the tenth Sunday after Pentecost: John C. Pope, ed., *Homilies of Ælfric: A Supplementary Collection*, vol. 2, EETS o.s. 260 (London, 1968), 552.

[3] For Scandinavian law, see Annette Hoff, *Lov og landskab* (Århus, 1997), a study of the Danish provincial laws as evidence for agriculture, including comparisons with Swedish and Anglo-Saxon law. Hoff argues that, although the Danish texts as they stand belong to the twelfth century, they contain strata of earlier material.

his code.[4] One would hardly guess that the Anglo-Saxon economy was almost entirely agricultural.

This literary contrast between Scandinavian and Anglo-Saxon cultures is interesting in itself, but, for the historian of agriculture, the important question is whether it reflects a similar contrast in social reality. Was it the case that important men in Anglo-Saxon society considered the cultivation of the soil, and the production of the food they ate, beneath their notice, while in contemporary Scandinavian society the equivalent figures had no such pretensions? This is important from an Anglo-Saxon point of view, since it affects the answer to another question: when the Anglo-Saxon Chronicle says that Viking[5] armies "divided the land and began to plough and to support themselves," did the men who had so recently been terrorising the inhabitants, and indeed rulers, of the English countryside, really start to cultivate it themselves?[6] Or did they at least concern themselves more closely with the practice and organisation of agriculture than did Anglo-Saxon landlords?[7]

Clearly these questions raise others, some of them very familiar, about the nature of Scandinavian settlement in Anglo-Saxon England: were the settlers in fact landlords only, or did the rank and file of the Viking armies become, as Stenton believed, peasant farmers?[8] If the former, did they acquire the inhabitants along with the land they took over, or did they perhaps settle it with slaves

---

[4] F. Liebermann, ed., *Die Gesetze der Angelsachsen*, vol. 1 (Halle, 1916), 36 (Alfred), 106–9 (Ine). I hope to examine the agricultural content of the Anglo-Saxon laws in a future publication; suffice it to say at present that the laws may in fact be somewhat more concerned with farming than they appear *prima facie*, due to the use of terms like *feoh*, which could either mean wealth in general, or more specifically 'cattle.'

[5] Because the ethnic origins of individual Vikings, other than named leaders, cannot be ascertained, I prefer not to refer to them collectively as "Scandinavian." The capital V is used to distinguish recognisable groups of raiders and/or settlers under Scandinavian leadership, often called "Danes" or "heathens" in Anglo-Saxon sources, from anyone else who might have been called in Old English *wicing*, 'pirate,' and hence in Modern English 'viking.'

[6] Anglo-Saxon Chronicle, MS A, *sub anno* 876: Janet Bately, ed., *MS A: A Semi-Diplomatic Edition*, The Anglo-Saxon Chronicle: A Collaborative Edition 3 (Cambridge, 1986), 50.

[7] See below for the suggestion that Scandinavian landlords' interest in farming was a result of the end of the Viking period, and therefore unlikely to be relevant to Viking settlement in England.

[8] F. M. Stenton, *Anglo-Saxon England*, 3rd ed. (Oxford, 1971), 519. See also idem, "Types of Manorial Structure in the Northern Danelaw," *Oxford Studies in Social and Legal History*, vol. 2, ed. Paul Vinogradoff (Oxford, 1910), 3–96, at 91. This is also the assumption behind idem, *The Free Peasantry of the Northern Danelaw* (Oxford, 1969).

or captives, or immigrant peasants from Scandinavia?[9] It seems to me likely that the surviving peasantry, if any did survive, would be left on the land in order to ensure maximum agricultural continuity and therefore productivity. Against this might be argued the known involvement of Vikings in the slave trade, but I suspect the Anglo-Saxon peasants of the "Danelaw" would have been more valuable to their new lords in their existing role than as mere merchandise. Farming must already have been severely disrupted in the areas settled by the Viking armies, and many peasants must have lost their lives. From the point of view of the settlers, the priority would have been to maximise production—after all, they themselves now had to make a living from this land on a long-term basis, rather than just consuming its products and moving on. To that end, they may have wanted to return agriculture, and its organisation, to the *status quo ante* as soon and as effectively as possible.

This, then, is one picture of what happened to Anglo-Saxon agriculture at the Viking settlement: any disruption was only temporary. It is a picture of continuity, or as much continuity as possible under the circumstances. Yet we know that major agricultural change did take place during the Anglo-Saxon period, and especially towards the end of it, that is to say, during and after the major period of Viking settlement in England. The best known of these changes is the beginning, at least, of the reorganisation of arable land, across large tracts of England, into open fields, and it is with this change that most of my paper will be concerned, since it has received a great deal of scholarly attention.[10] There were also changes, very possibly related, in both agricultural technology and the choice of crops. In the first case, the ard, or scratch-plough, was replaced by a larger, heavier plough with a coulter, to cut deeper into the soil, and a mouldboard to turn it over. This type of plough, heavy enough to need wheels, and several oxen to pull it, appears to have been in universal use in England after the Norman Conquest.[11] Meanwhile, barley, the commonest cereal in the early

---

[9] See, inter alia, Nils Lund, "The Settlers: Where Do We Get Them From—and Do We Need Them?" in *Proceedings of the Eighth Viking Congress*, ed. H. Bekker-Nielsen et al., Medieval Scandinavia Supplements 2 (Odense, 1981), 121–56.

[10] On the change to open-field farming there is an enormous literature, of which I shall cite only those items directly relevant to my argument. See Tom Williamson, "Debating the Open Fields," chap. 1 of his *Shaping Medieval Landscapes: Settlement, Society, Environment* (Macclesfield, 2003), 1–27, for a comprehensive review of scholarship on this topic.

[11] For discussion see David Hill, "*Sulh*: The Anglo-Saxon Plough," *Landscape History* 22 (2001): 5–19, although his conclusions differ from mine, and Grenville Astill, "An Archaeological Approach to the Development of Agricultural Technologies in Medieval England," in idem and John Langdon, eds., *Medieval Farming and Technology: The Impact of Agricultural Change in Northwest Europe*, Technology and Change in History 1 (Leiden, 1997), 193–223.

Anglo-Saxon period, declined in popularity, in favour of wheat, which was the most common bread-corn in lowland England by the time of the Conquest.[12]

The Open Fields

Historians have very reasonably asked why these major changes should have happened in the later Anglo-Saxon period (although it is fair to say that most of them have not worried unduly about the change in cereal usage). Given that we know that a widespread change in landlordship also took place across large parts of England at what may be the relevant period, various scholars over the years have suggested that open-field farming was introduced into England by Scandinavian settlers.[13] This is an attractive idea, but it seems to me that the precise evidence for their responsibility for this innovation has not been investigated systematically enough. This I propose to do in the main part of this paper, and to do so I shall adopt the traditional method of fictional detectives, looking for opportunity, for motivation, and finally for fingerprints.

---

[12] This change is discussed briefly in the standard works on Anglo-Saxon farming, and at slightly greater length in D. A. R. Banham, "The Knowledge and Uses of Food Plants in Anglo-Saxon England" (Ph.D. diss., University of Cambridge, 1990), 77–80; H. P. R. Finberg. "Anglo-Saxon England to 1042," in idem, ed., *The Agrarian History of England and Wales*, vol. 1.2: *AD 43–1042* (Cambridge, 1972), 385–525, at 421; Peter Fowler, "Farming in the Anglo-Saxon Landscape," *Anglo-Saxon England* 9 (1982): 263–80; H. E. Hallam, "England before the Norman Conquest," in idem, ed., *The Agrarian History of England and Wales*, vol. 2: *1042–1350* (Cambridge, 1988), 1–44. See also Debby Banham, *Food and Drink in Anglo-Saxon England* (Stroud, 2004), chap. 1, "The Staff of Life," esp. 13–16, and, for a rather longer perspective, Peter Fawler, *Farming in the First Millennium AD: British Agriculture between Julius Caesar and William the Conqueror* (Cambridge, 2002), 212–13.

[13] For instance, C. R. Hart, "The Origins of Huntingdonshire," paper delivered to the Centre for Regional Studies, Anglia Ruskin University, Cambridge, 28 October 1999 (Dr Hart is currently revising this material for publication). Finberg, "Anglo-Saxon England," 491–92, attributed the system's "egalitarian" character to "free and equal Danish farmers." On a more local scale, Edward Martin has recently attributed the distribution of open-field systems (much more common in the north and west) in Suffolk to the presence or absence of Viking settlement or influence: see "Medieval Settlement Surveys: Papers from the MSRG Spring Conference 2004, Oxford," *Medieval Settlement Research Group Annual Report* 19 (2005 for 2004), 5–8, at 6–7. As Christopher Dyer remarks on p. 8 of the same report, the tendency recently has been to concentrate on smaller-scale variation, rather than to seek general explanations.

Opportunity

To begin with opportunity, let us see whether the Viking settlers were in fact in the right place at the right time. The dates of their settlement are known fairly securely, by early medieval standards: the Anglo-Saxon Chronicle (its dates adjusted by modern scholarship) tells us that this happened in 875 in Northumbria, in 877 in the part of Mercia not entrusted to Ceolwulf, and in 879 in East Anglia.[14] Was this also the period when the open fields were laid out? It has to be said that, apart from some clusters of references in charters from the tenth century onwards,[15] the evidence for the existence of open fields in particular places is post-Conquest, and in most places late medieval if not modern.[16] For many parishes, the only evidence for their open fields is the nineteenth-century enclosure map that abolished them. However, it is clear from nearly all these references, even those dating from the twelfth century, that the field layouts they describe are not new, but have been established for some time. The question is, how long? It has not been seriously maintained for some time now that the system was brought to England by the original Anglo-Saxon settlers,[17] but David Hall, who knows the archaeological evidence for open fields, especially those of Northamptonshire, better than most people, proposes that the reorganisation may well go back before the middle of the ninth century.[18] His argument is that the ridge and furrow of the former open fields can in many places be shown to overlie the remains of earlier Anglo-Saxon settlements. The latest datable finds from these settlement sites are Middle Saxon pottery believed to have gone out of use around AD 850, and no subsequent Anglo-Saxon settlements are found in these parishes. Hall therefore believes that the inhabitants moved straight to

---

[14] Anglo-Saxon Chronicle, MS A, *sub annis* 876, 877 and 880: Bately, ed., *MS A*, 50–51.

[15] For a study of one such cluster, see Della Hooke, "Open-field Agriculture: The Evidence from the Pre-Conquest Charters of the West Midlands," in *The Origins of Open-Field Agriculture*, ed. Trevor Rowley (London and Totowa, NJ, 1981), 39–64. Finberg, "Anglo-Saxon England," discusses the charters at 487–95. However, it should be borne in mind that references to *gedal-land* or *communis terra* do not necessarily denote arable, nor therefore open fields. I intend to examine the charter references in detail in a future publication.

[16] For some of the earliest post-Conquest references, see Hallam, "England before the Norman Conquest," 42–43.

[17] See for instance S. Applebaum, "Roman Britain," in *Agrarian History*, ed. Finberg, 1.2: 3–277, at 262, and Finberg, "Anglo-Saxon England," 398–99. For earlier views, see H. L. Gray, *English Field Systems*, Harvard Historical Studies 22 (Cambridge, MA, 1915), and C. S. and C. S. Orwin, *The Open Fields* (Oxford, 1938).

[18] David Hall, *Medieval Fields*, Shire Archaeology (Aylesbury, 1982), 46–53. See also idem, *Open Fields of Northamptonshire*, Northamptonshire Record Society Publications 38 (Northampton, 1995), 130–31.

the sites of the present villages by about 850, and laid out their open fields at the same time, although he admits that this last step of the argument cannot be proven.

Most scholars would agree in broad terms with Hall's dating for the nucleation of villages, allowing for regional variation and local circumstances, but not all are convinced that the open fields were laid out at the same time.[19] Nucleation of settlement is probably a prerequisite for open-field cultivation, since it would be very difficult to reorganise a large area of arable land into subdivided fields if there were farms and hamlets scattered across it, but open-field farming is not a prerequisite for nucleation. It is perfectly possible for people living in one village to farm their land in separate enclosed fields, possibly at some distance, rather than in shares of two or three huge open fields surrounding the village. Admittedly, this does raise the question of why else people would move from their scattered farms and hamlets into nucleated villages, given the resulting inconvenience of reaching their fields. It is not my purpose in this paper to account for settlement nucleation, but the social disruption, and indeed physical dangers, of the ninth century in England could possibly have provided sufficient motivation, without concomitant agricultural reorganisation. Whatever the reason for nucleation, the fact remains that there is no evidence that the fields were reorganised immediately afterwards, nor in most cases for several centuries. Those villages with very early evidence for open fields could have been typical of the surrounding settlements, or they may equally well have been pioneers of agricultural innovation. The twelfth century, or even a later one, could be proposed as an alternative to Hall's ninth for the widespread change to open-field farming.[20] The case that Scandinavian settlers were responsible therefore remains not proven.

I have been dealing so far in broad geographical generalisations. This is to some extent unavoidable, in view of the paucity of evidence from most individual places, but it is possible to be a good deal more precise than I have been. Open fields are by no means universal in England. The areas in which they exist are shown, on a broad scale, in Figure 1.[21] The central zone of this map is the area of England typified by nucleated settlement and the classic "Midland system" of two or three open fields. There are, it is true, quite a few places within the central province, "village England," from which there is no evidence for open fields, and some in the other zones where open fields did exist. However, these latter are generally small systems in parishes with dispersed or semi-nucleated settlement

---

[19] On nucleation, see among others H. F. Hamerow, "Settlement Mobility and the 'Middle Saxon Shift': Rural Settlements and Settlement Patterns in Anglo-Saxon England," *Anglo-Saxon England* 20 (1991): 1–17.

[20] The chief proponent of a late dating has been Joan Thirsk, "The Common Fields," *Past and Present* 29 (1964): 3–29.

[21] This supersedes the frontispiece of Howard Levi Gray, *English Field Systems*, 2nd ed. (Cambridge, MA, 1959).

FIGURE I
Main zone of open field farming in England, based on enclosure records. Smaller areas of open field country, and places without open fields within the main zone, are ignored. Stars indicate pre-Conquest evidence for fields divided into strips, but this distribution owes as much to the survival of documents as to Anglo-Saxon farming practice. After Brian K. Roberts and Stuart Wrathmell, *Region and Place: A Study of English Rural Settlement* (London, 2002), figs 5.1 and 5.4.

patterns, where small enclosed fields held in severalty are also found. The western zone is mainly characterised by pastoral farming, where only small areas of land were suitable for arable cultivation, and an infield-outfield arrangement, with continuous cropping of the best or most sheltered land in the infield, and occasional cropping of parts of the outfield, was more common than an open-field system.

If we compare this map with one of Scandinavian settlement, however arrived at, it is clear that the two do not correspond at all well (see Figure 2). There are areas of the so-called Danelaw without open fields, and districts with open fields where no Scandinavians are believed to have settled. Moreover, some of the best known rural settlement sites from the Viking period in England, such as

FIGURE 2
The "Danelaw": main areas of Scandinavian-derived place-names in England (shaded), and the boundary drawn up by Alfred and Guthrum. Devon and Cornwall, which have no Scandinavian place-names, are omitted. After Else Roesdahl, *The Vikings* (Harmondsworth, 1991).

Ribblehead (Yorkshire), Bryant's Gill (Cumbria), and Simy Folds (County Durham), are not nucleated villages at all, but isolated farmhouses of the long-house type, with their own enclosed fields, miles, as far as we can tell, from anyone else's.[22] This is of course partly a matter of definition: these settlements are

---

[22] A. King, "Gauber High Pasture, Ribblehead: An Interim Report," in *Viking Age York and the North*, ed. R. A. Hall, CBA Research Report 27 (York, 1978), 31–36; D. Coggins, K. J. Fairless, and C. E. Batey, "Simy Folds: An Early Medieval Settlement in Upper Teesdale," *Medieval Archaeology* 27 (1982): 1–26; S. Dickinson, "Bryant's Gill, Kentmere: Another 'Viking Period' Ribblehead?" in *The Scandinavians in Cumbria*, ed. J. R. Baldwin and I. D. Whyte, Scottish Society for Northern Studies Occasional Publications 3 (Edinburgh, 1985), 83–88.

described as "Viking" or "Scandinavian" farmsteads, while conventional "English" villages of the same period, such as Goltho (Lincolnshire) or Wharram Percy (Yorkshire), even within the "Danelaw," are not usually distinguished by the same markers.[23] Nevertheless, it is clear that dispersed settlement continued to exist within the areas settled by Vikings, and in some places still exists at the present day.[24] If open-field farming was introduced to England by Scandinavian settlers, they did not introduce it everywhere they lived, and someone else must have introduced it to other areas. It would have to be argued that the practice was introduced first to some "Scandinavian" areas of England, but for some reason not to all, and then spread to other areas.

Motivation

We thus have a much less mechanical picture of the beginnings of open-field farming. Scandinavian settlers did not introduce it just because they were Scandinavian; if they did bring it in, presumably they had more complex reasons for doing so. Thus we arrive at the detective's next question, that of motivation. Why would these settlers, or indeed anyone else, have wanted to change to this method of farming? It would after all have entailed considerable disruption, as I have already argued, and consequent loss of production. Of course, there had already been disruption and loss of production. We really have no idea what state the countryside was in by the time Viking settlement took place. It might be the case that previous ways of managing the land had virtually ceased to function, and the situation was ripe for change. Indeed, it might be argued that, in order to derive satisfactory yields from the battered estates they were taking over, the former Vikings, never noted for overlooking opportunities for profit, would have felt compelled to introduce the most efficient agricultural system known to them.

Indeed, increased efficiency is the usual reason advanced for the introduction of open-field farming, irrespective of who introduced it. There are of course no yield figures for the Anglo-Saxon period, so any discussion of efficiency is of necessity qualitative, not to say speculative. I think it is also worth examining, briefly, what is meant by "efficient" in this context. In economic discussions, it

---

[23] For Goltho, see G. Beresford, *Goltho: The Development of an Early Medieval Manor, c. 850–1150*, English Heritage Archaeological Report 4 (London, 1987), and for Wharram Percy, M. Beresford and J. G. Hurst, *Wharram Percy: Deserted Medieval Village* (London, 1990). Now see also Julian D. Richards, "Finding the Vikings: The Search for Anglo-Scandinavian Rural Settlement in the Northern Danelaw," in *Vikings and the Danelaw: Select Papers from the Proceedings of the Thirteenth Viking Congress, Nottingham and York, 21–30 August 1997*, ed. James Graham-Campbell et al. (Oxford, 2001), 269–77.

[24] For a recent study of such an area, see Andrew Fleming, *Swaledale: Valley of the Wild River* (Edinburgh, 1998).

seems usually to be concerned with the ability to yield a "profit" for an owner.[25] Applied to early medieval agriculture, this would mean rents in money or kind for landlords from their tenants' land, as well as the surplus production of their own (the "demesne"). However, all the references we have to rents in the Anglo-Saxon period give fixed figures, and there is no indication of a mechanism for raising them if more efficient techniques, or any other cause, gave rise to higher yields.[26] As far as we can tell, then, any increase in productivity on tenanted land would be to the advantage of those working the land, rather than those receiving their rent, and landlords would only benefit from improved production on their demesnes. Unfortunately we cannot establish what size Anglo-Saxon demesnes were *vis-à-vis* tenanted land,[27] nor how easily they could be expanded or contracted if this suited the landlord, let alone how profitable demesne and peasant farming were in relation to each other.[28] However, it must be the case that, if landlords did not (or could not) raise rents, they only stood to benefit from a new system that included their own land. In other words, the demesne would have to be divided up into strips among those of the peasants in the open fields, and not kept as separate enclosures. In the Anglo-Saxon period it is likely that both "block" and scattered demesnes existed, as was the case later in the Middle Ages. If landlords with block demesnes were unable to put up rents, it is hard to see why they would want to introduce a system that would improve only the productivity of their tenants' land.

This brings us to an important point: so far we have been assuming that the new system was indeed introduced by landlords, and therefore that it is landlords' motivation that is relevant to the discussion. Most historians have also supposed that the innovation was seigneurial. However, we should not ignore the possibility that the new fields were laid out on the initiative of the people actually working the land concerned. There is no reason to assume that the early medieval

---

[25] For an extended exercise in the application of economic theory to English open-field agriculture, see Robert M. Townsend, *The Medieval Village Economy* (Princeton, 1993).

[26] See Sally P. J. Harvey, "The Extent and Profitability of Demesne Agriculture in England in the Later Eleventh Century," in *Social Relations and Ideas: Essays in Honour of R. H. Hilton*, ed. T. H. Aston et al. (Cambridge, 1983), 45–72, at 49 and 60, for suggestions of peasant rents being raised after the Norman Conquest.

[27] For the suggestion of a "standard inland" of 40 acres in 100, and some 11th-century figures for Northamptonshire, see Tony Brown and Glen Foard, "The Saxon Landscape: A Regional Perspective," in *The Archaeology of Landscape: Studies Presented to Christopher Taylor*, ed. Paul Everson and Tom Williamson (Manchester, 1998), 65–94, at 84.

[28] Harvey, "Extent and Profitability," discusses all these questions for the immediately post-Conquest period but, despite her title, offers little detail on profitability. In any case, she regards this period, quite justifiably, as being one of great change (70). She does offer some examples of estates with large demesnes in 1066, based upon number of demesne and tenant ploughs (57–58), but all these belong to very large landholders, including ecclesiastical institutions, and may thus not be typical.

peasant was incapable of making such a sweeping change. Collectively, peasants must have been capable of co-operation in order to operate the open-field system, and it need not have been a prohibitively greater challenge to co-operate in starting one. The decision could have been taken in some forerunner of the manor courts that administered the system in the later Middle Ages. If the change was indeed a peasant initiative, it might make sense to look to Stenton's Viking rank and file as the innovators. More importantly, perhaps, peasants might have a different conception of agricultural efficiency from their landlords. From their point of view, there might be a trade-off between productivity and labour input, once their own needs and renders to their lord had been taken care of. It should never be forgotten that medieval agriculture was relentlessly hard work, harder than twenty-first-century sedentary workers can easily imagine. There might come a point when peasant cultivators, whether co-operating or individually, might consider conserving energy more important than wringing more output from the land. But of course there is even less evidence for what was done by peasants, let alone why they did it, than for the actions of their social superiors.

Fingerprints

Another possible type of motivation would be cultural. Scandinavian settlers might have wanted to farm in this way in England because it reminded them of home. Open-field farming was indeed practised in Denmark and Sweden, so this argument has something to recommend it. However, it needs more detail, such as specifically Scandinavian features in English field-systems, since it has to be remembered that such systems were also pretty widespread in other parts of Europe. As far as field layout is concerned, such features are hard to find. There are variations in, for instance, the length of strips in both England and Scandinavia, as well as in Frankish systems. Indeed, the extra-long strips to be found in Yorkshire have been compared with German systems rather than Scandinavian ones.[29] In overall terms, however, layouts look pretty similar in all these areas, and indeed in Slavic lands, where in some cases they are known to have been introduced in the eighteenth and nineteenth centuries.[30] On top of that, the plans of nearly all known open-field systems represent centuries of development, not the situation when they were newly laid out. Thus later influences may have a lot more to do with what we see on the ground or a map than whatever may have influenced the original adoption of the system (see Figures 3–7).

One feature of English open-field systems which has been attributed to Scandinavian influence is the regular allotment of strips in the fields in turn to

---

[29] See for instance Hall, "Northamptonshire," 131–35.

[30] See Maria Dobrowolska, "The Morphogenesis of the Agrarian Landscape of Southern Poland," *Geografiska annaler* 43 (1961): 26–45; and Svetozar Ilesic, "Die jüngeren Gewannfluren in Nordwestjugoslawien," *Geografiska annaler* 43 (1961): 130–37.

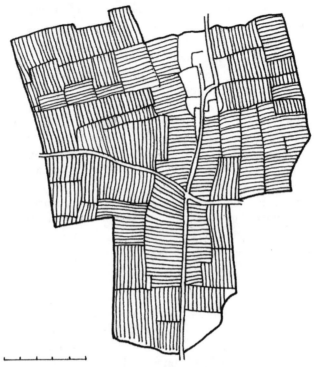

FIGURE 3
The open fields of a settlement in England: Etton, Cambridgeshire. Scale = 500 metres. After David Hall, *Medieval Fields* (Aylesbury, 1982).

the inhabitants of each house-plot in the village, so that each villager would have their neighbours' strips on either side of their own in the fields.[31] Associated with this regular allotment (in the minds of scholars, if not always on the ground) is the habit of referring to those strips at the south or east end of a particular furlong as *versus solem*, or some similar expression, and those to the north or west as *versus umbram* etc. These two features are combined in the *solskifte* system prescribed by law in parts of medieval Sweden. However, evidence for the regular allotment of strips to toft-holders in England is fairly rare, and most of it dates from long after the Anglo-Saxon period.[32] Moreover, documents using phrases such as *versus solem* do not necessarily refer to places where there is evidence for

---

[31] See George C. Homans, "Terroirs ordonnées et champs orientés: une hypothèse sur le village anglais," *Annales d'histoire économique et sociale* 8 (1936): 438–48; and Sölve Göransson, "Regular Open-field Pattern in England and Scandinavian *solskifte*," *Geografiske annaler* 43 (1961): 83–104.

[32] This rarity is recognised by Göransson, "Regular Open-field Pattern," 84.

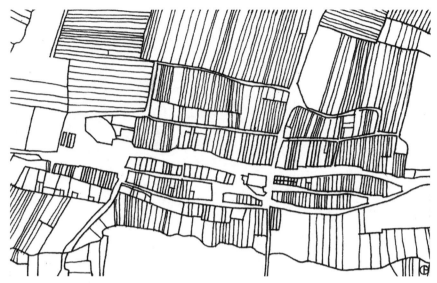

FIGURE 4
The open fields (central portion) of a settlement in France: La Neuveville-aux-Bois, Meurthe et Moselle. After J. Peltre, "Les Éspaces collectifs villageois: l'éxample des 'usoirs' lorrains," in *Villages, Fields and Frontiers*, ed. B. K. Roberts and R. E. Glasscock (Oxford, 1983), 93–101.

regular allotment (in fact, I am not aware of any that do). It is not therefore legitimate to infer that, where the one exists, the other must too. Again, all these documents are post-Conquest. I would therefore be cautious about assuming that there was ever a system in England analogous to the Swedish *solskifte*, and even more so in projecting its supposed existence back into the Anglo-Saxon period. If regular allotment of strips to the houses in a village ever was common in England (and there must have been some means of distributing the land in the open fields when they were first laid out), we hardly need to appeal to Scandinavian influence, let alone sun-worship, to explain it. It is a straightforward method, and might easily have occurred spontaneously to peasants or landlords in different parts of Europe. Similarly, the observation that the sun rises in the east, and is in the northern hemisphere normally to be seen towards the south, could have occurred to English villagers or clerks without anyone having to import it from elsewhere. The possession of strips with more or less sunlight would after all be a matter of practical concern. Sweden is, moreover, not a part of Scandinavia that we usually look to for influence on England. That role is taken by Denmark for the east of Britain, and Norway in the west.

If methods of allotting land are difficult to decipher, dating is even more obscure, if anything. The evidence for open fields in Scandinavia is as late as, if not later than, in England. Settlement nucleation also seems to have begun later

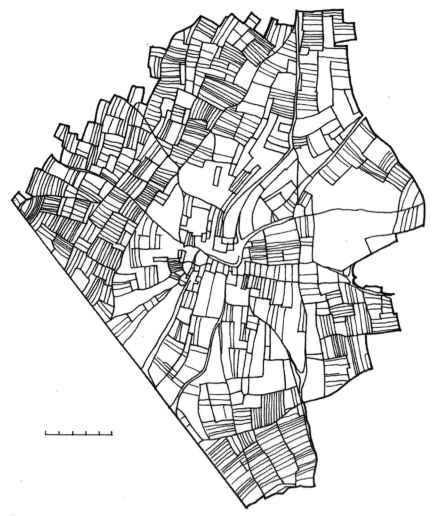

FIGURE 5
The open fields of a settlement in Germany: Raitenbuch, Franconia. Scale = 500 metres. After F. Eigler, "Regular Settlements in Franconia Founded by the Franks in the Early Middle Ages," in *Villages, Fields and Frontiers*, ed. Roberts and Glasscock.

FIGURE 6
The open fields of a settlement in Denmark: Brarup, Falster. Scale = 500 metres.
After K.-E. Frandsen, "Glebe and Vicarage on the Island of Falster, Denmark," in
Villages, Fields and Frontiers, ed. Roberts and Glasscock.

there than in England, and since there are no invaders to pin any innovations
on, few scholars would argue for open fields before the eleventh or twelfth century.[33] This is obviously rather late for them to have influenced a similar innovation in England. Bjørn Poulsen has attributed changes in Danish agriculture to
"the shift from a Viking economy to a more peaceful regime, where the leaders
of society had to earn their fortunes at home instead of in foreign adventures."[34]
In other words, this shift was very similar to the transition that happened earlier when the Vikings "divided up the land and began to plough" in England.
Poulsen does not pursue this point, but it might be argued that former Vikings

[33] One of the few is Mats Widgren, who proposes a date range of 800–1200 CE
for parts of southern Sweden: "Strip Fields in an Iron-Age Context: A Case Study from
Västergötland, Sweden," *Landscape History* 12 (1990): 5–24.

[34] B. Poulsen, "Agricultural Technology in Medieval Denmark," in *Medieval Farming*, ed. Astill and Langdon, 115–45, at 116. Eric Christiansen, *The Norsemen in the Viking Age* (Oxford, 2002), 194, states categorically that open-field farming "was definitely
not a feature of viking-age agriculture [in Scandinavia] . . . and attempts to link its appearance in England to Danish settlers are therefore pointless."

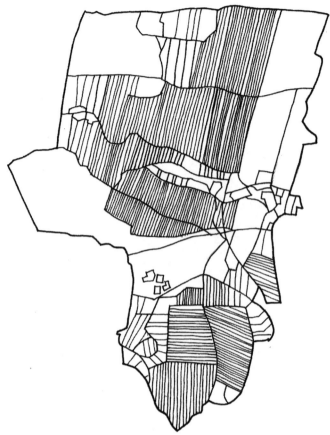

FIGURE 7
The open fields of a settlement in Poland: Rączna, Cracow district. After Do-
brolowska, "Agrarian Landscape of Southern Poland."

in Denmark imported new agricultural ideas from England, or that they looked
to England as a country where people like them had also made the change from
raiding to raising crops and livestock.

It has thus proved hard to demonstrate that Scandinavians had either the
opportunity or the motivation to introduce open-field farming into England, and
their fingerprints are even more elusive.

Ploughs

In the field of agricultural technology, we shall concentrate on ploughs. Another major piece of machinery, the water-mill, also came into use in the later Anglo-Saxon period, and may well have been connected in some way with the reorganisation of arable land, but the introduction of open-field farming into England has more often been associated with that of the heavy mouldboard plough. The argument is that this type of plough, which turns the soil to the side, worked best in a "spiral" motion, with the first furrow in what would be the middle of the ploughed area, and the others building up on either side of it, rather than starting at one side and travelling up and down until one reached the other, which would entail the plough-beasts walking on the ploughed tilth. Eventually the area produced would become excessively wide, and a new first furrow would be drawn, and the whole process started over again. Furthermore, the plough, plus the team of oxen required to pull it, needed a lot of land to turn around.[35] Oxen are apparently unable to cross their feet, which makes them much more difficult to turn round than horses. A single horse can also pull a plough which would need several oxen, two abreast.[36] A plough pulled by oxen is thus much more unwieldy than one using horse traction, and might, depending on the number of yokes, need many yards to change direction. The less the plough-team had to turn, the less land had to be set aside for this purpose, rather than actually growing crops. The way to avoid turning more than necessary was to set out the land in long thin strips, rather than the small squarish enclosures more suited to ard cultivation. This makes sense, but does not account for the fact that the mouldboard plough was apparently in use in Roman Britain, with its small enclosed "Celtic" fields.[37] We therefore need to be cautious about assuming that open fields necessarily mean heavy plough, and *vice versa*. Indeed, we should remember that parts of Sweden managed to convert to open fields while retaining the ard into the modern period.[38]

It is therefore necessary to look for specific evidence for the different types of plough in England. Of written evidence there is very little, and that little hard to

[35] Orwin and Orwin, *Open Fields*, 34–35.

[36] See John Langdon, *Horses, Oxen and Technological Innovation: The Use of Draught Animals in English Farming from 1066 to 1500* (Cambridge, 1986), 4–21, for the transition from ox to horse as the main plough beast, although he attributes this to a combination of technological changes rather than the agility of the horse.

[37] See, for instance, John Percival, *The Roman Villa: A Historical Introduction* (London, 1976), 114–16. Sian E. Rees, *Agricultural Implements in Prehistoric and Roman Britain*, British Archaeological Reports 69 (Oxford, 1979), discusses 26 Romano-British coulters (59–61), but no mouldboards.

[38] Janken Myrdal, "The Agricultural Transformation of Sweden, 1000–1300," in *Medieval Farming*, ed. Astill and Langdon, 147–171, fig. 7.1.

FIGURE 8
An ard. The iron share is shown in black.

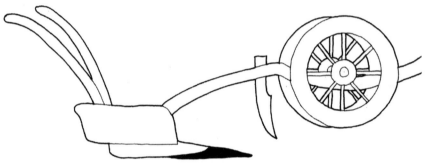

FIGURE 9
A heavy plough. Share shown in black.

interpret. Very few Anglo-Saxon texts describe a plough or ploughing at all, let alone in enough detail to distinguish an ard from the type with a mouldboard. For example the "Charm for unfruitful land" gives detailed directions for a series of arcane procedures, and ploughing plays an important part in the ritual described, but the only component of the plough mentioned is the beam, the main part of its wooden frame.[39] Thus we could be dealing with either an ard or a mouldboard plough. Ploughing was of course not at all an arcane procedure to an Anglo-Saxon audience, and that is no doubt why no detailed instructions had to be given. The plough itself, similarly, was a familiar object, and so there was no need to describe even the part of it centrally involved in the ritual, let alone the others.

It should be no surprise, then, that we are given little in the way of detailed description of either plough or ploughing in the late Anglo-Saxon estate management literature, nor in Ælfric's descriptions of the various rural trades in his *Colloquy*,

---

[39] E. van K. Dobbie, *Anglo-Saxon Minor Poems*, ASPR 6 (London and New York, 1942), 117–18.

dating from around the year 1000. The *Gerefa* tells us in what seasons ploughing should be carried out, and the *Rectitudines singularum personarum* by whom (mainly *geburs*), and Ælfric gives us a touching testimony to the hard work involved.[40] Of these, Ælfric is the only one to describe how the work is done, and even he gives little detail. He is also the only one to describe the equipment. He refers to share and coulter, but not to a mouldboard. This is undoubtedly because the share and coulter, being iron components, were detachable from the frame of the plough, and therefore attaching them constituted part of the ploughman's *mycel gedeorf.* The mouldboard was made of wood, and would therefore have been permanently jointed into the frame.[41] While coulter and mouldboard usually go together, ards with coulters did exist, and so it cannot be assumed that the one never existed in the absence of the other. Ælfric's smith also refers to share and coulter, as well as a goad, again the iron parts that a smith would have made, but he would have no interest in a mouldboard, if one were in use.[42] The *Colloquy* is therefore no more than suggestive as to whether a mouldboard was in use in England around 1000 AD. The *Gerefa* also has a list of tools, including plough equipment, interestingly giving the same items as Ælfric, share, coulter, and goad, but again no mouldboard.[43] The *Gerefa* in its surviving form belongs to the eleventh century, so even if its plough did have a mouldboard, its evidence would leave us agnostic as to when in the Anglo-Saxon period this device was introduced.

The one text, paradoxically, that does provide a reasonably clear reference to a mouldboard is a riddle, number 21 in the Exeter Book.[44] It does not actually name the component (riddles are meant to be enigmatic, after all), but, after describing the two points (share and coulter) inserted through its body, the plough (this being a first-person riddle) states that *feallep on sidan / pæt ic topum tere*: 'what I tear with my teeth falls to the side.'[45] This is not conclusively a reference to a mouldboard, since the crucial point is not made that the soil falls to one side only, and not to both as it would from an ard, but this distinguishing characteristic is identified earlier in the poem: *me bip gongendre grene on healfe / ond min swæð sweotol sweart on opre*, 'as I walk there is green to the side of me and, my track clear, black on the other.'[46] Since the Exeter Book dates from the second half of the tenth century, this also takes our evidence for a mouldboard a bit further back into the period of Viking settlement.

---

[40] *Gerefa* 12, in Liebermann, *Gesetze* 1: 454; *Rectitudines* 4.1b–2, in Liebermann, *Gesetze* 1: 447; G. N. Garmonsway, ed., *Ælfric's Colloquy*, rev. ed. (Exeter, 1991), 20–21.

[41] Indeed, Hill, *"Sulh,"* 14, assumes that they are cut from a single piece of wood.

[42] Garmonsway, *Colloquy*, 39.

[43] *Gerefa* 15, in Liebermann, *Gesetze* 1: 455.

[44] G. P. Krapp and E. van K. Dobbie, *The Exeter Book*, ASPR 3 (New York and London, 1936), 191.

[45] Lines 13–14.

[46] Lines 9–10.

Manuscript illustrations are hardly conclusive either. Pictures of ploughs are found in the Harley Psalter (three), in the Junius (or "Cædmon") manuscript of Old English poetry (two), and illustrating two calendars in Cotton manuscripts Tiberius B.v and Julius A.vi.[47] There are several problems involved in using these pictures as evidence for Anglo-Saxon farming practice. In the first place (*pace* David Hill) they are much more likely to have been copied from an exemplar than drawn from the life, and some of their exemplars were certainly continental.[48] This means that, if they are any guide to what happened in real life, it is not necessarily Anglo-Saxon real life. Such a caveat applies most strongly to the Harley Psalter, which is certainly copied from the Utrecht Psalter, but possibly to the two calendars as well. Secondly, none of these illustrations unambiguously shows a mouldboard. Coulter, wheels, and the general shape of a heavy plough are present in the two calendars, and probably in Junius 11, together with pairs of draught animals, but the eye of faith is required to believe that these ploughs would really turn the sod, rather than just digging into it.

The illustrations that have most frequently been identified as showing a "real" Anglo-Saxon plough are those in the two Cotton calendars.[49] Both of these belong to the first half of the eleventh century, but it is likely that Julius is the earlier. Its illustrations are similar in style to the Harley Psalter, and probably derive likewise from drawings of the school of Rheims (although whether these were attached to a calendar or not is far from clear), whereas those of Tiberius have been adapted to a full-colour technique. The content of the two cycles is extremely similar, quite close enough to suggest that one was copied from the other, and the similarity is particularly striking in the picture for January, which shows ploughing. Tiberius, then, has to be regarded as dependent on Julius, and the latter should be the focus of attention. As Figure 10 shows, its plough does appear to have a mouldboard, although one would hesitate to place too much

[47] I omit Cambridge, Trinity College MS. R. 17.1, listed by Fowler, "Farming in the Anglo-Saxon Landscape," 269, since this manuscript is dated to the middle of the twelfth century. I also leave out of discussion the Bayeux Tapestry, because of its late date, the possibility that it was not made in England, and the more disturbing possibility that the agricultural scenes have been "restored" in modern times. I should like to thank David Hill for pointing out this last caveat. The Harley and Junius illustrations can usefully be compared in Thomas Ohlgren, *Anglo-Saxon Textual Illustration: Photographs of Sixteen Manuscripts with Descriptions and Index* (Kalamazoo, 1992). For the calendars, see below.

[48] See Hill, "*Sulh*," 5–7, and for this problem in general, Martin Carver, "Contemporary Artefacts Illustrated in Late Saxon Manuscripts," *Archaeologia* 108 (1986): 117–45.

[49] Nos. 87 and 62 in E. Temple, *Anglo-Saxon Manuscripts 900–1066*, A Survey of Manuscripts Illuminated in the British Isles 2 (London, 1976). Facsimile of Tiberius B.v, with comparative illustrations from Julius A.vi: P. M. J. McGurk, ed., *An Eleventh-Century Anglo-Saxon Illustrated Miscellany*, Early English Manuscripts in Facsimile 21 (Copenhagen, 1983).

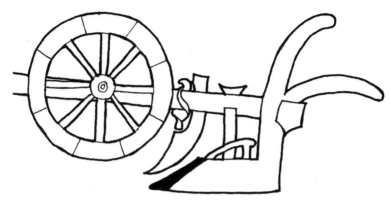

FIGURE 10

The plough shown in British Library Cotton manuscripts Julius A.vi and Tiberius B.v. The share is shown in black, as in the original. After McGurk, *Eleventh-Century Miscellany*.

weight on this conclusion. Of the other relevant illustrations, those in the Harley Psalter, following Utrecht, definitely show ards, while those in Junius 11 look like "heavy" ploughs, but are too stylised to allow detailed identification.

All these manuscript illustrations belong to the later part of the period, when we would expect to find heavy ploughs, but to accept that as evidence would be to beg the original question. Since some of the pictures show an ard, it must be true either that these continued in use alongside the heavy plough, or that manuscript illustrators copied their exemplars faithfully even when these were "out of date", and cannot therefore be used as evidence for agricultural practice in England at the time they were drawn. (Indeed, the Harley artists may have believed that the Utrecht illustrations were a reliable portrayal of the agricultural practices of biblical Palestine, in which case it would have been anachronistic to "update" them.) In fact it seems likely that both of these propositions are true, and that, moreover, "hybrid" or transitional forms, with some of the features of the heavy plough, were also in use in early medieval England. It is unlikely, after all, that Anglo-Saxon farmers were as concerned with distinguishing the two types of plough as modern scholars. They are much more likely to have adopted technical innovations gradually and piecemeal, as they became aware of them, as the necessary means became available, and as problems arose that could be solved as a result.

Archaeological evidence is also fairly ambiguous, in that, apart from a single coulter, the only excavated remains of Anglo-Saxon ploughs are shares, dating from the later part of the period (see Figure 11). While it has been argued that these are types characteristic of heavy ploughs, this is by no means certain.[50]

---

[50] See Astill, "Agricultural Technology," 201–2 and fig. 9.2.

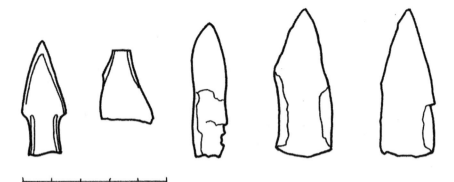

FIGURE II

Anglo-Saxon ploughshares. From left to right: Thetford, Norfolk (two); Nazeing, Essex; Westley Waterless, Cambridgeshire; and St Neots, Huntingdonshire. All probably tenth-century. Scale = 200 millimetres. After Astill, "Agricultural Technologies," and Hill, "*Sulh*."

The distinction seems to be made on grounds of size, ards being usually smaller and lighter than mouldboard ploughs, but this need not invariably be the case. Similar shares have been found in Scandinavia, but the shape of these items is functional, rather than culturally determined: equally similar shares were in use throughout Europe, throughout the Middle Ages and up to the introduction of factory-made ploughs in the nineteenth century. The surviving ploughshares therefore tell us neither what type of plough was in use, nor whether it might have been modelled on that of any other region. All of them date to the tenth or eleventh century, again the period when we expect to find heavy ploughs, but we should beware of circular argument here too. Furthermore, two of them come from urban sites, and two others from smithy assemblages, rather than from an agricultural context. No wooden parts of ploughs have been excavated from Anglo-Saxon sites, or, if they have, they have not been recognised. In the British climate, wood is preserved only in waterlogged conditions, and to date these have mostly been found at urban sites such as York and Norwich. These might seem unlikely to yield agricultural equipment, and if they did, it might be argued that it was not representative of rural assemblages. The likelihood of a whole Anglo-Saxon plough being excavated therefore seems rather remote, and that of its being classifiable according to the concerns of agricultural historians probably even more so.

Turning to the landscape, the existence of ridge and furrow is almost certainly evidence for a mouldboard plough, since it is produced by turning the soil; the ard leaves a very different criss-cross pattern. But ridge and furrow, like all landscape evidence, is very hard to date, and may not be coeval with the origin of open fields in the places where it is found. The only three examples of ridge and furrow archaeologically dated to the Anglo-Saxon period come from the tenth and eleventh centuries and, apart from Sandal Castle, Wakefield, from the very margins of Anglo-Saxon England: Hen Domen, Montgomery, and Gwythian, Cornwall. Of these locations, only Sandal seems likely to have been subject to much Scandinavian influence.[51] Intriguingly, it is also the only one within the "central province" of England, the *locus classicus* of the open fields. On the very limited evidence so far available, therefore, it seems that mouldboard ploughs and open fields were not necessarily associated in the Anglo-Saxon period.

Finally, a linguistic argument has been put forward for the introduction of the heavy plough into England from Denmark around the year 900,[52] but, while the names of this implement in the two languages, OE *ploh* and ON *pløgr*, are certainly related, this in itself does not entitle us to conclude that the word was necessarily introduced into English from the Danish, let alone that it was accompanied by the object it stood for.[53] In fact, the same evidence could just as well be used to argue for the opposite movement. Nor is it certain that *ploh* refers specifically to a mouldboard plough. Since it only appears at the very end of the Anglo-Saxon period, its predecessor *sulh* must have referred to both ard and heavy plough, and this may be true of *ploh* as well. Bringing all this material together, one has to conclude that, although the earliest evidence for the use of a mouldboard plough in Anglo-Saxon England does cluster in the tenth and eleventh centuries, this does not justify our pinning its introduction on Scandinavian settlers.

Cereal crops

Finally, the choice of crops. Although the precise relationship is obscure, I strongly suspect that there is a connection between the adoption of open-field agriculture and the move to wheat as the main bread-corn. In the classic three-field system, the fields were of roughly equal size: one fallow, one sown in the autumn, almost entirely with

---

[51] See Astill, "Fields," table 4.1.

[52] Lynn White, *Medieval Technology and Social Change* (Oxford, 1962), 51–53.

[53] *Pace* White, the OED is agnostic on the origin of *plough*. F. Holthausen, *Altenglisches etymologisches Wörterbuch* (Heidelberg, 1934), *s.v.*, regards it as a common Germanic word. In fact, *ploh* is not recorded in the meaning 'plough' until well after the Conquest (the entry for 1131 in the E manuscript of the Chronicle), but it appears with the meaning 'ploughland' in a charm for stolen cattle in a manuscript that may be pre-Conquest (BL Cotton Tiberius A.iii), and this usage probably implies that it existed in the meaning 'plough' as well. Both are cited by OED *s.v.* The charm is edited by [T.] O. Cockayne, *Leechdoms, Wortcunning and Starcraft of Early England* (London, 1866), 3: 286, and the chronicle entry by Susan Irvine, *MS E, The Anglo-Saxon Chronicle: A Collaborative Edition 7* (Cambridge, 2004), 132. Jane Roberts and Christian Kay with Lynne Grundy, *A Thesaurus of Old English*, 2 vols., Costerus n.s. 131–32 (Amsterdam and Atlanta, 2000), give only 'ploughland' for OE *ploh*.

wheat, and one spring-sown, mainly with barley, but also with any oats and legumes that were grown.[54] In other words, the amount of wheat sown was equivalent to near-ly all the other crops put together. It is unclear, however, whether this "classic" system was in use anywhere in Anglo-Saxon England, and therefore its connection with the "triumph" of wheat over barley must remain speculative.

The change to wheat was a gradual one, but it did reach its peak in the later part of the Anglo-Saxon period, also known as the Viking period,[55] and so it is reasonable to look for connections with Viking settlement. It has to be said, though, that if the settlers did increase the amount of wheat grown, it was not in order to replicate Scandinavian farming or diet. Wheat is close to its north-ern limit in the British Isles, and in Scandinavia it is even more difficult to grow successfully. In the Viking period, it seems to have been practically unknown there.[56] That it was eventually grown quite widely only shows that medieval Scandinavians shared the Anglo-Saxons' preference for wheat over other cere-als, not that they influenced it.[57] If Scandinavians did promote the cultivation of wheat in England, they might have been indulging exotic tastes picked up in continental Europe, but there is no evidence, apart from the coincidence of date, to suggest any connection between Viking settlement and this change in crop-ping practices.

If it is unlikely that Scandinavians were responsible for promoting wheat at the expense of barley, what about oats? These are and were a major crop in Scan-dinavia, indeed virtually the only cereal crop grown in early medieval Norway,[58] and they are also characteristic of the north and west of Britain. Whereas bar-ley was superseded by wheat in the so-called lowland zone of England, in the uplands it was oats that eventually became the major bread-corn. I have stated elsewhere that it is uncertain whether oats were in fact grown in Anglo-Saxon England, although they were certainly present as a weed, but this is to take a minimalist view of the evidence.[59] Even if we took a maximalist view, however, we could hardly maintain that the wholesale replacement of barley by oats in the

---

[54] For a clear explanation and diagram of such a three-field system, still in use at the present day, see J. V. Beckett, *A History of Laxton: England's Last Open Field Village* (Oxford, 1989), 43–45.

[55] See Banham, "Food Plants," 19–20.

[56] See Janken Myrdal, "Agriculture," in *Medieval Scandinavia: An Encyclopedia*, ed. Phillip Pulsiano (New York and London, 1993), 3–5.

[57] Bi Skaarup, "Diet and Nutrition," in *Medieval Scandinavia*, ed. Pulsiano, 134–36.

[58] See Myrdal, "Agriculture," 3.

[59] Debby Banham, "*Be hlafum and wyrtum*: Food Plants in Anglo-Saxon Society and Economy," in *From Earth to Art: The Many Aspects of the Plant-World in Anglo-Saxon England. Proceedings of the First ASPNS Symposium, University of Glasgow, 5–7 April 2000*, ed. C. P. Biggam (Amsterdam and New York, 2003), 119–31.

highland zone took place in the Anglo-Saxon or Viking period. The evidence is minute compared with that for wheat in the lowlands (partly because far less archaeological research has taken place in upland areas), and there are plenty of references to show that barley was still being made into bread as late as the eighteenth and nineteenth centuries in Scotland, Wales, and the north of England.[60] In any case, the fact that Wales is in the oat zone shows that traditions regarding the choice of bread-corn are not connected to Scandinavian settlement so much as to climate, terrain, and soil. The use of the Norse-derived word *haver* for oats in many parts of Britain with an oatcake tradition does not of course mean that Scandinavians introduced oats to these areas, any more than *kirk* means that they introduced Christianity.[61] It is merely one of numerous such vocabulary items in the dialects of "Danelaw" areas, most of which relate to aspects of life that were not affected by Viking settlement.

Livestock

For the sake of completeness, it ought to be said that it does not look as if the Vikings introduced any significant changes in livestock husbandry, either. It has been supposed that British White cattle, with their black or red "points" (ears, nose, feet, etc.), were related to the Swedish Fjällras, which have a similar colouring, and that therefore the Vikings must have had something to do with the origins of the British White. However, there seems to be nothing beyond the physical resemblance between the two breeds to support this tradition. Presumably on the basis of this supposed relationship, Fjällras bulls were imported in the early twentieth century to "improve" British White stock, and thus it will not be possible to elucidate the matter by DNA analysis. Furthermore, it was only in the same decades that British Whites were fully distinguished from White Park cattle, and the two acquired separate herd books.[62] Since the link being made is

---

[60] For a brief discussion of the oats/wheat divide, see Laura Mason and Catherine Brown, *Traditional Foods of Britain* (Totnes, 1999), 14–15: for the use of oats and barley in Scotland, see under "Scottish oatcake," 264, "Beremeal," 332, and "Oatmeal," 332–33, and for English traditions, "Staffordshire oatcake," 266–67 and "Yorkshire oatcake," 270–71. For Welsh oat and barley bread, see S. Mynwel Tibbott, *Baking in Wales* (Cardiff, 1991), 7–13.

[61] Joseph Wright, *The English Dialect Dictionary* (London and New York, 1902), vol. 3, lists *haver* from Scotland, Northumberland, Durham, Cumberland, Westmoreland, Yorkshire, Lancashire, and Lincolnshire.

[62] See G. Kenneth Whitehead, *The Ancient White Cattle of Britain and their Descendants* (London, 1953), 92–94. I have been unable to discover any more recent research on the subject.

again with the "wrong" part of Scandinavia, it does not seem worth pursuing the matter exhaustively.

The number of sheep kept in England, *vis-à-vis* other stock such as cattle and pigs, probably increased during the ninth and tenth centuries, since they were the basis of the main export industry of the time (not counting that in slaves), but the evidence is not particularly clear. In any case, this was a process that had been going on since at least the time of Offa, and continued with some interruptions throughout the Middle Ages, so it is unlikely that the initiative of Scandinavian settlers played a major part.[63] Indeed, it may be argued that, since a fair proportion of England's wealth was based on sheep, they constituted one of the elements that attracted the Vikings to England in the first place.

Conclusions

This paper should not be regarded (perhaps counter-intuitively) as completely negative. I ought to stress that I am convinced that Scandinavian settlers must have influenced agriculture in the areas of England where they lived, but such influence may have varied greatly, even at a very local level. Given that many members of the Viking armies may not have been of Scandinavian origin, however, there may well have been influence from others areas of Europe, too, and perhaps even from further afield. Furthermore, Scandinavians themselves would have been quite capable of introducing innovations from other places. If my search for Scandinavian influence has taught me anything, it is that such influence looks very different in different places. The Vikings were nothing if not culturally adaptable, perhaps sufficiently so to introduce open-field farming to England from, say, Frankia. The agriculture they had left behind in Scandinavia was evidently inadequate to keep the Viking leaders in the style to which they became accustomed, and so it might have served their interests better, when they took over their English lands, to emulate the farming of more prosperous regions. England itself was of course a prosperous region, even if, by the time the Vikings settled, its productive base was not what it had once been. It may be that Anglo-Saxon agricultural techniques were the most productive they had come across, in which case they are unlikely to have introduced any major changes. Then again, it may in fact be the case that they were not particularly interested in the details of estate management, despite the evidence of Scandinavian laws and sagas. These sources belong after all to the twelfth century and later, even if they do contain earlier material. If we accept Poulsen's dating[64] of new agricultural practices in

---

[63] See Julian Richards, *Viking Age England* (London, 1991), 71–73, and Pam J. Crabtree, *West Stow: Early Anglo-Saxon Animal Husbandry*, East Anglian Archaeology 47 (Ipswich, 1989), 83–94.

[64] See n. 34 above.

Denmark to the end of the Viking age, it may be that the laws and sagas reflect a new social reality, in which Scandinavian landlords, deprived of the profits of their enterprises abroad, were forced to retrench and exploit their lands at home as fully as possible. If they were looking for models of how to maximise agricultural profits, they may have looked to England, as somewhere with which Scandinavia still had links, and as having a climate not too different from their own, for an example. While I would not like to suggest that Anglo-Saxon influence on Scandinavian agriculture is any more than a possibility, it does seem to me at least as plausible as that the major influence was in the opposite direction.

Acknowledgements

I should like to thank Lesley Abrams, Rosamond Faith, Laura Mason, Susan Oosthuizen, John Sanderson, and Elina Screen for variously discussing with me the ideas in this paper and suggesting references. None of them is to be held responsible for the use I have made of their contributions.